PULLING DOWN THE SUN

THE PUEBLOS, THE GREAT HOUSES AND THE CLIFF DWELLINGS

Pulling Down the Sun

The Pueblos, the Great Houses and the Cliff Dwellings
2008 - 2016

by

J. M. White

Anomolaic Press

Anomolaic
Press

91 Vantrease Road
Brush Creek, TN 38547
www.futurenothingnessalready.com
michaelwhite@dtccom.net

Editor Emeritus: Lamont Ingalls
Senior Editor: Susan McDonald
Graphic Design and Layout: Anthony Blake

International Standard Book Number
978-0-9989809-2-8
All rights reserved
First edition 2018
Cover photo: Sunset at Taos
Jewelry design – Otto Lucio

Table of Contents

PREFACE

The tribal heritage of our nation is ignored and overlooked by the great majority of Americans. While all of us share an indigenous tribal heritage, for most it is lost in the haze of prehistory, buried in our psyche, unreachable after hundreds or thousands of years of Westernization. However, there are avenues, ports of entry, to learn about our tribal heritage. It is possible to visit the indigenous people who have managed, by various quirks of fate and sheer determination, to bring their culture and traditions into the twenty-first century. There are presently twenty living pueblos located in the deserts of New Mexico and Arizona. Taos is the northernmost, Zuni the southernmost, Hopi the westernmost. All but Hopi form a line starting with Taos at the northern point following the Rio Grande River south to Albuquerque then heading west to Acoma and ending at Zuni on the Arizona border. Of the twenty living pueblos, Taos, Hopi and Zuni are outstanding examples of those who have retained their traditions in special ways. Taos and Hopi still have multistory adobe buildings that preserve the ancient architecture as a remnant, a revenant, of prehistoric times. It is marvelous to visit these buildings and see the multistoried adobe buildings with the great plazas that serve as a reminder, like an echo, that the old ways are still alive. However, while members of the tribe have apartments in these buildings, no one lives in them full time. Whereas at Zuni while the old multistoried adobe buildings are gone, the old town area with the traditional plazas still in place, is a living villages.

Another avenue into this heritage is to visit the monuments of the past and see the great ruins of the cultures that preceded ours. There are countless ruins left by the ancestors of the pueblo peoples. They are scattered throughout the deserts and canyons, they stand as incredible reminders of the civilizations of the past. The buildings and the roadways they created are architectural and engineering marvels. We are still uncovering the mathematical and astronomical principles of their construction and use.

Another point of entry is found in the books written by the earliest Europeans describing their first contact with the myriad indigenous cultures throughout the Americas. Here we see them at the cusp between the prehistoric and the historic. After European contact things would never be the same. Once the ravages of genocidal fury and rampant disease passed, they were followed by a deluge of ethnologists, anthropologists and archaeologists who have written voluminous tomes about our indigenous peoples. There is also a growing body of literature written by the indigenous people themselves.

This book chronicles some of the living pueblos in New Mexico and Arizona and visits the greatest of the massive ruins of their predecessors. This glimpse into the ancestral past is an attempt to see the tribal past as a part of our collective psyche. We have lost touch with our indigenous past, most people are woefully ignorant about the indigenous people who occupied this land before the European invasions. Most are equally ignorant about their descendants who are with us today. Yet not so many generations ago we all lived in indigenous tribal cultures and this heritage is deep inside us. Certainly there is no going back. But these journals offer a glimpse into the indigenous past that, for uncounted millennia, was our heritage.

THE PUEBLOS

ZUNI

HAWIKKU, HALONA AND THE CENTER OF THE WORLD 2010

THE A:SHIWI

At Zuni the sun is the father of all things, the earth the mother, water the grandmother, fire the grandfather and all growing things are our brothers and sisters, none of whom can live without light, without warmth, and without water, which taken together, bring forth the great abundance which is cooked over fire to sustain us. In the beginning the light from the sun vanquished the sublime darkness and brought forth the waters, those above and those below. The light revealed the great ocean, the earth and the sky. The sky father joined with the earth mother so that mankind and all the creatures were conceived in the womb of the earth and came forth from the caves. Then the sky father used grains of corn to create the stars, to be their guide when the sun was gone. The earth mother created the mountains to demarcate the land and clouds to bring the rains.

The great sun pitied the first humans while they were still deep in the womb of mother earth. The sun cast his gaze upon the water and created two brothers, the clouds, and gave them arrows of lightning and a bow made of many colored lights which is still visible in the sky after a rain. They fired their arrows breaking open the earth so the humans could see the night sky high above. Then the priests built a ladder and climbed up into a higher cave. When dawn came they followed the light and emerged from the earth where they discovered many gods and strange beings and the gods taught them how to pray and do ceremony.

While the Zuni were in the innermost womb of the earth they found themselves in deep subterranean caves, they eventually discovered fire and began to find their way upward. Before they emerged their hands and feet were webbed, they had a covering of slime and their reproductive organs were on their foreheads. Upon climbing out they washed away the slime, spread their fingers and toes, and rearranged their sexual organs.

When the Zuni came out of the earth they were deep in the Grand Canyon and began a migration in search of the center of the world, the middle place, where they could live. From their place of origin they moved south into the sacred mountains where the kachinas gave them herbs to use as medicine. Then they moved along a great river and after living there a while they divided, one group went south, while another continued to follow the river untill two rivers came together, near a beautiful lake where the gods live in an underwater pueblo. During their journey they found other people and wars began. The war gods provided assistance and the people settled at Haloma:wa, the middle place. A spider showed them the right spot by reaching its legs to the waters on each side so its heart was just over the center of the world. At Haloma:wa they were divided into clans and still live there today.

Paleo points dating back thousands of years have been found around Zuni. By 2000 BCE the people began to grow corn and beans; about 1000 BCE they were living in pit houses that were dug into the earth. They began to grow excess crops and created subterranean storage spaces. Then about 200 CE they started making pottery and by 700 CE small villages began to form with groups of pit houses congregated on the mesas. Large trade networks developed and by 900 CE they moved the houses above ground, establishing multistoried adobe villages with large plazas and ceremonial kivas.

This evolution from subterranean pit houses to above ground masonry pueblos mimics the mythology of the Zuni coming up out of the earth. By 1000 CE they began to congregate into larger villages on the model of the great houses at Chaco Canyon. These villages were congruent with agricultural areas and larger areas for hunting and gathering wood. Around 1250 CE the smaller pueblos were abandoned and the population shifted into larger plaza-centered settlements with multistoried pueblos. By 1300 CE some pueblos had up to a thousand rooms. The Zuni built over thirty plaza-oriented villages at various places up and down the Zuni River from 1250 to 1540 CE.

By 1500 CE the Zuni were living in six main villages scattered along a fifteen mile stretch of the Zuni River. You can still visit the ruins of these villages. Then in 1539 the Spanish showed up and life would never be the same. From then on the Zuni endured multiple assaults from the Spanish to the south and from the Indian tribes that surrounded them, especially the Navaho and Apache who raided their lands. The first Spanish expedition to Zuni was lead by a black Moor named Estaban in 1539. When he arrived at Zuni they did not appreciate his attitude toward the women or his avarice regarding their possessions and swiftly executed him. They immediately sent word to other pueblos that the invaders were human and could be killed like any other person. The next year Coronado followed Estaban's trail with a huge army of Spaniards backed with hundreds of native soldiers.

This marked the end of the prehistoric period for the Zuni. The southernmost of the six cities was named Hawikku and it was the first place the Spanish invaded. When tales of seven cities of gold incited the Spanish to come north, Coronado invaded with armored troops on horseback. The Zuni watched their approach and met them with 250 warriors who fought, for the first time, against the guns of the Spanish. The Zuni were forced to withdraw along with the residents of the pueblos and hid on top of a nearby mesa while the Spanish occupied the village. This was the only major battle as the Zuni negotiated peace and allowed the Spanish temporary access to their villages. Coronado soon moved on and no Europeans came back for another thirty years. This, however, did not protect the Zuni, who numbered about six thousand when first contact was made. The Zuni suffered terrible losses as epidemics of smallpox and measles greatly reduced their numbers.

After Coronado returned to Mexico the next Spanish entrada to reach Zuni was in 1581. It wasn't until 1598 that any real settlements were established and these were along the Rio Grande far from Zuni. However, the Spanish demanded vassalage and considered the Zuni Spanish subjects. Spanish missions were established in Zuni by 1632 but soon thereafter the Zuni executed two priests and their escorts and burned the church. In 1680 the Zuni joined the Pueblo Revolt and drove all the Spanish out of New Mexico. The Indians in all the pueblos joined together in a synchronized attack on the same day. After this the Zuni, anticipating the swift return of vengeful Spanish soldiers, retreated to the old village on top of the mesa. At this time there was one Catholic priest at Zuni who was recognized by the tribe as a decent man and, rather than kill him, they offered him the opportunity to become a Zuni. They said if he would wear Zuni clothes and learn to live like a Zuni they would adopt him into the tribe and he could live with them. This was apparently an offer he could not refuse and he became one of the first Spanish priests to "go native". However, nothing is reported about what happened to him. The Spanish returned in force in 1692 and re-established their control of the region. Even during this time the Zuni were facing constant raids by the Apache and the Navaho who were their traditional enemies. Once they made peace with the Spanish they decided to consolidate all their scattered villages into one for better protection. They continued to use the abandoned villages that were in fertile farming areas, especially in the summers. They built a multistoried village which was five stories tall on the ruins of the old village of Halona, and they are living there to this day.

Zuni agriculture centered on corn. In the 1880s they had up to 10,000 acres under cultivation in fields that had elaborate embankments that damned and channeled the water to prevent erosion. They made scary, bizarre looking scarecrows and hung dead crows on strings all over the corn fields. The Zuni harvested thousands of pounds of corn, along with peppers and squash, in an environment that got eleven inches of rain per year. In the Zuni River valley, where they had access to more water, they made "waffle" gardens which had mud walls around every plant to direct every bit of water to the roots. They had sealed storage bins and kept up to two years of corn in reserve.

The Zunis' knowledge of the plant life in their area was extensive and ancient. They had profound religious veneration for all the plants and would speak with them, pray to them and make offerings to them as a part of gathering them. They used the local plant life for food, for medicine and for dyes. A variety of plants were used for healing; for anesthetics to treat headaches and toothaches, for childbirth, for wounds and sore throats. Some were used for divination. During times of drought they could live off wild foods, things like pine nuts, berries, sunflowers, wild rice, wild beans, fungi and potatoes.

Plants were used for their fibers, to make clothing, mats, baskets, rope and trays. Plants provided paints, perfume and soap. The Zuni gathered it all in a way that was sustainable and showed respect for the plants, which were considered higher life forms than humans.

Hunting was a religious activity that involved the use of fetishes that were kept in special containers and regularly fed with cornmeal. When a Zuni killed a deer or any animal they would rush up to it, put their face next to its face, and breathe in the last breath that escaped from the animal thus assuring renewed life for the animal. The dead animals would lie in state in the pueblo adorned with jewelry and covered with a fine blanket. All hunting was accompanied by prayers with offerings of elaborately decorated prayer sticks and ceremonies.

Zuni ceremonialism is one of the most highly developed in all of North America. For the Zuni every object, animate or inanimate, has spiritual power. There are great hierarchies of clans, subclans and secret societies. When the elders die they go to the kachina village and join the council of kachinas and return to the village to dance at the ceremonies to help bring the rain. Certain of the priests in the village are designated to become lightning-makers when they pass on. There are great powers which are celestial, terrestrial and subterranean including the plumed serpent and many others in each realm.

The Zuni have six kivas, one for each of the kachina societies, each associated with one of the six directions, all located on a plaza. The main kiva is a square building with no exterior door and the entrance through the roof. The kivas have ledges running around the walls for seating. There is a chief kiva where they set up the great solstice altar and hold ceremonies to usher in the new year. It is here they create sand paintings to initiate the youth. The main kiva is located on tsia'awa plaza, in proximity to the ceremonial house of the town chiefs. This is considered the center of the world and the most sacred place in Zuni.

Present day Zuni consists of two main population centers: one is the village of Halona and its suburb of Black Rock and the second consists of four seasonally-occupied farming communities scattered around the reservation. The Zuni have around 700 square miles which was carved down little by little by encroachment by Navaho and American land grabbers who ruthlessly acquired Zuni lands by any means at their disposal. The Zuni reservation has shrunk considerably from the old times when they held an area many times larger and would hunt big game in Utah, conduct religious ceremonies in Colorado, chase the buffalo across the plains, trade all over Arizona and into Mexico, and make pilgrimages to the Pacific Ocean.

The existence of the Zuni people is something of a miracle in modern America. The Zuni are a small tribe living in the middle of a barren desert. They have been the target of over four centuries of concerted efforts to destroy their culture, suppress their language and religion and appropriate their land. Yet in the face of incredible obstacles they have survived and have kept their language, their religion and their homeland to a greater extent than nearly any other tribal body in America. In 1600 there were about 6,000 Zuni living in six pueblos scattered along the Zuni River. By 1850 the population was reduced to 2,000 and by 1900 the census reported only 1,400 Zunis in New Mexico. In 2010 the population in the village had rebounded to over 6,000 with several thousand more living off the reservation. Current estimates have the population at over 10,000. The Zuni now have seven medicine societies, seventeen clans and two religious fraternities.

The pueblos have managed to survive partly due to the circumstances of geography, living in a part of the country that was inhospitable to most invaders. This aided their determined efforts to maintain their culture and traditions in the face of centuries of Spanish and then American imperialism. Zuni is one of a few small pockets of traditional Native American culture that have managed to survive into the twenty-first century.

INDIAN TIME

The journey starts airborne from Nashville to Denver and then to Albuquerque and on to Zuni to reenter the long ago. The Zuni have experienced wave after wave of Europeans who have been, with a few exceptions, out for their spiritual and cultural, if not their physical destruction. But the Zuni have a remarkable history that, even in the face of the onslaught of destructive forces, has allowed them to maintain their homeland as well as their language and religion.

In Albuquerque Susan and I rented a car and took off west toward Zuni. We followed Interstate 40 along the old Route 66 and in about an hour headed south on Route 53. Before long we were driving through an unearthly phantasmagoric landscape, vast and foreboding, of black lava rock. I pulled over and walked among the lava stones in an immense plain filled with a jumble of black shards of lava that are harsh and unrewarding to walk on, rough and jagged, where it is difficult to keep your footing. It is a landscape of ten thousand years ago still laying in wait, stretching into some vague and unmapped future. The New Mexico landscape is ever changing and, one of the delights of exploring it, is that you can find yourself in distinctly different landscapes and eco-systems in the course of an hour or two. We started in a harsh desert and then came into heavily forested hills before we came to the lava fields. Next we saw a sign telling us we were on Navaho land and within a few more miles came to the Zuni reservation. Here is where the familiar was no longer in charge, where we were departing from the everyday, where the landscape has a quality that is foreign to our eyes. The beauty of it is so intense it is like some form of primeval poetry, a lyricism of the earth, a harkening back to when everything, even the landscape, was expressed in poetic harmonics. The landscape itself seemed removed from time, a throwback to a geologic dream time, to a mythic prehistoric past, atavistic, yet still with us.

When we drive into Zuni the main street is a dusty two-lane road in the middle of a desert. There are a few houses, a couple of deserted looking businesses, mesas and buttes in the distance. We came to a solitary stop sign and continued on, not knowing whether we were on the outskirts of Zuni or where. We quickly became aware that we were heading back out into the desert. There is only one hotel in Zuni and our directions said it is on the main road. We drove back through slowly, a couple of restaurants, one gas station, a Zuni Community Center and a couple of little Zuni jewelry shops, but they were closed and that was all we saw. I came back to the stop sign and turned this time and then felt more like we were in the pueblo. The street was lined with one-story houses built of buff-colored stone that looks like adobe and matches the desert landscape, all of them flat roofed. And then another stop sign and what appeared to be a little grocery store but it had no signage on it and there was no indication of a motel anywhere. There was an old couple at the end of the porch on the store and I pulled over next to them, they were speaking in Zuni. They looked at me, "Where's the hotel?" He gave me a quizzical look and pointed at the store without saying a word. "That's it?" I queried, he nodded. "Park around back." I pulled around to the little parking area and we went in the store. As we walked up on the porch I could see there was a sign over the door and it said Inn at Halona, only most of the letters were missing and until I was able to figure out what it said it remained an indecipherable ideogram.

The store was a strange little place. It had a few rows of groceries, mostly snack foods and sodas, and then there was a counter where you could buy supplies for making jewelry with trays of turquoise and coral. In the back was a little deli serving fried chicken and French fries, then in one corner was a little desk where you check into the hotel. We signed in and they told us where to park, right next door to the store in the back. We moved the car and parked in front of a fence with a sign that said, Parking for Blue Corn Pancake Lovers Only.

I called Otto who was going to show us around the next day and let him know we had arrived. He said he would come over and meet us in about half an hour. When he arrived we sat on the porch of the hotel. Otto said he made jewelry and that he really wasn't a guide but that he was glad to show us around and that he occasionally gave talks about Zuni culture. Otto is a full blood Zuni, who describes himself as a progressive who has served on the Zuni council. He is about forty, well spoken, raised off the rez till he was eighteen. We stand in the courtyard at the Inn at Halona and talk about Cushing and Stephenson, two of the most famous ethnologists who had written about Zuni. Otto tells us about a year he spent working at the Smithsonian as an archivist, going through all the pictures of Zuni and making copies to bring back. He couldn't believe the amount of Zuni stuff in the back rooms of the Smithsonian and describes a warehouse full of pottery, not just little pots but very large pots on shelves ten feet tall that fill a complete warehouse. We laid out a plan for the next day to see the ruins where first contact had been made, to see a fetish carver, to visit the museum and meet a kachina carver. I asked if there was anything we should do this evening, he said many of the Zuni liked to walk on a little trail around the base of Corn Mountain about this time and told me how to find it. So when he left we drove out to watch the sunset from Corn Mountain.

CORN MOUNTAIN

There is a dirt road that goes out to Corn Mountain with a place at the foot of the mountain to park. There are a bunch of cars and trucks parked by a walking path that seems to be very popular. A smaller dirt road, only one lane wide, cuts off and seems to wrap around the base of the mountain. We drive along it very slowly watching the sunlight play on the red sandstone, an incredible site, glowing a deeper red as the sun sets lower in the western sky. There are wildflowers in profusion all along the road and the face of the escarpment changes from moment to moment, twin spires appear on the far southwestern side, beautiful red monoliths that are separated from the mesa by a short distance yet firmly a part of the mountain. Then there are places where the side of the mesa has curtains of stone, side by side lining the base of the escarpment. Then we come to a place where the face of the mesa is like a gigantic cathedral entrance, pillared on both sides and domed, all embedded in the sheer rock of the mountain side. I had read an account of an expedition up to the top of Corn Mountain that described numerous small caves and shrines along the way, all decorated with petroglyphs. On another occasion an archaeologist named Fewkes reported there was a cave at the base of Corn Mountain with hundreds of petroglyphs, some of monstrous size, some very small. Nearby, he found a rock face honeycombed with small openings where people left offerings.

I would like to climb up to the top where the Zuni went for protection in times of war. There are ruins there of the village they built to live in while they were under attack. On several occasions they retreated to the top of the mesa and lived there for many years. They went there when Coronado invaded and the whole population retreated to the mesa top while the warriors faced off the invasion at Hawikku. Then again after the 1680 pueblo revolt they moved to the top of the mesa and lived there for twelve years until the Spanish returned in force and they negotiated a new peace and came down and consolidated all the population into Halona.

Once the sun went over the horizon the brilliant red glow of the mountain began to fade and, at the same time, the vista of the western sky suddenly fired up in a brilliant array of metallic gleaming bright shades of red and orange, then in the gradual creeping darkness it was as if all the colors of the spectrum pooled at the vanishing point of the distant skyline and were sucked over the curve of the earth, pulled by some spectral gravity dragging the colors with it as the sun disappeared over the far western rim of the earth. We marveled at the psychedelic display of colors until darkness seemed to overcome them with its inevitable fate and we headed back to

Halona Inn. After dinner my cell phone rang. It is Otto who says the fetish carver and the kachina carver are both at home and would like for us to come this evening if that is ok. I told him that was great and to come pick me up. Susan decided to stay in and get organized. I was waiting on the porch when Otto showed up a little after dark.

FETISHISM

I had read Frank Hamilton Cushing's book about fetishes written in the 1880s [1] and he had several pages of illustrations of all the types of fetishes the Zuni had at the time. I copied the illustrations and circled the ones I liked the best and sent them to Otto a few weeks ago asking if he could find a fetish carver who could carve fetishes in the old style. When Otto showed up he seemed excited and said he had found someone who could carve fetishes in the old style and we were set to go meet him right now. Otto said the carver and his brother were both waiting for us. We climbed into his truck and took a short ride to a concrete block house in the village. Otto knocked on the door and in a minute we saw a little girl's cherub face looking out at us, a slightly older boy finally opened the door and told us to come around back. Otto told him to show us the way and he came running out and led us around to the back porch where a couple of men were waiting with a small table set up under the porch light. They are brothers, the older one with a mustache, the younger a bit heavier. The older brother's name is Delvin Leekya and the younger is Freddie Leekya. There are several fetishes laid out on the table. Each one matched one of the traditional designs from the book. The little girl from the front door reappeared and then a couple more little kids, all under age six. She was shy and hanging back just inside the back door but a couple of the others were curious enough to venture out and hang around the table but when they started reaching for the fetishes they were gently shushed back inside.

I couldn't believe the fetishes. They were exact replicas of the traditional pictures in every way. They were beautifully done with a variety of stones. I had indicated I wanted them made of certain types of stone and they were, several made of turquoise and amber. Then I started getting worried about the cost. They were really exquisite and I could imagine him wanting a high price, especially for the ones made of turquoise. I told him that I loved to read about Zuni and had read everything Cushing had written and a bunch more and it was a privilege to come here and experience Zuni firsthand. I said I appreciated him making these in the traditional manner. He called for someone in the house to bring out a picture of his grandfather. A woman quickly showed up at the door with a framed photo of an old Indian wearing a scarf around his head with multiple strands of turquoise around his neck. He was holding a fetish in one hand. Then she came back with another picture and this one was the father of the two carvers. He was also holding up a fetish but not wearing any turquoise. His name was Francis Leekya and both he and his father were famous carvers in their day. They told me Francis only had one arm. I was amazed at that. They showed me how he carved with a grinder and could hold the stone with his one good hand and use the grinding wheel to shape it. Delvin told me that once the old man made a bunch of fetishes and got ready to go off to a show and then died before he left. There were four brothers in the family and they divided the fetishes and kept them as remembrances. The woman disappeared and came back with a really big bear that was among the last he made.

I was intently studying the fetishes. There are a set of six fetishes that are related to the six directions: the bear, the mountain lion, the badger and the wolf are associated with the four directions; north, south, east and west. The eagle and the mole are for the heavens above and the earth below, representing the directions up and down to complete the six directions. I wanted to have all the directions covered and there they are in front of me, along with several others. I am nervous about the cost and wondering what he is going to want for them. I have to split my money between the fetish makers, the kachina carver and the potters and jewelers so I am quickly counting my money and ask him to price them. He lines them up and then starts in pricing the larger ones at $30.00 and the smaller ones at $25.00. I am thrilled and thought that he might want significantly more for them so I pull out my wallet and count out the money without trying to bargain. Delvin starts putting them all away, each one in a separate little bag.

Freddie has been standing nearby watching the transaction. He has a small plastic box under his arm so I ask him if he has anything he would like to show me. He opens the box and brings out four figurines. Two of them are human shapes, a man and a woman, made of white buff stone, each of them with turquoise beads around their necks, and they each have polished stones on the bottom of their shoes, the man has a walking stick and is wearing a scarf around his head. Otto is really impressed and indicates that these are really something special. I agree. Freddie also has a couple of very nice animal fetishes. He stands all of them on the table, very impressive. He says the man is a priest. I look closely, both the man and the woman have little bits of turquoise inlaid on them and are very nicely done. Delvin jokes and says Freddie just looked in the mirror and then carved the man to look like him. The priest has fat cheeks and does look a little bit like Freddie and we all get a laugh out of that. I get my wallet back out and ask the price, again it is very reasonable, although this time, I bargain with him just a little and quickly settle on a price and pay up.

Then I tell them, "Listen, I am very happy to have these fetishes and I want to understand how to treat them properly and how to display them or use them. What should I do, what are they used for?"

Delvin starts in, "They are for protection."

"Do you use them?"

"Oh yes, when I am getting ready to go deer hunting I take the fetish with me on the hunt. When I go out, we do prayers and ask the fetish to help us find the game, and when we find game we feed the fetish to show it respect."

"Do you keep them in a special way here at your house?"

"Oh yes, there is a special pot we keep them in, they have their own house and we make sure they have corn meal offerings."

"Where do you get the stones?"

Freddie spoke up, "Some of these stones come from Corn Mountain."

"Wow, which ones?"

He pointed out the light brownish stones that included the priest and the woman.

He said that they would go out early in the morning and go up to the top of the mountain and do prayers and ask for guidance to find the right stones and make offerings of corn meal in return for taking the stones. Then they would look around and find the right stones. He said that if I needed protection I should use the priest and the woman and they would help me.

By now all the fetishes were packed up, several more kids had been appearing and reappearing, beautiful little kids. I asked if I could take pictures and they didn't seem to mind so I took a couple of portraits and we took our leave.

When we met Otto the next morning he said I had gotten really good deals on those fetishes. He had looked them up on line and said that the prices on line were four and five times the amount I had paid. He said that their father and grandfather were famous carvers and well known for carving in the traditional manner. I couldn't believe my luck and thanked Otto for steering me to them. The magic of the fetishes is an enigma to me.

In Zuni mythology in the long ago the world was covered with water, then great arrows of lightning shot across the earth and the waters boiled and the oceans receded leaving behind the scorched earth. All the great beings of that world were shriveled and dried and changed to stone and even today you can still find their strange forms embedded in the rocks. To the Zuni stones are the abode of great forces which can provide services to those who know how to access their powers. These stones can belong to a person, to a clan or to the tribe. Each carved stone is considered a living being and kept in a fetish jar where they live on a bed of down that has been sprinkled with powered turquoise and mother of pearl. The fetishes face their feeding hole where they can breathe and eat the corn meal and drink the water that is offered to them. The jar is kept covered with deerskin and the lid covered with a flat stone.

In ancient days the Makers of the Paths of Life, the great supernatural forces of the universe, created the mountain lions, the black bears, the badgers, the white wolves, the eagles and even the moles as the guardians of the six directions: the mountain lion for the northern realms, the bear for the western, the badger for the southern, the white wolf for the eastern, the eagle for the upper realm and the mole for the lower realms. Each animal serves as the guardian for all the medicines in each of their respective realms. Messages were conveyed to these animals on prayer sticks which are striped with paint and plumed with feathers and deposited where the Makers can respond to them. The fetishes are exhorted with ritual and ceremony and on the full moon of each month they receive sacrifices as offerings for the medicines they provide.

In the Zuni creation myth the people are born out of the earth. They start life in a subterranean realm and eventually work their way up to the surface. When they emerged from the earth the great beasts, the bears, the mountain lions and the wolves attacked and devoured them. The supreme beings took pity on them and turned the animals to stone so that only the hearts of the animals remained alive in the rock. The Zuni honored these fetishes, keeping them in special places, performing ceremonies for them, feeding them and giving them water. They would call on their powers to protect them and to help in all their endeavors. The wolf, the wildcat, the coyote and the mountain lion helped the hunters and when a kill was made, the heart was cut out and the fetish bathed in its blood as an offering of thanks for their help in the hunt.

The Zuni carry their fetishes on their bodies in a small buckskin bag. When the hunter went off hunting, or the warrior to war, offerings were tied to the fetish, in some cases with the sinew of a mountain lion. They fastened a small arrowhead and a variety of shells, beads and feathers to the body of the fetish. They used beads of turquoise, coral and black stone alternating with seashells, small univalves, known as "heart shells", which are emblematic of the supernatural. The arrowhead tied to the fetish is called the "Knife of War" and is used as medicine to protect the owner from unexpected attack. The fetishes are believed to have the power to erase foot prints so a person's trail cannot be followed.

MASKOLOGY

Once Otto and I were back in the truck he offered to take me to the house of the kachina carver who lived close to the Inn at Halona I had asked Otto to have him carve a kachina for me and I ended up ordering a fire god and a mudhead. When we got there a barrel-chested young man was outside in the yard and he waved us in. Otto introduced me to Alvert who invited us in. There was the fire god kachina and a mudhead kachina on the table and he said he had been working on them all day. I asked if the kachina still came to the village and he said oh yes and when they came all the people had to fast for four days from certain types of food and from all sex to prepare for their arrival. The kachinas were beautifully done and I was delighted. We settled on a price with a bit of bargaining. Later that week when we were in Albuquerque in a store that sells native crafts from different reservations and there was a very similar kachina of the fire god, only not as tall, and it was priced at nearly five times what it cost me so I appreciated the deal he gave me.

The mudhead is a bizarre-looking kachina that is associated with the Shalako which is one of the biggest kachinas in more ways than one. The mask for Shalako is over ten feet tall and when Shalako comes to the village it is one of the most important ceremonies of the year. When Otto first talked to him about carving a mudhead, they called me and asked which mudhead I wanted. It turns out there are ten of them but it is difficult for me to distinguish between them so I asked Otto to pick one for me. The mudheads are called Koyemci and each one has a separate name like Kyalutsi (the suckling), Tsalashi (old youth) or Potsoki (the pouter), Muyapona (wearer of eyelets of invisibility) and Ecotsi (the bat), and each has subtly different features regarding their funny knobbed mask. They have seeds they bring to the village each year, including several different kinds of corn: yellow corn, blue corn, white corn, red corn, black corn and speckled corn, along with squash and gourds.

The mudheads are deformed creatures who are impotent. There were times during the old dances when they would end up nude but they are considered like little children without shame. Yet they are highly skilled at love magic. They are the clowns of Zuni and stir up all kinds of mischief. They provide ludicrous, uncouth games, guessing games and play tag with a bean bag and sometime play obscene games that involve mock lovemaking with exaggerated motions. Their actions are typically greeted with great hilarity and merriment. It is considered dangerous to refuse the mudheads anything.

We are sitting in the living room and I ask Alvert about the mudheads and he says that the fur bag over the shoulder is made from the skin of a fawn and explains that the chief picks the best hunters who go out and kill the fawns for each of the mudheads and they skin them from head to tail and treat the skin and make a special pouch that the mudheads use as part of their apparel.

"How many mudheads usually come to the village to dance?"

"Oh it can be five usually but can be up to ten, especially for the shalako dance."

I ask Otto to tell me the story of how the mudheads came to be.

He started right in and said, "A brother and sister kachina were traveling and when night came the sister laid down to sleep and then the brother got aroused and had sex with her and the mudheads were the result of this incestuous relationship. Their grotesque shape is a warning to everyone about what happens if you have incest." But he also said that since they are kachinas they have special powers.

"Do all the people in the village believe in the katchinas or have a lot of them been converted to other religions?"

"Oh yeah, maybe forty per cent have adopted some modern religion, they are all kinds, there are Mormons and Catholics and Baptist and all that."

I am a bit befuddled, I thought Zuni were nearly free of Christianity and am surprised at his answer, but on reflection, thinking of over 400 years of constant effort on the part of missionaries of every variety they are lucky to have sixty per cent of the village still holding to the traditional religion.

"Are there kachinas at all the pueblos?"

They look at each other.

Otto speaks up, "I don't think so, mostly here and Hopi and Acoma."

I had read that the kachinas live under a lake that is west of Zuni so I asked if that was the case.

Otto spoke up again, "Yes, but only in the old days, the lake is dried up now."

I am shocked. I want to know about the kachinas coming to the village. "Do the kachinas come into town?"

"Yes, sometimes, they come from the west."

"Are there dances in all the plazas or is it just in the tsia'awa?" the place they consider the center of the world, the enclosed plaza at the center of the old village.

"They dance all over the village." he tells me.

Alvert had a book about the kachinas and he brought it out, a big picture book by Barton Wright. I looked in it and was surprised to see pictures of Shalako and processions of kachinas coming into the village. They were obviously old pictures from the early 20th century when the Zuni decided, for a very short time, to allow photographs during the dances. I ask Alvert if he dances, a question which both of them understand to mean, does he have a mask and wear it at any of the dances. He says he believes in his religion and prays but has only danced once many years ago. He said that if you say you are going to dance and then you don't, bad things can happen. Now I wonder if I am intruding in an area where he is not at liberty to discuss. Then we started discussing our next project, I asked if Alvert would mind if I took a picture and he posed with the mudhead. Then we settled up on what I owed him and Otto and I were off into the Zuni night. We agreed to meet the next morning at 9:30 as he dropped me off at the Inn at Halona.

I had looked into the kachina cult to try to figure out where it came from and how it got started. There is evidence on pottery shards, petroglyphs and kiva murals that shows the earliest evidence for the kachinas comes from the Mimbres Valley in southwest New Mexico on the border with Mexico. Archaeological evidence from both pottery and rock art dates back to 1000 CE. This Mesoamerican cosmology and its attendant ceremonialism and dance cycles apparently started in Mimbres and in the next two hundred years was adopted by the pueblos in the Rio Grande valley and in Zuni and Hopi. The imagery associated with kachinas includes masked figures, four-pointed stars, anthropomorphs, corn images and various animals, especially serpents and cloud designs.

Then starting in the 1200s there was widespread drought that drastically affected the Anazazi culture, forcing the people in the Chaco Canyon and Anazazi outliers to move toward the Rio Grande valley to have enough water to grow their crops for survival. Some of the scholars suggest that the kachina cult became a way of integrating these people as a whole with a new societal bonding mechanism. They built much larger villages, many with 500 to 2,000 rooms, all with large enclosed plazas and community kivas. The kachina dances and ceremonies were a tribal-wide ceremony that served to integrate migrants from different villages in such a way their clan affiliations did not exclude them. The fact that the entire ceremonial tradition is built on bringing the rain would have appealed to people escaping from a drought. In the next few hundred years the kachina ceremonialism was present in all the pueblos in the Rio Grande valley and to the west. Kachina imagery appeared on the pottery, in the murals in the kivas, and was widespread on the rock art sites. The kachina religion focuses on rituals designed to bring the rain, rituals that maintain the balance between humans and the forces of nature and evoke clouds and cloud imagery. But the kachinas are also associated with the ancestors and the afterlife. The kachinas served as intermediaries between the village and the more mysterious forces of nature.

When the Spanish consolidated their power in the 1600s they suppressed the kachina ceremonies and did everything in their power to eradicate kachina ritualism from the pueblos. They came very close to succeeding and it appears that most of the eastern pueblos no longer have kachina dances, at least not publicly. However, the western pueblos, further from Spanish influence, still maintain kachina dances, some of which are open to the public, both in Hopi and in Zuni.

The legends tell that the place where the people came out of the earth was a watery environment and the people looked more aquatic, were covered with moss and their fingers and toes were webbed. Before this they had no knowledge of death and their emergence marked the birth of death. The birth of death is the birth of self-knowledge, of the ability to recognize the past and the future and to know that you, like all living things, will die. And with this comes the birth of religion as a means to overcome death, to find a place in the presumed afterlife. The people came to a place called Moss Lake and there the gods saw them and decided to help them, so they washed them and removed all the moss and severed the webbing so that their hands and feet look like they do today. Out of the depths of time the people began searching for the middle place where they could live. In this search, at one point, they were crossing a lake they called Whispering Springs Lake when some of the infants squirmed loose and fell into the lake and drowned. When the people found the middle place they were mourning the loss of the children. Then the first kachinas came to the village and danced and explained they were the spirits of the dead children and they were living in a village at the bottom of the lake. But when they returned to the lake it was their wish to take someone with them. After that a life had to be sacrificed every time they came to the village. Eventually they reached an agreement that the Zuni could make kachina masks and, when they put on the masks for a dance, the kachinas would come to life but would no longer require anyone to return with them to their village at the bottom of the lake.

The "impersonator" had to make proper offerings including elaborately decorated prayer sticks planted at shrines and on the shores of the lake, and the masks had to be treated with reverence and ceremonially fed with corn meal. The kachinas represent or impersonate the great mysteries of life; these are the spirits of the ancestors and the spirits of the forces of nature, primarily the clouds, the stars, the Corn Mother and the six directions. They believe we share the same breath with all of nature, with the rocks, the trees, the water, all the animals, everything. The kachinas evoke the powers of all these mysterious forces and enlist them to help in this journey and in the transition that takes places when it is over. They are intermediaries, messengers, representatives, even psychopomps of the invisible mysterious forces that govern this life and this universe. The kachina's main role has to do with fertility and fecundity. The kachinas are mysterious invisible forces, they are the great beings who personify these forces, and the masks that represent these beings, and the people wearing the masks, and the carved images of these beings. They can be animistic, anthropomorphic, mythological beings with beaks and horns. They can have abstract artistic representations as clouds, as stars and as lightning. They can be part human, part animal or part bird. When a dancer dons a mask that person is transformed and transfigured. They are invested with mysterious powers. They manifest the invisible forces of the cosmos to become the spirit of the clouds and the winds and the very breath of life. This is the animating source of life itself, it is the inherent power of the universe to transform itself and bring forth life and awareness at all levels of presentation.

An anthropological paper published in 1929 by The Bureau of American Ethnology at the Smithsonian [2] reported there were six "cults" at Zuni. It said the kachina cult was the predominant of the six and that it had "beautiful and spectacular ceremonies" which all the men took part in, unlike some of the other cults which are specific to some clans or groups. Kachinas came to the people on special days to dance for their "daylight" fathers who feed them sacrificial foods and communicated with feathered prayer sticks. The first kachinas were humans who died and became ancestors and now when a Zuni dies they go to live in the kachina village and become kachinas themselves.

Maskology is the study of the veneration, through impersonation, of these supernatural beings. Another story tells that the first kachinas were the spirits of humans who were sacrificed as offerings for the mysterious forces of the world. When a Zuni passes away they become kachinas, although there is not a person-to-person correspondence and no one kachina can be identified with any individual person. The kachinas are also associated with thunderclouds. The powers of the kachinas are inherent in the masks which, when worn in a ceremony, become the kachina and are treated with complete reverence. They believe the masks have the very substance of death and if anyone dons a mask other than for ceremonial purposes they will die, in some cases choked by the mask itself.

The people believe the kachinas are affectionate and kind to the Zuni. They enjoy coming to the village and dressing up and dancing with the people. But the kachinas can quarrel among themselves and end up meddling in human affairs and squabbling over the feathers offered to them on solstices. Pautiwas is the leader of the kachinas and determines the timing of all the dances. If the people want to schedule a ceremony they must bring prayer sticks and plant them on the shore of the lake four days prior to the dance. Hamokatsik, the mother of the kachinas, prepares their costumes. Kachinas often come unannounced and in disguise to discipline the proud and reward the pious and the outcasts. However, should anyone violate their sanctity or shirk their responsibilities the kachinas can be swift in their punishment and can cause sickness or even death. Before putting on a mask the impersonator must make reverent prayers and once the mask is on, if anyone touches the dancers while they are wearing the regalia of death, it can have dangerous consequences. When the masks are removed the impersonators must go through a ritual bath before they reestablish human contact.

They believe that when the mask is worn the person wearing it is transformed into the supernatural being it represents. The mask itself is of great value and protects the person who wears it. The mask actually secures the owner a proper venue in the afterlife. Each mask represents a priest of the kachina village. Some masks are ancient and are the property of the village. Newer masks are the individual property of their maker who must keep it in a sealed container with proper ritual and respect and with sacrifice of food for the kachina village and for all the ancestors. When it is put away the wearer must plant prayer sticks and refrain from sex for four days. Each person of any means owns a mask which is used at the dances and is distinct from the priestly masks. These individual masks are created as soon as a person has the means so that he can dance in his own mask. When he dies it is dismantled and buried with him so that he will have it to use in the kachina village.

When a new mask is created the maker sings a song,

"Now I have given you life
Bless us with your spirit
Call the rains for us
Now it is finished
I have made you into a person." [3]

The mask has powers of transformation. It transubstantiates into the presence of the supernatural so that the mask corporeally is the god. Having a mask in your house is considered a good thing, it can be a source of supernatural protection and succor.   To make a mask is no simple undertaking. It is a costly, time-consuming process and once the mask is done the new owner is called to the kiva where he goes through a ritual beating by the four leaders of the kiva who take long branches of yucca and whip him four blows on each arm, four on his chest and four on each leg. After the kiva chiefs give him a full round of blows his family shows up and brings a feast of Zuni stew and bread. The new owner takes the first bites of the food and offers it to the "people of the sacred lake". After the feast the head kiva priest takes some of the food to the river and, as he sends the food into the current, he recites a prayer telling the koko they are sending a "new person" to the village. The next day the man dances in the mask for the first time.

Others report that kachinas are venerated at all the pueblos except Taos. The remaining pueblos believe in these supernatural beings who live in nearby lakes or in the mountains. The kachinas call the rain. All adult males go through initiation where they are whipped to teach them to know the kachinas. The masks are used during elaborate rituals involving offerings of corn meal, prayer sticks, altars and shrines, sexual abstinence and music and dance.

The next morning Susan and I stood under the small tree in the courtyard of The Inn at Halona waiting for Otto. The Inn at Halona is the only place to stay on the Zuni pueblo and there are just a few rooms. We had blue corn pancakes at the breakfast table and sat with a couple from Texas who were Buddhist and we talked about the Dalai Lama and our trip to Tibet in 2011. Once we got outside Otto showed up and we loaded into his truck and went to the visitor's center to get our photo permit. Just as we arrived the guy who runs the tourist business for the tribe pulled up – Tom Kennedy. We looked at the books and got a nice t-shirt with a Zuni design, paid ten dollars for the photo permit and headed out.

HAWIKKU

We were going to the ruins at Hawikku. I asked Otto what the word Hawikku means and he said it means a bundle of weeds wrapped or tied up, like a sage bundle. Otto remarked how difficult it is for an Indian to start a business. That when it comes to business dealings Zuni are not as aggressive about making profit and they have little money to start a business and getting a loan is nearly impossible. The principles of capitalism are just not compatible with Indian ways. He said if you do it get off the ground and start making money then a whole horde of relatives and relatives of relatives descend on you each needing money and it is very bad form not to give them the money. Susan was interested in how the land on the reservation is divided or used by the tribal members. Otto said the whole reservation is held in a trust status with designated lots passing on from generation to generation in the same family.

It is a short drive to Hawikku which is at the end of a deeply rutted old dirt road that is washed out at one spot so Otto had to drive around on an improvised roadway. Then he parked on a knoll overlooking a broad valley and we were there. I jumped out of the truck and there, right beside where he parked, are a couple of red sandstone boulders about a foot tall and both of them are covered with pottery shards that have been gathered from the site. The site consists of a series of small knolls that are obviously the ruins of the buildings that once stood here. Some of the buildings were three or more stories tall. The ground is covered with pottery shards, many of them with fragments of design work, some red, some black, some brown. Frederick Webb Hodge [4] did the excavation starting in 1917 and his field notes remark that the number of pottery shards littering the ground were more intense at Hawikku than any other ruins he had visited. The same seems to hold true today. We worked our way out to the end of the ridge and looked across the valley toward the low hills in the distance.

I had acquainted myself with the history of this place since it is one of those rare sites where we know first contact was made between the invading Spanish and the natives. When Coronado was appointed governor of the provinces in northern Mexico he took with him Fray Marcos de Niza and Esteban de Dorantes. Esteban was a black Moor who had survived incredible adventures. He was part of a crew that was shipwrecked in 1528 on an expedition to explore Florida. As they approached the coast they ran into a hurricane and lost their ships. They were immediately attacked and quickly built rafts hoping to make their way around the coast to Mexico. The rafts were a disaster and all but four of the survivors of the hurricane died. Those four were Cabeza de Vaca, Dorantes and Castillo Maldonado along with a slave of Dorantes, the black Moor named Esteban. De Vaca wrote a famous report about their adventures that still makes good reading.

They made their way along the coast of Texas and into Mexico and finally went south far enough to find a Spanish settlement. They were the first Spanish to report about the Native Americans of the Gulf Coast and the first to see a buffalo. Along the way they heard reports from the local Indians about large cities with multistoried buildings in the deserts of the Southwest. They also heard that these cities contained great wealth. When they wandered into the first Spanish settlement in Mexico they were quickly escorted to Mexico City to report to the governor and written reports were send back to the King.

When Coronado was appointed governor he took Esteban with him from Mexico City. Esteban was still a slave and had been purchased from Dorantes by Mendoza so that he would help lead the way to the "Seven Cities of Gold". Fray Marcos was recruited to lead the expedition. He was a French speaking Savoyard who had been in Peru in 1534 just after the conquest by Pizarro. In 1536 he moved on to Guatemala and then to Mexico City in 1537 and from there he accompanied Coronado to his new office in Nuevo Galicia. Coronado quickly put him in charge of an entourage of about 600 local Indian warriors from Sonora and he and his newly-acquired slave Esteban were commissioned to explore beyond the northern edge of his territory. Coronado accompanied them to the northern boundary of the territory and sent them on their way.

Hawikku is the site where Fray Marcos' guide, Estaban, which would be translated as Stephen in English, made first contact with the Zuni in 1539. Hawikku was the name of one of the six cities of the Zuni at that time – all six of them lined up along the Zuni River. It was Cushing who figured out that these ruins were the place where Estaban, leading the way for Fray Marcos, made the fabled first contact. Otto tells us the ruins were excavated around 1920 and have been backfilled to protect them and at that time they discovered a number of graves. One of them had bones of a man much taller than the Zunis and those may have been the bones of Estaban. Otto said that the people let Estaban set up camp just outside the village but that he made constant demands on the people in an arrogant way and wanted a different Zuni woman each night and they quickly got fed up with him and killed him. The Indian guides with him returned to Fray Marcos and reported the death of Estaban. The Fray claimed he only came close enough to see the village from a distance. Otto says the people used to put corn on the roofs to dry and that it made the village look like it had roofs of gold and that he must have seen that because he reported the people had gold and silver and turquoise. At its height Hawikku consisted of six separate buildings. It was the largest of the six villages occupied by the Zuni in 1540 when Coronado arrived. It is estimated that it held about 700 inhabitants and was founded about 1200 CE.

Looking out across the wide plain it wasn't hard to imagine the multistoried pueblo behind us with a cadre of warriors standing in front of it, where we now stood, watching Coronado's approach across the flat floor of the valley. Otto pointed to the place, off to the southwest, where there is a break in the distant ridgeline where Coronado's army came through. The armored horsemen in the front were armed with an early form of firearms called arbutuses. These were as intimidating as tanks and armored vehicles are today. Coronado stopped at the base of the hill just outside the pueblo and had a priest come forward with a translator to read the demand from the King that they surrender and become his subjects. This included the warning, "If, you do not do as I ask or you maliciously delay, I assure you, with the help of God, I will attack you mightily. I will make war against you everywhere and in every way I can. And I will subject you to the yoke and obedience of the Church and His Majesty. I will take your wives and children and I will make them slaves. As such, I will sell and dispose of them as His Majesty will order. I will take your property. I will do all the harm and damage to you that I can, treating you as vassals who do not obey and refuse to accept their lord and resist and oppose him. I declare that the deaths and injuries that occur as a result of this would be your fault and not His Majesty's, nor ours, nor that of the soldiers who have come with me." [5] This was greeted with a hail of arrows. Coronado's overwhelming forces made short work of the Zuni warriors who retreated to Corn Mountain after nearly killing Coronado with rocks thrown down from the roofs of the pueblo.

Looking out over the plain I felt a shiver go down my back. This was one of those times in history that marked the first contact between two irreconcilable forces. The Zuni surely knew what was coming, they had commerce deep inside Mexico and knew that the Spanish had occupied the country. They had traveled to surrounding tribes that knew very well the existence of horses and armor and firearms at the Spanish disposal. Now it was here in front of them. They knew these were not supernatural beings but were humans with weaponry far more advanced than their flint-tipped arrows. The Spanish were blinded by greed that had been fed by the incredible riches of Peru and Mexico and assumed they would find more of the same at the pueblos. They were driven by a misshapen religious evangelism that would go to any lengths in the name of religious conversion. To the Spanish the indigenous cultures were a resource to be exploited for tribute and slave labor. The Zuni clearly saw the Spanish as an invading force that would irrevocably alter their culture and lifestyle. They were determined to withstand the onslaught and have done so from then until now. It was the forceful eclipse of one culture by another, enforced with incredible torture and violence, with the assumption of complete dictatorial power. The decree they read at the foot of the hill was no idle threat and the Zuni knew it. For their part they used strategic retreat. The population at large had already moved to the top of Corn Mountain and once the warriors were driven out of Hawikku they joined the rest of the tribe and negotiated from their stronghold.

I found a detailed line drawing by an architect who had studied the reports from the excavations. Otto and Susan and I studied it and oriented it to see how and where the building stood on the end of the ridge. We could plainly distinguish where each of the main buildings had once stood. We examined each of the mounds with the drawing in hand and stood in the ancient plaza which is still clearly discernible. On one of the mounds a baby rattlesnake slithered across the ground and disappeared into a hole, little brother death, black eyes fixed and empty harboring eons of night, a forked tongue testing the desert air. At the edge of one of the mounds I saw something black and picked it up. It was about the size of a large grapefruit and when I looked at it I could see grains of corn. It was a blackened burned hunk of corn from a storeroom. When the village was destroyed by an Apache attack around 1670 the Apache burned the entire pueblo. The excavation field notes indicated they found rooms full of charred corn in some places over five feet deep. I could hardly believe that parts of it were still surfacing. I showed it to Otto and Susan. Each mound was composed of loose heaps of sandstone that had been the walls of the buildings. In a couple of places there were small fragments of walls still intact and on the top of the mounds you could see the outlines of the rooms plainly visible.

There are cattle grazing in the wide fields at the base of the hill where we are standing and there are cattle fences to keep them out of the ruins. I ask about the cattle and Otto says the cattle farmers can lease fields for their herds. He says his grandfather had big herds of cattle and went off to fight in WW II and came back and the government had cut his herds in half saying that the Zuni were overgrazing their land. The government agents told the Zuni they had the authority to order them to cut their herds back according to a formula so that only so many cattle per acre were allowed and in many cases this meant they had to cut their herds in half or more. His grandfather had been considered rich by Zuni standards and went off to serve his country and came back to find half his wealth taken away by the government. And while he was away he learned to drink and became addicted and when he got home he couldn't stop and, as a result, he lost the rest of his herds.

I had copies of some of the photos taken during the excavations by Hodge in 1917 and we stood there and studied them. With a bit of orientation we were able to find the exact spot where the photos were taken and see where the building being excavated at that time had stood. Hodge had unearthed graves and sent the bones to museums in DC and NYC where they apparently remain to this day, to the disgust of Otto.

Coronado had wintered at Hawikku in 1539-40 and had stopped again on the way back to Mexico after his expedition up the Rio Grande and into the plains. After that the Zuni were left in relative peace until nearly 1600 when the Spanish assumed control of all the pueblos and soon thereafter they were forced to build a mission church at Hawikku. The remains of it are still visible at the foot of the hill.

Hodge found some wooden combs that were inlaid with turquoise and these are now in the museum in the village. Otto remarked how the ancients knew enough of the jewelry arts to inlay turquoise. We were continually picking up pottery pieces and finding pieces with different colors and intricate designs.

Standing at the center of the ruins Otto tells us the story about when a famine hit. It got so bad that the parents of a boy and girl left them in the pueblo and went off to a neighboring village to try to get some food. The kids were scared and the boy made a dragonfly out of corn husks and sprinkled corn meal on it and it came alive and flew off. They followed it and it led them to their parents. Since that time the dragonfly has been a special image associated with Hawikku. An abstract butterfly design can be found as one of the motifs on the pottery they excavated at Hawikku.

We could discern the Zuni River meandering through the plain in the distance defined by a line of willow trees. I asked Otto how far down the river it was to Whispering Lake, where the kachinas had their village before the lake dried up. He said it was about thirty miles and that the place where the Zuni think the Kachinas live now, what he called Zuni heaven, is near where the lake had been.

Otto told us how he made a pilgrimage to the Grand Canyon. The Zuni legends report that when the first Zunis came out of the ground they were in the Grand Canyon so he went there to be at that spot and to make offerings. He climbed all the way down to the bottom of the canyon and had cornmeal and prayer sticks. The prayer sticks were made to carry his prayers to the ancestors. He said the cornmeal is a good food for the dead and they appreciate having it, so he offered cornmeal to his parents who are both gone.

I ask, "Do you go to their graves to make the offerings?'

"No," he says, "I do it whenever I feel like it and it doesn't matter where."

Hawikku doesn't take up much space. Only a few acres at most. There was a book written incorporating Hodge's field notes into a manuscript. Hodge had intended to write it himself but died before he finished. The book is a fascinating account. Hodge hired a crew of Zuni diggers and one of them was Pedro Pina, a highly respected member of the tribe. They provided Hodges with insights into the items they were digging up. They identified the artifacts and indicated those that were ceremonial. They dug up hundreds of graves and found the Zuni often buried their dead with food offerings in the graves. Some graves were nearly filled with corn, some with seeds of other plants like gourds or wild seeds that were part of their diet, and some had a thick layer of pollen over the body. They found several crystals, along with lots of turquoise and shell beads. When they excavated the buildings they found rooms filled with corn, many of them with the corn charred by the final conflagration that destroyed the village around 1670. They found lots of pottery, both in the graves and in the various rooms of the pueblo. The book has beautiful line drawings of the pots as if you are looking down at the pottery from above and the graphic designs are incredibly beautiful, swirling patterns that are eye dazzlers with psychedelic patterns that have an intricate intensity and artfulness in the flow of the lines. In one room they found a life-sized statue. The upper body was ceramic and the lower body was a mannequin. There is a picture of it in the book, it is stylized and primitive and abstract yet primordially human.

We walked through the whole site from back to front and then around the perimeter and then back to the center where we could clearly distinguish the plaza and then it seemed we had covered the whole site. It was hard to leave. The sky was a clear blue, the view to the south and west was open with a distant horizon, behind us a desert landscape covered with low scrub. I reluctantly climbed into the truck for the ride back.

LITERARY ARCHAEOLOGY

There is a wealth of literature starting with the earliest chronicles of first contact. As more and more information becomes available the pictures continue to be filled out. The literary archaeology of Hawiku includes the reports from the excavations, along with information from other ancient sites of the Zuni, and then the information gleaned from the chronicles of the Coronado entrada and the rest of the various missions that followed, and finally the great hoard of ethnographic information starting with Cushing.

When the Spanish invaded the Zuni territory they had a very organized bureaucracy that maintained written records and reports that had to be sent back to Spain to apprise the court of everything they discovered. As a result there is an incredible paper trail of documents that detail every move they made. These documents provide firsthand accounts of the first contact with the Zuni. Richard and Shirley Cushing Flint have done a remarkable job of scholarship in bringing all the documents that mention the exploration of Zuni together in a large book called, *Documents of the Coronado Expedition, 1539 to 1542*. These include the accounts of Fray Marcos, the first Spaniard sent to make contact with the Zuni, several accounts of Coronado's entrada, a letter written by Coronado while he was still at Zuni and several others that illuminate different aspects of the entrada. Looking at the observations of the Spanish chroniclers, prejudiced and chauvinistic as they are, still provides the first glimpse into the life of the people as they are thrust into history.

Events unfolded rapidly. Columbus landed in 1492 and on his subsequent voyages he established his capital in Cuba. From there the next generation of Spanish conquistadors fanned out in all directions. They explored the geography and figured out the boundaries of Florida, Mexico and South America. They captured Indians wherever they landed, tortured them and sought out the largest cities and any treasures they could capture. They quickly learned about the riches of Peru and the great capital of the Aztec nation. By the 1530s they had taken advantage of their vastly superior weapons of war and their horses to conquer both Cusco and Mexico City and with it they hauled off riches far beyond anything they could have imagined and established themselves, with Royal sanction from the Spanish court, as rulers of a vast domain.

The Spaniards who had taken part in the conquests of Peru and Mexico naturally assumed there were other cities filled with comparable riches in other parts of this great unexplored expanse. By the late 1530s they were vying for Royal permission to lead great armies of conquest to raid the presumed untapped riches of these undiscovered countries. Desoto won the right to go to Florida and Coronado got the royal nod to invade the lands north of Mexico. It was like a land rush of speculation where everyone wanted to take part. These conquistadors took their booty from Peru and from the Aztecs and invested it in these new ventures. fully expecting to find even greater wealth in these new lands. Both Coronado and Desoto were to become completely disillusioned. Desoto died on his venture but not before covering a great territory and being the first European to see the great mound builder civilization that ruled over southeastern North America. It is remarkable how much devastation one person can wreak. Desoto's invasion force marked the end of a whole cultural tradition that occupied a significant section of the southeastern United States. The military invasion certainly had its effect but it was the plagues that followed that were the most devastating. It was nearly a hundred years before any other Europeans came into the southeast and during that time wave after wave of plague swept across the continent and there are estimates that up to ninety per cent of the population died as a result. The survivors gathered together and consolidated into what we now call the Seven Civilized Tribes and, in 1838, most of them were moved west of the Mississippi in the infamous Trail of Tears.

Coronado was the rich son of a minor official in the court of Spain. Vazquez de Coronado arrived in the New World in 1535 along with the new viceroy of the northern-most reaches of the Spanish empire, a man named Antonia de Mendoza. Coronado was a native of Salamanca, Spain where his father was chief administrator in 1515 and was close to the Mendoza family. In 1537 Coronado got his first assignment when Mendoza sent him to quell an uprising of blacks and Indians at a silver mine southwest of Mexico City. He accomplished his mission by executing the perpetrators in the most extreme manner: he had them drawn and quartered. In 1536 he married Beatriz de Estrada, daughter of the former royal treasurer and received a dowry of extensive land holdings. In 1538 he became governor and judge of Nueva Galicia on the far northwest edge of Mexico. This province had been conquered with great cruelty by Beltran de Guzman. He was assigned to investigate these cruelties and issued a finding favorable to Guzman. The impact of his entrada changed forever the way of life for the pueblo Indians and the other tribes in the Southwest. But it did not have the overwhelmingly destructive impact of Desoto's expedition. Coronado had a chronicler who wrote a detailed account of the invasion, and Coronado himself wrote letters back to the King, the first one while he was still at the Zuni pueblo. In it he reported, "They are not familiar with His Majesty, nor do they wish to be his subjects."

FIRST CONTACT - FROM PREHISTORY TO HISTORY

Coronado had some idea of what to expect during his invasion. A person named Malchior Diaz had been sent by Mendoza to seek information about the possibility of wealth in the Indian cities to the north. He went north but when he hit the Sierra Madre Mountains he was stopped by the severe winter weather and turned back. But he did manage to interrogate the Indian population who informed him about a place called Cibola. He found informants who claimed to have been there many times. He wrote a letter to the King describing his findings. He reported that there were buildings at Cibola three and four stories high. He was told they eat human flesh. And those whom they capture in war are kept as slaves and finally that they have large quantities of corn, beans and melons. He learned they wear head scarves and have turquoise jewelry. They had cotton cloth and made earthenware vessels and lived in numerous scattered villages that were included in Cibola. He thus gained the distinction of being the first European to write about Zuni. Next came Fray Marcos who wrote a report of his expedition in 1539 and described what he saw and heard. He had Estaban lead a band of three hundred warriors. Estaban was traveling with "a beautiful woman which the Indians had given him" and many turquoise stones. He dressed in native dress and had a gourd decorated with bells and red and white feathers. He had natives from Mexico who had been to Hawikku, the first Zuni village north of Mexico, and they knew the way and served as guides. As he was coming near he sent two of his native warriors ahead of his troops with his gourd. It seems that a gourd was considered a special talisman.

This gourd had quite a history. When Cabeza de Vaca and Estaban and their two companions were making their way across Texas the natives had given them two gourds that were used as rattles, decorated and filled with tiny pebbles. De Vaca reports that they were "instruments for the most important occasions, produced only at dances or to effect cures, which none dare touch except those who own them. They say there is a virtue in them, and because they do not grow in the area they say they come from the heavens." He says these gourds, "added to our authority and were a token highly reverenced by the Indians which had been our principle insignia and evidence of rank." [6] The two advance guard Indians informed the chief that Estaban was coming and gave him the gourd as a token of his approach. The Zuni chief was well aware of their approach and took the gourd and threw it to the ground, "with much wrath and anger". The chief told them that if they continued toward the village they would kill them. When they reported this back to Estaban he replied that he was not deterred as this had often been the case in his previous travels as well. So he and his troops proceeded to the village of Hawikku.

When he arrived they put him in a building outside the village and stripped him of all the goods and turquoise he had carried with him. He told the Zuni, "that behind him were coming two white men, sent by a great lord, men who were well versed in the things of heaven, and they were coming to instruct them about things divine". [7] The Zuni weren't buying it and believed they were coming to conquer them. They held Estaban for three days, interrogating him. Then they killed him. Reports vary but they may have also killed many of his retinue, while at least some of the people traveling with him returned to find Fray Marcos. The Zuni immediately sent word to all the other pueblos that the men coming up from the south should not be treated as gods.

The friar reported that survivors of the massacre came back carrying a message from the Zuni chief that, "they must go back immediately or else not a man of them will remain alive". It stopped him on the spot; he was afraid for his life. He was carrying a variety of gifts to give the Zuni and he immediately dispersed them to the Indians in his entourage and prepared to return to Mexico. Yet something apparently changed his mind and he writes that he "begged some of them to go to Cibola to find out whether any other Indian had escaped and that I had to see the ciudad of Cibola". He goes on, "I continued on my way until I was within sight of Cibola. It is situated in a plain, on the lower slope of a round hill. As a town it has a very handsome appearance, the best I have seen in this region...the settlement is grander than the Ciudad de Mexico". He says that he had positioned himself on a hill where he could see the "houses all made of stone with their upper stories and flat roofs". Justifying himself that, if he went on they would surely kill him, and then he wouldn't be able to make this report. He turned back and hightailed it for Mexico. He wrote that he "erected a large mound of stones there with the help of the Indians. On top of it I set a small, thin cross, and declared that the cross and the mound were being erected in token of possession in the name of don Antonio de Mendoza, viceroy and governor of Nueva Espanaqne on behalf of the Emperor, that by this act I was taking possession of all the seven ciudades...so I turned around, with very much more fear than food. I traveled as quickly as I could across the whole distance." [8] He immediately returned to Coronado who directed him to write his report. This is a highly unlikely account since there are no mountains in the vicinity of Hawikku that would provide such a view and everything he reported he knew from reports of the Indian guides who had years of experience visiting and trading with Hawikku. These guides told other tales of populous areas further to the north where there was gold, emeralds and precious stones and the dishes were made of silver and houses decorated with gold.

After seven months on the trail the friar reported to Coronado and then to Mendoza and, while the news was not what they expected, it none-the-less set off a flurry of speculation and preparations for an invasion force. Rumors circulated that the Seven Cities of Gold had been found. There were a number of contenders to lead the force but Coronado was able to best even Cortes and at age twenty-nine was appointed to lead an invasion force to conqueror what was then known as Cibola. News of Fray Marcos' expedition set off a sensation in Mexico. The Fray described Cibola as "a wealthy and populous place" and indicated he had seen it only from a distance. The expedition was financed largely by Mendoza and Coronado. Coronado's stake in the expedition was based on the wealth of his wife. They invested heavily and obviously expected great returns.

Coronado recruited 358 Spaniards, 6 priests and over 1,300 Indians plus an unknown number of slaves and servants. This comprised six companies with 127 horsemen. Coronado himself had seven slaves, four men and three women. At least 45 of the men had helmets and armor. They also took large herds of cattle, hogs and horses so the whole entourage must have been quite impressive on the move. They traveled along the trail established by Fray Marcos, who accompanied them. When they were nearing Zuni they encountered their first hostilities. Coronado decided to go ahead of the main troops with 75 horsemen, a few footmen and over a thousand native warriors so this was not a small contingent of Europeans facing off a hostile force of indigenous warriors. They came in force and used advanced weapons, horses and an overwhelming force of mercenary Indian fighters.

In 1540 Coronado wrote a letter to Mendoza reporting on his progress. The letter was written from Zuni about thirty days after his arrival. In it he gives his report on the details of the battle at Hawikku. He claims that when he arrived at Hawikku he sent two Indians into the pueblo ahead of his force carrying a cross to negotiate a peaceful settlement. They quickly returned and told him to prepare for war. He then sent his maestre de campo don Garcia Lopez and one of the priests to approach the village with an interpreter. They were to read aloud the "requerimiento", the formal demand from the King of Spain ordering them to become his subjects.

When he grouped his troops on the plain in front of the village he was attacked by two hundred warriors who were defending the pueblo. He reports that the Indians quickly retreated into the villages where they continued shooting arrows at his troops from the roofs of the flat-topped buildings. Coronado responded with crossbows and arquebuses. Coronado led the assault into the village and nearly lost his life when the Indians threw down large stones from the upper rooftops. Because his armor was different from everyone else's he made a distinctive target and it was only by the intervention of two of his soldiers that he escaped being killed. The battle lasted only one day and the Zuni retreated, leaving the Spanish to take over Hawikku. He reported that he only lost two men killed and three wounded. He also said that three horses were killed and eight wounded.

The Zuni have a detailed oral account of the Coronado invasion that is still remembered. They report that Coronado came with over three hundred Spanish soldiers, many of them on horseback, along with hundreds of native warriors and a few Catholic priests, along with huge herds of cattle and sheep. The Zuni knew they were coming and monitored them as they approached their land. They launched their first attack in a narrow canyon where the Zuni River meets the Little Colorado River. They continued to harass them with guerilla tactics until they reached Hawikku. Here they were met with a force of six hundred Zuni warriors. The Zuni were very well organized by their War Chiefs, who used horns and smoke signals to direct the battles. They report they drove back the first assault by the Spanish on the village with the loss of twenty warriors and had a large number of wounded in what was their first battle against firearms and horses. While the Spanish were regrouping, the Zuni abandoned the villages and retreated to the top of Corn Mountain where they negotiated a peace settlement and moved back into their pueblos.

Coronado's chroniclers say he quickly made peace with the other villages and stayed at Hawikku from July, 1540 to December before he moved on to the Rio Grande area around what is now Albuquerque. Fray Marcos was with him and in the letter he reported that Marcos had, "not spoken the truth in anything he said. Instead, everything has been quite contrary." When Coronado realized that there was no gold or silver he, and everyone with him, was severely distraught and blamed Marcos for his reporting. They seriously questioned whether he had actually seen the place or had exaggerated his claims. As a result Marcos quickly headed back to Mexico, leaving Coronado to continue his travels. Marcos apparently was ostracized and his reputation was in ruins until his death in 1558.

Coronado described the villages as "very good houses, of three, four and five stories. In them there are good lodgings, rooms with galleries, and some underground rooms that are very excellent and paved". He described Hawikku as having two hundred houses with a total of five hundred hearths and reported "they have turquoise in quantity". He said they grow corn, beans and eat small game and that they have, "the best tortillas I have seen anywhere...and have excellent granular salt". [9] He stopped by again on his way back to Mexico. After that the Zuni were left more or less to themselves until Juan de Onate arrived in 1598. There were other expeditions that visited without trying to establish a permanent base; Chamuscado and Rodriguez came to Zuni in 1581; Espejo in 1583; then Onate in 1598 and again in 1604-05; and Zaldivar in 1599. Coronado returned to Mexico severely disappointed and deep in debt. He eventually petitioned the King to try to recoup some of his losses and died in 1554 at age 43.

It wasn't long before the Spanish were in firm control of Zuni. By 1629 the Zuni were forced to start construction on two churches, one at Hawikku and the other at Halona. The church at Hawikku was called Mission La Purisim Concepcion. The Zuni did not appreciate the continuing payments of tribute to the priests and in 1632 the two priests in the area were killed. The Zuni, expecting retaliation, abandoned the villages and lived on Corn Mountain for the next three years until the Spanish negotiated for their return to the villages. The church was subsequently rebuilt in 1650 but suffered repeated attacks from the Apache. In 1670 Apache attacked Hawikku and burned the church and killed many of the residents. This marked the end of Hawikku. All that remains are the few mounds of loose stone debris littered with pottery shards we find today.

In 1680 the Zuni joined the pueblo revolt and killed or chased out all the Spanish, who returned with a vengeance in 1692. Once again the Zuni moved to Corn Mountain to escape the extreme cruelty of the Spanish who used crushing brutality with all the pueblos. When they decided to come out of the mountains they built one large village instead of going back to the six smaller villages they had before. And to this day they still reside in that village.

Since Zuni is in the middle of a desert and travel was difficult they were, to some extent, left to themselves. Remarkably, the Spanish gave them legal title to their land which helped immensely when they had to start dealing with the American government after 1848. This gave them a unique legal standing since they were one of the very few North American tribes that had legal documentation for the ownership of their land. As a result they, still to this day, live on the same land where the Fray first discovered them in 1539.

Driving back from Hawikku we came up over a low hill and there in front of us was the place they call Twin Mesas, two similarly shaped huge mesas standing side by side. We stopped the truck and got out to take pictures and enjoy the view. Otto said we would be going there later to see petroglyphs in the vicinity of the twin mesas.

Back at the village we dropped Susan off at the Inn. She was interested in hearing a presentation about the murals in the old mission. The man who painted them was giving a lecture in the mission at 3:00 and it was already afternoon so it was obvious that we couldn't make it out to the petroglyphs and be back in time for the lecture so she decided to stay in the village and visit the shops and hear the presentation.

Otto wanted some lunch so we went in the grocery store beside the Inn where they have a little deli with a few tables in the back of the store. I looked at the food, all of it fried, with big trays of chicken and potato wedges and Otto and I sat at one of the tables in the back of the store, there on the wall by the table was a small metal plaque that had the name of a former patron who had eaten there every day. Otto said the man was extremely obese and died of a heart attack.

TWIN MESAS

Otto and I loaded up in his truck and took off. Just west of the village we turned north on a dirt road and in just a few minutes the twin mesas loomed large on the eastern horizon. And there between the two mesas was something that I had not seen from the distance, a large monolith, a single pillar of stone rising up from the desert floor, a sheer, narrow stone pinnacle twisting as it rises from between the two mesas. It is a totally unexpected sight. We drove back a dusty dirt road, little more than a path, until we came to a line of red sandstone cliffs about fifty feet tall. Otto says the petroglyphs start here and he drives back along the cliffs quite a ways and parks.

As we walk up to the red sandstone the first petroglyph appears out of the flat stone panel. The sandstone is a uniform orange red and when we were still a few feet away images carved into the stone begin to emerge and come into focus. We slowly move to the left, both of us with our cameras taking pictures, one after another images appear out of the stone. From a distance they are invisible but when you approach the cliff they materialize out of the rock. They are pecked or cut into the red stone and since they have little color gradation they are easily overlooked but as you examine the stone face, more and more of them appear. Some are cut deeply into the stone and stand out dramatically, others are little more than scratches which you have to stare at intently before you can configure them into images. We found no Kokopelli images but many of the standard petroglyph motifs appeared again and again. The spiral and even a double spiral appeared several times and I wondered if any sun daggers appeared on the spirals to mark the solstices or equinox. The twin mesas with the accompanying monolith loom large on the eastern horizon. I could imagine a sun priest coming to this spot to mark the movements of the celestial bodies across the horizon. Then at one spot there is a large stone, about six feet tall that has a dramatic point and this seemed like the natural place for measuring the movement of the sun, the moon and the planets as they rise over the Twin Mesas on the eastern horizon. I suspected this spot was an ancient observatory to measure the cycles of the heavenly bodies. They understood very well the movement of the sun north and south on the horizon, stopping at the solstices with the equinox midway between, and they measured more subtle cycles like the movement of the moon, which makes an 18-year journey along the horizon and back again, and of course the movement of the stars and planets, great wheels within wheels playing out the harmonic patterns of the heliosphere.

At another spot I picked up a black stone about the size of baseball cut in half. It fit perfectly into my hand and I assumed I had found a hammer stone used with an antler or other pointed stone to peck and cut the designs into the cliff face. We found panel after panel, occasionally marred by graffiti of one kind or another. At one spot we found a series of cattle brands carved into the soft red stone. At other places there are people's names and initials interspersed among the petroglyphs. There are antelopes, horses and anthromorphs. Some panels have corn plants, others have voyage lines and some have sun signs and four-pointed stars. We found several big squares filled with abstract lines. In some places the designs were high up where they had to build scaffolds or hang from ropes from above to make the designs. Then at one place there was a big rock on the ground and under one lip of the stone we found a large skeleton that appears to be a big cat. The head was turned away from us with the body stretched out in the space under the stone with a very long tail.

"Are you superstitious?" Otto asks.

"No, not really."

He obviously wanted me to pick up the skull so I reached under the stone and pulled it out. I put it on the rock and we both examined it closely. The skull has long canine teeth and a short cat face. It is bigger than a fox, maybe a small cougar, not a coyote or dog type. I put the skull back in place and aligned it with the backbone and ribs so it was in the natural place. We both marveled at it before passing on.

Before long we came to the end of the cliff where the boulders round out and the cliff face makes a turn. It is a hot day and I am just as glad since I was ready to stop. It is well after three o'clock. I am ready to turn back after taking a hundred or more photos and seeing hundreds of others that I didn't deem dramatic or clear enough to photograph. We walked back to Otto's truck and I climbed back into the truck seat to relax.

As we drove back to the village I watched the twin mesas on my left. They are monumental landmarks that stand out of the desert, plainly visible for miles around on all sides. What a landscape! On the east of the village stands Corn Mountain, a mesa that rivals Fajada Butte at Chaco Canyon for its beauty. Now to the west of the village here are the twin mesas, with an enormous natural megalith between the mesas. And finally, just a few miles to the east of Corn Mountain, is a line of ridges one of which ends with a series of red sandstone pinnacles that reach toward the sky like giant uncapped columns. The landscape is as rich and vibrant here as in the famous Monument Valley, or around Sedona, or Taos where they have the Rio Grande gorge, the great granite mountain overlooking the pueblo and the deserts filled with sage.

MODERN POTTERY

Otto arranged for us to meet a potter who had agreed to make me a pot with a traditional design. He took me to the potter's house and we parked and walked through a complex of trailers and houses to his home. He came out to greet us and said his name was Carlos. He took us into the living room. His mother was also home. He brought out several of his pots and said he was getting ready to go to a show. He had about a dozen pieces, some with handles made of three strands of clay woven together, most of them with the house of the deer design.

Then I pulled out the two sheets of paper I had sent Otto with traditional designs and asked if he could make one with the design I had circled. He said yes, no problem. He pointed out the design features which he said represented clouds and rain. I was surprised since the designs are totally abstract and have no resemblance to clouds or rain.

Then he brought out a cardboard box and it had his tools and samples of all his clays and paints. He showed me a chunk of white clay and let me hold it. He said he got it here at Zuni not far from the village. It is hard as stone. Otto takes it and puts his tongue to it. He indicated I should do the same so I do. It has a smooth distinct taste of a wild elemental earth flavor, not exactly sweet but deeply nostalgic, eerily familiar. Carlos says that in the old days this type of clay was used like we use sheetrock and the interior walls of the adobe buildings were plastered with a thick coat of this white clay. Otto says he can remember going to houses that had it as a kid and he and the other kids would go up to the walls and lick them. He said it is still used as medicine by some people. Carlos says that when he goes to gather it he has to crawl back into a small hole and when he gets back in there it opens up into a small room and the walls are so white that he doesn't need any other light. I can see it in my mind's eye and marvel at the vision of the subterranean room with its own inner illumination.

He shows me other clay he gathers over by Acoma and then a couple of stones that come from Corn Mountain. One is a piece of mica. He brings out a stone bowl that appears to be a broken grinding stone they used in old times to grind corn and he says he uses it to grind the mica and then puts it in the clay to make it sparkle. He also has a couple of other small stones, one that he grinds to make brown paint and one that makes black paint. He describes how he gathers yucca leaves and boils them and uses the yucca paste as a base for the paint he makes to paint the pots. He has a couple of small brushes that he made himself. He says he buys little brushes and pulls out all the bristles and then uses squirrel fur to make his own brushes. The ends of the brushes are quite long and must be the hair from the tails of the squirrels.

We then discuss the shape of the pot and I ask if he can make the pot for me in the same shape as in the pictures, he says it is hard but that he can. All the pots he has are open bowls and the one I want closes in toward the top with an aesthetically pleasing shape. He goes into the kitchen and brings out a pot that is unfinished that has this same shape. I ask if it is done with coils or if he pours it, he says it is all done by hand using coils of clay which he smoothes and shapes. He shows me two small stones he uses to polish the pots. They are extraordinarily beautiful. Both small, basically pebbles, one about as thick as my little finger. The other even smaller. The longer one is banded, dark brown with lighter brown bands. It is really exquisitely beautiful. The other is a black pebble with a high sheen. They appear gem-like with a gleam that radiates light.

I have been curious about how the potters put the designs on the pots and get them to meet as they go around the circumference of the pot. The designs are all highly intricate and often form both positive and negative images, and it is impossible to tell where the designs start or end in an endless circle of perfect symmetry around the bowl.   He sits the unfinished pot on the little coffee table and stands up over it and shows me how he looks down and says he makes two slight marks on opposite sides of the pot and then from those points he reaches around the pot with one hand on each side to measure half way around and makes another mark and then just uses those marks to place the design on the pot. I am amazed that he can eyeball the pot and place the design on it with such perfect symmetry. Then we discuss the price for my pot and shipping and shake hands on the deal and Otto and I take our leave.

HALONA:WA

Otto and I drive back to the main part of the old village and park in the area where the old five-story adobe building used to sit on the top of the small rise that overlooks the Zuni River. The river is now the ghost of a river marked by a line of small willow trees. We sit in his truck and I pull out a series of old maps. In 1890 an architect named Mindehoff came to the village and did an architectural rendering of the buildings. He took his drawings back to the Smithsonian and made a three-dimensional rendering of the village. I tell Otto about it and we speculate about whether they still have it.

Otto had done a summer internship at the Smithsonian and he told me about going in a warehouse full of old Zuni pots. But he didn't remember seeing the reproduction of the village. So I had Mindehoff's sketch and then another one done in 1915 and then a street map from 1948 and finally an aerial view of the village from 1972. We looked through them in order and watched the evolution of the village. By 1948 all the old adobe buildings were gone. But the mission was there in each of the drawings and served as a point of reference to show how the architecture of the town changed over time. We orient all the various maps to the mission and overlap them to watch how the village changed. In each of the maps we see how the various plazas kept their places. There is the main plaza by the mission but the most mysterious plaza is one that is perfectly square which, in the old village, was totally enclosed with multistoried buildings surrounding it. I asked Otto about it and we looked at some old photos and drawings and I asked him how people got to it and he told me there had been two passageways that were enclosed walkways, like tunnels that led to it and he showed me one of the entrances in an old photo.

We got out of the truck and walked up a narrow alley that leads to this plaza. The alley was littered with dog shit and we had to watch our step. In a little ways the alley leads to a set of stone steps that go to a roof. As I climb up these steps I am surprised, even shocked, to find myself on the roof of a building looking down into the plaza. There it is, the center of the world. I had been studying these maps for the past few weeks and had assumed that this alley, which was easy to see on the 1948 and 1972 maps, led straight into the plaza at ground level and instead I was one story above the plaza looking down into it. It was like stepping back in time. I had seen several drawings done by Cushing showing views down into this plaza with masked dancers in a row, and Zuni people sitting on the edges of the roofs watching the spectacle below. Now I stood here, on the same platform, with a different set of buildings that still look down into the plaza and present stadium seating for the Zuni just as it had since the inception of the village. The plaza appears squared below with abstract panels perpendicular to it and irregularly stepped like a crazed painting by Albers or Escher. It has held this shape and configuration since the first rendering in 1890 and surely long before that, as long as the tribal memory of the Zuni includes this village. The rooftops wrap around the plaza on all four sides with two narrow alleys that lead into it on ground level. The roof where we are standing is lined with metal chairs, all folded and laying down in a row.

"Reserved seating, huh?"

"Yeah, I suppose so." Otto responds.

We walk around the rooftops which connect on three sides of the plaza, taking pictures from every angle. And there, where we walked up, is an old-style ladder poking up through the roof. I point to it and ask if it is a kiva and he nods. There is also a ladder coming up from the plaza. In Cushing's day the governor lived here and the kiva was a shrine. I ask if the governor still lives here but Otto says no. I ask if the shrine is here and he says it is inside one of the houses at ground level. A couple of the buildings are two-story and on the north side the buildings rise three stories, so the image of the plaza in the old drawings with Indians standing and sitting on the roofs of the multistoried buildings is still intact; but, in the old days, some of the buildings were four and five stories.

There is another set of steps at the other end of the building and they lead down to another alley where there is an old dilapidated adobe building with no roof. It appears to be the only adobe building still standing, albeit only barely. We walk down the steps and along the narrow streets that lead out to the old mission. In the back side of the mission there is another plaza, this one even larger.

We walk around the old mission building. The plaza behind the mission is a famous spot that had been photographed in the old days and I have one of the photos and want to get a contemporary photo from the same place to compare them. Otto and I looked at the photo and he showed me where to stand, saying that the old photo was probably taken from a rooftop but we have to settle for ground level. The old pictures taken in this plaza show the old adobe pueblo that framed the plaza climbing up the hill, taking advantage of the rise of the ground to give the buildings a greater sense of height. Otto told how the Catholics had to lease the land where the mission sits and they actually gave up the lease since so few people came to mass and now the church is deteriorating. It is poetic justice that the Catholics had to pay to lease the land since in the early days they enslaved the Zuni and used forced labor to build the original building. When we walk to the back of the mission building we see the outer layer of adobe buckling and starting to fall off in places, and it appears the wall is about to fall down. He said it was affecting the murals inside and there is a lot of controversy about how to preserve the murals. He says the artist is trying to claim the murals for his own and take them down and move them to a museum. But a lot of people aren't happy about that since the tribe paid him to paint them and they can't see how he can claim ownership of something he was already paid to do. The murals depict the kachinas and some people feel it is a sacrilege to depict them and that the murals should be destroyed.

Otto and I wandered the streets with the old maps under my arm, stopping at the other plazas to orient ourselves. We ended up at the top of the little hill, on its knoll. We can plainly see foundation stones from the older buildings that once stood here. They are at ground level and trace the outline of the rooms in the ancient buildings. On the maps this was the part of the pueblo that had five stories stacked one on top of the other.

I call Susan and it turns out she is at a craft store that is only a few blocks away so she comes and joins us. Otto leads us back up the hill, known to the Zuni as the "ant heap", which is the highest point in the village. There are narrow alley-like streets that demarcate the inner geography of the village and when we reach the top of the little hill there is a woman hanging out laundry on a clothesline just outside her house. It is Otto's wife's aunt so Otto takes us over and introduces us. She has three clotheslines almost full of laundry. There is a little boy about two years-old playing at her feet. We have a great view from her yard. You can see the old church just to the east and she shows us a new two-story building sitting just down the slope from her and says it blocks the old view she used to have down into the main plaza beside the mission church.

From time to time we could hear men talking and laughing, their voices drifting over from one of the nearby buildings that had its windows open. She starts telling Otto about all the problems in that part of the pueblo. She points to one of the buildings and says they busted a couple that live there for selling cocaine. That they came out carrying the scale and took them off. She says there are people making crystal meth in the neighborhood. Otto is shocked and later tells me he can't believe they are doing that in the oldest, most sacred part of the pueblo. The little boy with her is really cute and she introduces him but says his mother died when he was only a few months old so she is raising him. She is done with her laundry and we move on, continuing our tour. As we walk down the hill toward where we left Otto's truck we pass a little house and Otto stops and says to wait here. He goes up to the door and knocks and speaks to a woman inside. It turns out he wants to introduce me to the man of the house who has a lot of knowledge regarding the ceremonies but he is out doing chores. There is a big backhoe parked beside the house and it looks incongruous, like a metallic monster from a different age, crouched beside the little house on the slope of the hill. It is almost malevolent, like a time shift that leaves me feelings anxious and nauseous.

We have followed most of the streets and alleyways that divide the buildings into small warrens and at each intersection I pull out the maps to see what has changed in the past hundred and twenty years; the configuration of the streets and plazas are nearly intact but the old buildings have been torn down and rebuilt, some of them several times and now the old adobe structures are extinct, replaced with the red sandstone that still echoes the color of the adobe. There are houses with sloping roofs but most have pueblo-style flat roofs. Otto comments that at some point they started using sloped roofs but they haven't worked out and most of them are in disrepair and are being replaced with flat roofs that fit into the old architectural style of the pueblo.

The sun is getting low and our day is nearing its end. Otto drives us back to the Halona Inn. We agreed to meet for dinner with his family at Chu Chu's. He asks how many of them he should bring and I tell him to bring anyone who cares to come. I realize that Indian families are extended and this could end up being a lot of people but that is fine. I look forward to meeting all of them. We agree to meet at seven as he drops us off. When we get to Chu Chu's Otto and the family are there and have assembled several tables to seat us all. I had hoped for some Zuni stew but the only cook that makes it is not available so we have to deal with the typical menu items. Otto and his wife are there and his oldest son is with him, along with a daughter and her husband and their infant plus Otto's two grandchildren. We do introductions all around and I sit next to his son and get him talking about his life working with the education system on the reservation. He helps the high school kids find financing to go on to college. He has a degree in science and wants to find something more related to his degree but is happy to have a job here at home. He has a child at Acoma and talks about the problems of working with the mother since she lives there and the child is learning Acoma language instead of Zuni. When we leave the moon is high in the sky, its silver light shining on Corn Mountain.

FRANK HAMILTON CUSHING

I had mentioned the early ethnologist, Frank Hamilton Cushing, a number of times and had asked Otto if they still remember him. Otto said that they called him Cushy and told how Cushing was a frail man and they decided to toughen him up and made him sleep on the floor. He said when Cushing left and went back to Washington he took all kinds of things with him including some masks that they had made for him and he posed for pictures wearing a mudhead mask. The old people thought Cushing died an early death because the Kachinas didn't like it and brought about his early demise.

One of the most remarkable occurrences in Zuni history happened in 1879 when Cushing visited Zuni as part of a Smithsonian expedition to study the pueblo culture. The Bureau of Ethnology had just been established as a branch of the Smithsonian and there was, at that time, no academic training in the field. Cushing was marked by genius from his youth and had avoided all formal education due to his fragile health, which plagued him all his life. His desire for knowledge and his focus on Native American culture was an obsession from his earliest days. As a boy he wandered the woods and collected artifacts and took it upon himself to learn how to recreate arrowheads and pottery out of the raw materials he could find at hand. He was also a gifted writer and published his first paper, on the antiquities of upstate New York, at age seventeen. At age nineteen he was hired by the Smithsonian and at twenty-one was sent on the first expedition of the Smithsonian in search of the pueblo Indians.

The rail lines ended at Las Vegas, New Mexico (long before the advent of Las Vegas, Nevada as a gambling capital) where the party proceeded on horses and mules. Cushing was the youngest member of the team and the most rambunctious and he rode ahead exploring ruins on either side of the trail and leading the way. Consequently, he was the first to see the Zuni pueblo in the distance and met a Zuni herder who took his hands as if to shake them and then held them to his face and breathed on them in the time-honored Zuni greeting. So Cushing went on to Zuni and when he arrived at the plaza he likewise took the hands of the elders who greeted him and breathed on them. This opened the door for him as the first visitor to honor their customs, surprising them all.

He was so enraptured with Zuni that, when the expedition returned to Washington, he stayed and lived with the Zunis for four years. During this time he lived in the pueblo, ate Zuni food, wore Zuni clothing, spoke Zuni language, and absorbed the culture. When he first moved in they declared they had to "harden his meat" and forced him to endure fasting and hardships. He was slowly initiated into the rich ceremonial life of the Zuni; he participated in all the dances and was allowed into the kivas where he watched the initiations. He wrote a series of books and articles and was the first anthropologist to go native, for which he was roundly criticized by his academic peers who looked with absolute disdain on the idea of actually living a "primitive" lifestyle, and complained that it compromised his academic credibility.

After nine months living at Zuni, Cushing mastered the language. One of the first things he realized when he was able to speak Zuni was that for each aspect of life, be it cutting fabric to make clothing, building a wall, re-enacting a ceremony or going out hunting, there was an ancient formula, in verse, that was repeated as you did the activity. This served as a form of instruction, like a guidebook, and each person was initiated into this and memorized the instructions as they learned the activity.

In 1881, Cushing received a distinguished visitor from the Hopi nation. Cushing was, by this time, recognized as a Zuni chief and had previously visited the Hopis. The Hopi chief expressed his desire to be friends and when it was time for him to leave Cushing said to him, "May you be happy on your journey to the house of your people and when you are there may you be with your children and your people and live to see each sunset happily as one day succeeds another."

Cushing was able to rise through the ranks of the Zuni tribal chiefdoms and became the First War Chief, a title he used proudly on some of his correspondence with the Smithsonian Institute. In order to be a War Chief you had to kill an enemy in battle and bring back his scalp. Cushing accompanied a Zuni raiding party and returned with the scalp of an Apache; however his scalp was immediately declared ineligible since it was harvested with an iron blade. Then a strategy was devised wherein Cushing was taken into the wilderness where the scalp was hidden; he had to stalk it, and then take it with a flint knife, after which he qualified and was the first, and only, member of the Smithsonian Institute to be a War Chief of the Zuni nation.

At one point Cushing took a contingent of Zuni elders and did a tour of Eastern cities where they caused quite a stir in the local press. The Zuni were also impressed and gathered ocean water to take back to use in their ceremonies. Cushing would appear along with them in his Zuni clothes and act as interpreter.

I found a passage in one of Cushing's books describing how a child born in Zuni was secluded for the first nine days of its life and remained isolated from the world of daylight. On the tenth day it was introduced to the sun. A divination was performed to determine the child's name. The Zuni believed that since all life has form, consequently all form must have life, and that all the forces of nature are derived from some form of life, thus the wind is the breath of a living being. When it is time to have the child's naming ceremony wands are painted with colors symbolic of the various directions and feathers of appropriate colors are tied to the wands. Then the wands are embedded in clay balls and set outside, each in its appropriate direction. During the ritual it is noted which feathers are most agitated by the wind. This indicates the source of the child's totemic ancestor from which it will gain its powers. Later, at the time of puberty, the child goes through a period of purification with isolation, fasting, emetics and purgatives. During this time the child must "still the heart" in order to enhance spiritual perception and gain a sign in a vision from a spiritual guide.

Cushing described how the Zuni had games that all the adults and children played and they believed these games had a divine origin and had been first played by the gods. The games were considered sacred and betting was a religious duty. The games were regulated by the priests and could be played only in certain seasons and only by order of the chief and even then they had to be accompanied by elaborate ceremonies, sacred songs, recitations of ancient instructions and prayers to the sun.

Cushing did all he could to help the Zunis with land disputes and other problems and eventually he crossed a prominent Senator who was involved in a land grab to acquire the rights to Zuni land for big cattle interests that he represented. The Senator threatened to pull the funding for the fledgling ethnology department at the Smithsonian and as a result, in 1884, Cushing was called back to Washington. He eventually led another archaeological expedition to Zuni for the Smithsonian and went on to do archaeological work on a site in Florida, where he unearthed amazing wooden sculptures from a bog. These still remain some of the most exquisite wooden sculptures ever unearthed. He died while still a young man but left an impressive array of writings that are still available.

Cushing wrote a series of articles about Zuni that were published in the early reports of the Smithsonian Institution. These have been collected and reprinted. He wrote one long series of articles titled *Zuni Breadstuffs* which cover Zuni agriculture and food preparation practices, including the myths and ceremonies that accompanied all these activities. These were first published in a magazine called *The Millstone* in successive volumes from January, 1884 to August, 1885. It was reprinted in one volume in 1920 by the Museum of the American Indian and was subsequently republished in 1974. It is a fascinating account that starts with the creation myths about corn. Each chapter is accompanied by drawings made by Cushing. The book *Zuni: Selected Writings of Frank Hamilton Cushing* includes many of the Smithsonian publications in one volume. There is also a collection titled *Zuni Folk Tales* with over 400 pages of stories from Zuni. One piece titled *Zuni Fetishes* was first published in the *Second Annual Report of the Bureau of Ethnology, 1880-1881*. It is one of the best pieces of ethnological research done by Cushing and shows remarkable insight into the Zuni way of thinking and their religious attitudes, all reported without condescension or cultural judgments. It has been reprinted many times and is Cushing's best known piece of writing. The scholar Jesse Green has collected Cushing's correspondence with the Smithsonian along with the journals he was keeping while he was at Zuni and it is available as *Cushing at Zuni: The Correspondence and Journals of Frank Hamilton Cushing, 1879-1884*. While he was living at Zuni he traveled far and wide, often with the Zuni, and he made an expedition to the Grand Canyon where he contacted the Havasupai Indians in 1882. He was only the second white person ever to visit their tribe. His book *The Nation of the Willows: The Narrative of Frank H. Cushing's Journey to the Havasupai Indians in 1882* was published in 1882 in the *Atlantic Monthly* and then reprinted in one volume in 1965.

When he was recalled to Washington he continued his work at the Bureau of Ethnology but was plagued with bad health and was slow meeting his deadlines for publications. In 1886 he returned to the West as the leader of the Hemenway Southwestern Archaeological Expedition and was in charge of archaeological explorations to find the earliest expressions of Zuni and pueblo culture in the ruins in the area.

This lasted two years before he was again forced back to Washington by bad health. The rest of the expedition was headed by J. Walter Fewkes, who diverted the effort from archaeology to ethnology. Cushing remained in Washington, working on his various publications until 1895 when he was asked to go to Key Marco, Florida with a full-scale expedition. From this he published *Exploration of Ancient Key Dwellers' Remains on the Gulf Coast of Florida* in 1896. He explored and documented a number of ancient village sites up and down the west coast of Florida before settling at Key Marco, where he unearthed a remarkable collection of wooden articles from the bottom of a bog. These are exquisite and beautiful to a remarkable degree. Subsequent research by Phyllis Kolianos and Brent Weisman unearthed Cushing's letters, journals and research notes, and these have been published in two volumes: *The Lost Florida Manuscript of Frank Hamilton Cushing* and *The Florida Journals of Frank Hamilton Cushing.*

He died in 1900 while planning his next expedition to excavate shell mounds in Maine.

VILLAGE OF THE TWIN KIVAS

We are up early the next morning to meet Otto. This morning we have breakfast with a table full of hunters who are here to kill elk in the surrounding mountains. Quite a contrast from the morning before. When Otto shows up we are scheduled to see a fetish carver named Alex. Alex had his tools set up on the front porch. He showed us the various kinds of stone he works, which are all cut in rectangular blocks. All the work is done with small electric grinders and buffers. He pulls out a big chunk of turquoise about the size of a soft ball. He had started cutting it but he offers it to Otto for his jewelry shop because he says it was too hard. Otto seems happy to get it. Alex lives in the oldest part of the town, close to the old mission church.

Standing there in the plaza Otto told how in the 1930s the WPA started constructing houses of red sandstone blocks. Eventually they replaced all the old adobe buildings. Then he thought of another carver in the vicinity and took us inside a house where we met an old woman with graying hair and a slight build. We shook hands and I bowed and breathed on her hand, she smiled. The traditional greeting at Zuni is to take both hands and hold them in yours and breathe on them. She is one of the traditional healers. They have a nice hospital run by Indian Health Services and I asked if she was allowed to practice there and she said, "Yes if the patients requested it".

During lunch Otto had been in touch with the Zuni rancher who has the grazing rights to a site called the Village of the Two Kivas. It is considered an outlier of Chaco Canyon and possibly the furthest south of all the outliers. On the drive out I showed Otto my journal. It is leather-bound and has the emblem of New Mexico embossed in gold on the cover and is full of pictures of scenes at Zuni from various books I have read.

Otto wants to talk about the Aztec and Maya and about the practice of human sacrifice in those cultures; how the Aztec would sacrifice hundreds of people at certain festivals and what that meant in their religion. We discussed how they believed you had to make sacrifices to the gods to show that you honored and respected them and gave thanks for them bringing good weather, good hunting, good crops, victory in battle and all the good things in life. Each person had to make personal sacrifice and even the Emperor had to make blood sacrifices, sometimes letting blood from his penis. The Emperor's blood was let onto special paper and then burned to carry the offerings to the heavens. Human sacrifice was the highest sacrifice you could make and the Aztec had elaborate ceremonies that involved hundreds and maybe even thousands of human sacrifices where lines of people came through the temple and the priest would cut out their hearts and lay them on an altar to the gods and their body would be cannibalized.

As we were driving by Corn Mountain, Otto said that the people had lived on top of it at least three times, the last being when the Spanish came back after the pueblo revolt in 1680. But the first time was when there was a great flood. He showed us the high water line on the face of the mesa. It is a line clearly demarcated around the mesa, which is red sandstone with striations of white that define the various geological strata on the cliff face. He told how the people retreated to the top and watched as the water got higher and higher and finally a priest started making prayer sticks and put them into a big bundle and climbed down the edge of the mesa and planted the sticks and then did some ceremony and sacrificed two children. The water came up to where the prayer sticks were planted and stopped. He said even now you can see the two children, which is the name for two big sandstone columns that are on one side of the mesa.

I started telling him that human sacrifice was not just practiced in Mexico and South America but all over North America as well. That took him aback and he said,

"Well there goes the romantic image of the Native Americans."

"Yes Otto, it was hard for me to accept when I first heard about it and I vehemently denied it when the first person told me about it."

I told him there is now clear evidence that it was a part of the Chaco culture and was probably practiced all over the Southwest. He said he couldn't believe his ancestors could have done such a thing.

"Well Otto, if you go back far enough you can probably find that all our ancestors practiced human sacrifice; it was part of the religion in the old days and seems like it was practiced all around the world. So my ancestors are just as likely to have practiced it as yours when it comes down to it. It is just a matter of time."

I said Cushing strongly suspected that the Zuni had practiced human sacrifice but that it had been discontinued a hundred years or so before he was there. He suspected that if the circumstances were right they had been doing it right up to his time, but very discretely. Otto was taken aback by this and expressed disbelief. We talked about how sacrifice and making offerings was part of Indian culture and each person was expected to show their courage and their commitment to their people. That if you weren't willing to make sacrifice you were a selfish person and had no commitment to your religion or your people. And when it came to human sacrifice they used captives but, at other times, a person was expected to give up their life, or the life of their child, for the people or to placate their gods.

We talked about how cultures around the world had made the transition from human sacrifice and how this was reflected in their myths and how there is a jump made at a certain stage in religious development when there is a break with human sacrifice. You can see it in the Jewish religion in the story in the Old Testament about Abraham and Isaac. God asked Abraham to sacrifice his son, and then at the last moment Abraham found a sheep caught in a bush nearby and took it as a sign from God that he could use animal sacrifice in place of a human. After this the Jewish people were no longer required to give a human life but had a substitute that was acceptable. Something similar happened in ancient Tibetan culture. Any hint of human sacrifice is buried deep in the prehistory but they still remember when their priests were making animal sacrifices and at some point in their development they started making dough effigies called torma that were acceptable in lieu of animal sacrifice. It seems the Zuni reached a similar conclusion when they started making masks and impersonating the gods. Before this they believed that when the gods came to the village they required a human sacrifice to take back with them. But when the Zuni started wearing masks they were no longer required to provide a human life. At some point in our deep prehistory human sacrifice was considered a necessity as part of religious practice. We got ourselves into that mess and it took thousands of years and some new myth making to transition out of it.

As we were pulling up to a crossroad there was a blue pickup truck pulled off to the side near a gate. It was the person who leased the grazing rights to the land and he was there to open the gate for us. He and Otto talked for a few minutes and then Otto came back to our car and said he was asking for a twenty-dollar access fee. We paid him and he held the gate open while we drove into the field and across the desert landscape toward a cliff face in the distance. We went through another gate and climbed up a small rise and parked the car. It was blazing hot by this time. When we got out, we could immediately see two large depressions that were all that marked the sites of the kivas. Above this were the remains of a couple of stone walls and the visible stone work was very much in the manner of the stone work at Chaco.

The remains of the village sat on a small knoll overlooking a beautiful valley with a dry streambed running through it. Behind us were tall cliffs broken into two terraces, stairstepped, one above the other.

The ground around the stone walls and the kivas was littered with pottery shards and we picked up a handful of them and took pictures. Otto didn't seem to care but we had no interest in keeping them. We found several kinds of shards, a few were red with black lines showing ancient designs. The old village had been excavated in the 1930s with the help of Zuni laborers but in the past eighty years the kiva walls had disintegrated and the whole area was covered with desert scrub and there were signs of grazing animals everywhere.

The temperature had been climbing all day and was now well over one hundred degrees. But we headed up the mesa side and had to scramble over boulders and when we got up to the first cliff face there were petroglyphs with panel after panel along the cliff face, including a nice kokopelli and spirals, human hands and sun signs and animals and weird geometric designs. I was stunned looking at them. The kokopelli was outstanding and it was surrounded by wavy journey lines, stylized insect shapes and intricate patterns.

I looked at Otto and said, "Susan and I have been to museums around the world but this is, to me, as spectacular as any of them; it is the beginning, the golden age of art." I could tell Otto was absorbed in it himself and we all stood there delightfully captivated, in an aesthetic trance. Otto led us from panel to panel and then said that during the excavations in the 1930s the Zuni workers had come up here and painted some of the panels and he lead us around the cliff untill we came to a panel with kachina masks painted on it. Beside one of the two painted panels they had pecked 1935 into one of the sandstone boulders in big bold letters. From here we had a beautiful view of the valley with mesas and buttes in the distance. The little stream had been dammed and there was a scenic lake in the upper part of the valley surrounded by greenery reflecting the clear blue sky.

The heat was blazing and when we got back to the car the temperature on the car thermometer was 108. On the way back to Zuni we passed by the north face of a sheer mesa. There is a window in one of the cliffs and just below the window rock is a white sandstone spire thirty feet tall standing alone in the flat plain in front of the mesa. Otto said that in ancient times there had been a salt lake here in Zuni but that the people had not respected it and had taken salt from it in ways that were not appropriate and the goddess had warned them and when they didn't heed her warning she had risen up one day and had gone through the cliff face, creating the window. Before leaving she pulled a feather out of her headdress and stuck it in the ground and the white sandstone column is her feather. Then she traveled seventy miles south and made a new salt lake and now the Zuni people have to travel all that way to get their salt. He said if you were in a plane you could clearly see the trail she left, going straight from here to the salt lake.

I asked about marriage and whether they followed Christian rituals of marriage. He said the Zuni have resisted this aspect of Christianity and despite the best efforts of hundreds of years of Spanish priests, followed by a couple of hundred years of Protestant missionaries, the Zuni still liked their own ways. He said there were no real marriage ceremonies but after a couple lived together for at least six months they could go to the tribal council, who would sanction their union.

Next I asked about Zuni burial customs. I knew at Taos they had a graveyard in the old mission plaza and people were buried there and after a few years they would bury someone else in the same grave. He said when someone died they were brought to the house and there was an all-night wake and when the sun came up the female relatives would wash the body and they would take a few of the person's favorite things and put them with the body and wrap the body in a blanket. Then they take it to the graveyard and the grave would be prepared and they would bury the body and that, like in Taos, they might use the same grave as someone else who had been buried there years before. Here at Zuni they stand no stones, inscribe no names; all are equal in death. In America we suffer under the myth of individuality; in the graveyard there is no illusion. Here each person is all persons, every man all men, every woman all women, unrecognized in the darkness of night or the darkness of the grave. None have special rights to their wretchedness or their riches. Earlier in the day we had stood in front of the graveyard in the courtyard of the old church. Here the specter of things past sings. Here it becomes clear. It is the end of the journey where we repent of our vanity. We looked over the old crosses littered about, in various stages of decay. Seeking a hidden system of life, my questions remain unanswered. Here I am looking for the news of the universe denied in the day-to-day commerce of passing life. I am watching time unspool in a series of sunrises, as fleeting as a dream. Wondering if there is not some cryptic intelligence in this graveyard, waiting for the bones to step forth and dance me a new dance; something raw, unshaped by the constructions of a mind obsessed with the desires of the ego, obsessed with possessions, obsessed with greed, all ridiculed by the truth of the grave.

WITCHES

The Zuni have a long mythology regarding witches. It begins with the origin tales that report when the people emerged from the earth a pair of witches came up with them and brought up from the underground two gifts. The first was death, an unseemly gift for sure, and the other was corn. So witches can bring benefits as well as causing any number of calamities such as drought, epidemics or floods, or even problems between people or clans. While human they are a people "of a different breath" and, to survive, have to take the breath from living people to continue to live. In ancient times witchcraft was the only crime punished by the Zuni Council of High Priests. When a witch was prosecuted and found guilty the Bow Chief was responsible for their execution. Cushing has an illustration of the trial of a witch showing a man with his hands tied behind his back hung from a peg on the wall suspended by the cords holding his hands together until he confesses.

The belief in witches and the methods of their prosecution remained in effect during the Spanish occupation. When the pueblos were forced to accept the reservation system the American government attempted to intervene in the cases of torture of witches. However, reports of this kind of torture continued, with the last reported case in 1925. In the late 1800s and early 1900s the Zuni elders held that anyone who provided information to Americans regarding these practices or any of the Zuni beliefs was a witch and would be prosecuted accordingly.

WE'WHA

As we were pulling back into the village I mentioned to Otto there was another famous ethnologist who spent time with the Zuni and published her findings with the Smithsonian. Her name was Stevenson, I asked if they still remembered her as well. He mentioned that no one liked Stevenson much and that she wasn't a very nice woman. I asked about We'wha and whether the people still had berdache and he said that yes there were homosexuals in Zuni but he wasn't familiar with the person named We'wha or the term berdache.

I knew about berdaches because I had read an account from 1904 about Matilda Coxe Stevenson who published a famous report detailing the mythology and ceremonies of the Zuni. While living at the pueblo she hired a Zuni to be a maid, a person named We'wha. She plied We'wha with questions about her religious practices and had her act as her guide to show her the shrines and sacred caves in the area. Stevenson invited We'wha to come to Washington D.C. as her house guest. We'wha was quite a sensation in Washington. She set up a loom on the mall and demonstrated how to weave, donating the blankets to the Smithsonian. She attended numerous receptions, and even met President Grover Cleveland at the White House. She stayed six months and acted as the prime informant for the 600 page book that Stephenson published in 1904. But unbeknownst to Stevenson, or the Washington society, We'wha was a berdache, a person the Zuni considered a third gender. A male who lived and acted like a female, the role they called "twofold one kind". The Zuni referred to her in the feminine and she passed for a woman with the local missionaries and other whites who visited the pueblo. We'wha even had a role in one of the sacred ceremonies where she wore the mask of a captured god who was forced to dress like a woman to placate the other gods.

LAST NIGHT IN HALONA

It was getting late so Otto dropped us off and we went to ChuChu's. After dinner one of the cooks at the Inn at Halona had said her family carved fetishes and she gave us the phone number and invited us to come by her house. We called and they invited us over and gave us directions to find their house.

We knocked and were invited in; there were little kids everywhere, and a TV blaring in the living room. There was a large flat screen TV against the wall with cartoons on, and a couple of kids on the couch watching. We sat at the kitchen table with the woman who had invited us and her brother. She was working on her fetishes, tying on the offerings. I watched intently, asking what type of thread she used, to which she replied "sinew", a thin brown thread. She had several turtles, each with a baby on its back, and said that turtles were all she carved. Her brother is a well known carver, a young man in his thirties. He sat at the table with us. They were adding onto the house and there was an unfinished room on one side and as we walked in we could hear a grinding tool running in that room. The brother and sister at the table were both busy with their fetishes so I asked if we could see the younger brother who was running the grinder and they gave us the go- ahead. The new room was only walls and a roof and there was the other brother and a friend. He greeted us and showed us the small fetish he was working on. Then he went back with us to the kitchen table and they had some fetishes for us to choose from. I asked if the Shalako would come when the room was finished and they said yes and talked about how much work was involved in having them come to the house. Then we stood all the fetishes up and I asked Susan to choose. She picked out six fetishes. Everyone seemed happy. We thanked them for inviting us into their home and they thanked us for coming and we were off.

Otto had invited us to see more of his jewelry. We found his compound and went in. His sister was there, the mother of the two small kids. She took them off to the playground which thrilled both of them. Otto had a table set up with a few trays of earrings. He showed us his little room where he makes his jewelry and talked about going up to Taos to sell at the festival. He pulled out little drawers and showed us the pieces of coral, turquoise, lapis and shell he used and the bits of silver. I asked if there were any clues for us to tell real turquoise from fake and he said a lot of what passes for turquoise was plastic or composite and that I should take a needle and heat the tip of it and touch it to the stone. If it went in, it was plastic or composite.

Back at the Inn at Halona Susan and I organize our stuff and get packed to leave the next morning. I get out the kachinas and the fetishes and figure out ways to pack them safely for their travels. The room has a bookshelf and I get to spend a little time looking at the books. They have a copy of the old Smithsonian reports written by Stevenson. I was reading a Zuni folk tale in one of my Cushing books, a coyote tale, and the phone rings. It is Otto, he has a local potter he wants to introduce me to, and will come over and take me. I said sure and was delighted to be off on one more adventure in the Zuni night. I got dressed and went up the narrow steps and there was Otto on the porch. He had his truck out back and we went to his trailer. I went in and there are two more small kids, a boy about three and a girl five. They are

Otto's grandchildren, not his kids, as I first thought, and in a minute a man walks in with two pots, one big one and a smaller one. The smaller one has two deer on it and they are each framed with a traditional Zuni motif. The pots are very thin and painted white on the outside and adobe brown on the inside. Then the outside is painted with two shades of brown. He has a deer with a heart line on each side and geometric motifs around the deer. The geometric designs meet and form a negative image.

I buy the small one and Otto shows me a few more of his pieces. Otto tells me the potter is a special guy, that he teaches in the high school and can make traditional-style pottery. In some of the pueblos making traditional style pottery has made a comeback. I felt lucky to have found another Zuni pot. I interacted with Otto and his wife for a few minutes. He has a poster on the kitchen wall with a collage of rock-n-roll musicians and I pointed out a few of them that I especially liked and compared notes on our tastes in music. Turns out Zunis are big fans of heavy metal and you can hear it coming out the open doors of the houses in the pueblo; anytime you hear a radio you hear heavy metal. I tell Otto not to worry about driving me back as the hotel is only a few blocks away; so he walks out and points me in the right direction. As I walk away I can see Otto's trailer is part of a family compound and from what he has told me there is a matriarchal family structure with his wife's mother as the elder member. There are three trailers positioned like a horseshoe so there is a courtyard with all the family members just a few feet apart. I hurry back and show the pot to Susan and call it a night.

EL MORRO

Next morning we eat quickly and take off. We are heading to Albuquerque and take the road east out of town. Just a few miles east I see a break between two big buttes and there is a road that runs between them. There are spectacular formations at the end of one of the buttes so we drive back to get a closer look. There are a series of stone spires, some twisted in impossible shapes, sentinels, clustered in a variety of heights. The bright red sandstone has eroded out of the face of the mesa, leaving dramatic stone formations like jagged obelisks. We take pictures and then in a few miles come to El Morro, also known as Inscription Rock. It has a visitor's center. We stop in, look at the books and then walk back to where the inscriptions are located. It is a beautiful spot. El Morro is a dramatic butte with sheer stone faces that shoot straight up hundreds of feet. And at the base of the cliff face there is a lovely pool. It has been there for centuries and has marked a watering hole where travelers have stopped since time immemorial. All along the cliff face are panels of petroglyphs; they are not only from the ancient prehistoric cultures but it looks like every visitor who came by carved their name in the soft white sandstone. There are several left by Spanish explorers in the early 1600s. There are hundreds of them, mostly ancient. I see a bear's foot with stylized claws, along with all the usual petroglyph designs, and intermingled are names and dates starting with the Spanish continuing up until the park service took over and stopped people from carving their names. I want to read them as an ancient gospel, older than our written testaments, with constellations of meanings lost to us now. These were scriptures to the ancients, relating their history, their legends, their myths, their clans, their travels.

There is a sidewalk that runs around the base of the butte with a trail that leads up to the top. It is a great walk and when we get to the top there are ruins of an early Zuni village. It has been excavated and restored and we can distinguish the buildings and the rooms in each building. The ruins are just back from the edge of the cliff. Walking up we had a view across the arroyo and could see for miles into the distance. One side of the village is looking out across the arroyo and the other side is looking down into a box canyon. The mesa has a canyon that reaches into the interior and there in the middle of the box canyon is another amazing spire, this one a solitary megalith that comes up from the floor as tall as the top of the mesa. And across from us, on the other side of the box canyon, is a table rock balanced on a pedestal poised there, perfectly balanced to hold its own weight. The trail leads around the top of the mesa and then back down behind the visitor's center. It is one of the most dramatic and scenic walks we have ever been on and we reluctantly get back in the car and continue back to the airport in Albuquerque.

It is hard to think about leaving. It requires a jump in time and I wasn't comfortable with the time shift, nor was I too comfortable with leaving the little bit of the ancient world I was experiencing, a little pocket still surviving where they follow the logic of analogy, believing that since all life takes form, that all forms have life. From this it follows that any form has the powers of the life that it resembles. Thus, by reproducing a form they embody that life and become that thing. Their masks, body paint, kachinas and fetishes are means of incarnating the mythic totems to become the deity and enact its purpose in a primal theater. In modern times we see gods in the image of humans; the Greeks, the Romans and the Jews all pictured the gods in human form and thought that humans are the closest to god while animals, insects and plants are lesser forms of life. But to the Zuni it is reversed. Humans are the weakest and the furthest from the gods; the animals have more powerful teeth, more powerful claws, they have fur to keep them warm and are closer to the mysterious supernatural forces of nature that are the rulers of this world.

In the Zuni worldview the sun, the moon, the stars, the plants, animals and humans are all conscious and interrelated in a great web of life. Humans are the lowest form of life. In their hierarchy those things that have greater degrees of mystery are more powerful and closer to the supernatural. Those things partaking of greater degrees of mystery are more advanced, more powerful and more immortal. The animals, having instincts not present in humans, are higher forms of life. The forces of nature are even more mysterious and consequently are even higher than the animals. The extent of relationship between different forms is based on the extent of the resemblance they bear one another. The forces of nature are personified and endowed with the features of the forms of life whose operations they most resemble; for example, the snake zigzagging across the ground resembles the lightning and is thereby more closely related to the power of lightning than are humans who bear it less resemblance. The forces of nature are superior in wonder and power; existing before animals or humans, they are ever-recurring immortal causes and conditions for all other forms of existence and are called "Silent Surpassing Ones".

Driving away from Zuni, away from El Morro, I mourn for the lost wonder and know that we have sacrificed nature and our relationship with nature to the forces of greed, traded our birthright for a few shiny coins.

ZUNI

THE DANCING GODS - 2013

"To the Zuni the whole world appears animate." Ruth Bunzel

To the Zuni even the wind and the clouds are alive. Even objects made by humans, like pots and furniture and clothing, are alive and have a distinctive essence. These essences are not anthromophs and are not imagined in human form, but are alive and conscious yet they have no personality. According to the literature on the Zuni, which begins in earnest in the latter half of the nineteenth century, all beings are harmonious components of the whole, helping to preserve and sustain one another. Among these beings some have more influence on human affairs and are referred to as those, "who hold our roads". When they withhold their gifts the humans must regain their confidence with prayers and offerings.

The Zuni remember a time when the earth was malleable and animals could become human and humans change into animals. In those times the kachinas came into the village but once the world hardened all was established as it is now.

The landscape coming into Zuni is incredible. On the way from Albuquerque we pass by Acoma and come into ancient lava beds and then into the Zuni Mountains and the high conifer forests. At the ridge line of the mountains we cross the continental divide at something over eight thousand feet above sea level. Once we cross the mountain range we come down into a desert with steep mesas and buttes that shoot up out of the flat desert floor. Along the sheer edge of the mesas and buttes are pinnacles of stone, some standing in groups. There are red sandstone spires and in some places there are lone stone sentinels away from the base of the mesas, standing up out of the desert floor. Then we pass El Morro, a huge white mesa with a pool at the base of the massive white cliffs and ruins on the top of the mesa and a box canyon inside it. Then we are near Zuni and before long Corn Mountain appears, a deep red sandstone mesa with white striations that stands as a guardian and place of refuge for the Zuni village that reposes in its shadow.

I had been in touch with Otto about coming for the kachina dances that are associated with the summer solstice. It is an annual event but there is no announcement about it and it is not a tourist attraction; it is a religious ceremony that the Zuni have been performing for centuries and it continues into the present and the foreseeable future. There are over a hundred kachinas and various ones come to the village at different times of the year. For summer solstice the rain gods come with the mudheads. Once Otto knew the date for the event he called and Susan started making travel plans to be in New Mexico. We had seen dances at several other pueblos but had never seen the kachinas, so this trip was surrounded by a bit of mystery.

LITERARY ANTHROPOLOGY

I had read several accounts from early anthropologists who attended the mid-summer rain dances, the first by Matilda Coxe Stevenson who was there in the 1870s and 1880s, and then another by Elsie Clews Parsons from the 1920s. Following in their wake Ruth Bunzel visited in the 1930s. These exceptional women were pioneers in their fields and had done extensive research at Zuni and had informants who provided them detailed information, much more than the elders and priests wanted. They all published large and detailed accounts that eventually made their way back to Zuni. Inevitably someone would show the Zuni priests the published accounts and they were shocked when they saw the information being published in the annual reports of the Smithsonian Institute. The informants could expect to be beaten or possibly killed for talking about ceremonial information so it took a powerful incentive to get them to talk.

These anthropologists reported how ritual activities played a part in the everyday activities of the Zuni. Offering food to those who have gone before was a part of any meal, like saying the blessing for modern Christians. Cushing reports that a bit of food from each meal was thrown into the fire as an offering and that this type of offering, along with the prayer that accompanies it, was one of the earliest rituals learned by the children and was even a requirement, or graduation exercise, for them when they are weaned. It was only when the child was able to offer the food and recite the attendant prayer that they were ready to move away from mother's milk. The food offering was made by priests and by the matriarchic head of the household before any meal. Other food offerings were made in the evenings with the food tossed into the Zuni River so that it would flow downstream to the village of the gods. At the indoor offering only a few words were required; "Eat, may our roads be fulfilled and blessed with life." The outdoor offering required a longer recitation. These offering were not made, according to Bunzel, to one's own ancestors but rather to the ancestors as a whole.

In old Zuni all aspects of life involved an initiation which followed a standard paradigm. The process of initiation began at birth. When it was time for a baby to be born the mother went into a secluded room and all the men had to leave. The midwives and female relatives covered the windows and door with a blanket and the entrances were posted with downy white eagle feathers from the eagle's breast as a sign to stay away. At the time of birth the attendant picked up the newborn and breathed into its mouth, giving it "the breath of life". Then a large pile of sand was brought into the room, heated and mounded on the floor. Blankets were thrown over the sand and a depression was made where the mother and baby lay facing to the east. Corn meal was rubbed on the baby. If it was a boy the grandmother placed an ear of yellow corn behind its head. If it was a girl she placed two ears of white corn that had grown together behind her head. The mound of sand symbolized the earth and in Zuni gardens each stock of corn grows out of a small mound of earth, mounded up by the farmer. Thus, the infant was sprouted like an ear of corn into the village. A woman from the father's clan brought the baby a blanket and mother and child stayed secluded for ten days. On the tenth day mother and child followed a path of cornmeal to the east side of the village and watched the sunrise. As the sun comes up above the horizon the mother held up the baby to greet the sun and prayed for its health, happiness and long life. This follows the standard paradigm for initiation which included first isolation, then liminality or realization, and then incorporation. All of these phases were accompanied by long recitations of various myths, legends and accounts of the ancestors, along with prayers, propitiations and supplications.

In a paper titled, *Zuni Ritual Poetry*, published by the Smithsonian Institution in the Forty Seventh Annual Report of the Bureau of Ethnology in 1929-1930 Ruth Bunzel provides transcripts of many of the Zuni prayers.

One of the most common was the "Prayer at Sunrise". I will paraphrase Bunzel's translation.

(The Invocation)

On this day

the sun father

appears on your sacred path

(The Offering)

I am giving to you

the prayer meal

from which we draw life

(The Request)

Please grant your long life

                waters

                       seeds

                              riches

                                    powers

and your strong spirit. [10]

THE SUMMER SOLSTICE RAIN DANCE

According to Stevenson's account from the 1880s, the summer solstice started when the setting sun strikes a certain spot on Corn Mountain and holds that position for five days. That marks the end of the sun's journey to the north. At this time the sun priest, also known as the deputy of the sun father, gathers the people in the kiva of the north and makes prayer sticks as offerings to the sun and moon. Then, from the roof of the kiva, he announces summer solstice. Altars are erected and embellished with fetishes. Medicine water is consecrated, prayer plumes are prepared, songs are sung accompanied by drums, rattles and flutes. Special pottery is freshly fired, gourds covered with eagle plumes are filled with water from a sacred spring in the nearby lava fields. Paintings are made with corn pollen while special priests stay in retreat in the kivas, keeping their thoughts pure and praying for the rain. They are preparing for the kachinas to come to the village. These kachinas include: Sayatasha, Yamuhakto and Hututu, along with the mudheads who dance through the village while women on the rooftops pour water mixed with corn meal over their heads. Reeds filled with tobacco are painted black and wrapped with corn husks and given to the men who personify Shalako at the next winter solstice. The great Beast Gods are invoked to intercede for rain and pathways of cornmeal are laid out through the streets. Great processions are made to deposit prayer sticks at sacred caves in the mountains. These caves are considered passageways to the meeting hall of the Council of the Gods. Others go to the Lake of Whispering Waters where the kachina dwell at the bottom of the lake and leave yucca stalks called fire sticks. Then they build a new fire of cedar and use it to set fire to trees and grass and create as much smoke as possible to make cloud masks for the rainmakers. These processions are accompanied by thunder sounds made by whirling flat bits of wood at the end of a string. Back in the village they present cattails from the lake to the Priestess of Fecundity at which time thirty gods and eight goddesses appear in the plaza. After dancing at each of the four plazas they enter the kivas and break their fast with a great feast. After this, the women wash the hair of the dancers with suds from the yucca plant as a ritual cleansing and they reenter the mundane world.

In the 1920s Elsie Clews Parsons attended the dances and wrote a major work about the Zuni. She was a renegade ethnologist who visited all the pueblos and hired informants. She spent a lot of time at Zuni and wrote an account of the summer solstice dances calling it itiwana, which means the middle place or the middle of the ceremonial year. During this time the priest watched the sunrise from a petrified stump on the east side of town. When the sunlight hit a certain place on Corn Mountain he informed the Rain priest. After which prayer sticks are planted; first for the Sun and the Moon, then for the deceased priests. During the time of the ceremonies, the priests must stay sexually continent and refrain from eating meat. When the prayer sticks are all offered they announce the dances will take place in ten days and all the people make and plant more prayer sticks. Images of the War Gods are made and the people come and sprinkle them with cornmeal and make prayers. On the ninth day, a representative of the badger clan collects cedar fire sticks from each house and makes a fire in one of the kivas at sunset. Meanwhile, the priest makes a sacred design out of cornmeal on the kiva floor and the next night collect the images of the War Gods and bring them on a path marked by cornmeal accompanied by the sound of whirling whizzers. The War Gods are installed in the kiva and given offerings of food. The next day the War Gods move to a shrine on Corn Mountain where a fire is built that is visible to everyone in the village. From this time no more fires are allowed outside the houses and no ashes can be taken from the hearths. The fire in the kiva must be kept burning for the next ten days, when more prayer sticks are planted and everyone has a ritual hair washing.

For the next four days there is no commerce and no eating meat or grease. After fifty days there are all-night dances and prayers for fertility and rain. Two nights later, the leader of the kachinas, Pa'utiwa, comes to town and visits each of the kivas, after which the impersonators of the katchinas for the next year are appointed. Spring water is collected in medicine bowls and the kachina of the Big Firebrand and the Blue Horn dance and sing all night to "send out the old year". With the rising of the Morning Star a fire is kindled as a procession of the gods parades through the village with Shitsukya and Kwelele and Kupishtaya and Poshaiyanki. And as they leave the kiva the people sweep out all the old ashes and deposit them in their gardens, praying that in one year they return in the form of fresh corn. During this time the kachinas Shitsukya and Kwelele dance on the roof of the kiva, handing down cooked sweet corn strung with yucca. Next Pa'utiwa comes to town with more prayer sticks and the implements needed for the hoop and stick game. Then, as Pa'utiwa is leaving town, a woman from the Dogwood clan presents him a knotted fringe and many prayers. That night a Chakwena kachina woman comes to the village and enters the kiva, making an anti-sunwise circuit of the town, giving a special blessing to all the pregnant women. She is followed by Atoshle kachina who runs around frightening the children and the Thlelele, maskless nude figures, who run through the village and are pelted with embers from the houses. Baskets of seeds are distributed to all the kivas and as the morning sun rises the last of the kachinas leave the town.

JUNE 30, 2013 SUMMER SOLSTICE AT ZUNI

I called Otto on the way to town and he said to meet at the visitor's center. When we walked in there was a big sign saying no photo permits were being issued on this day due to the ceremonies. I spoke with Tom Kennedy who runs the center and discussed etiquette and procedures for the day. He told us to go to a certain place to watch the procession into town and thought they might be coming as early as two or three in the afternoon. In a few minutes Otto walks in. He tells us that he doesn't expect the kachinas to come into town until five or six so we have time to do other things during the day. We toss around a few ideas and Otto suggests we go see a new set of ruins that have been discovered just west of town. We pile into his truck and are off. The tribe wanted to build a new runway for the little airport they maintain and had picked out a place in the desert. Since there was going to be federal dollars and it is on the reservation they had to do an archaeological survey as part of the environmental clearance to use the money. Sure enough, when they did the survey they found a significant site, so much so that they decide to excavate it.

Otto took us back to his place before we headed out to see the ruins and as we drove in he pointed out all the outdoor ovens lined up in a row in the family compound. There are eight of them standing there and there were flames shooting out of them. I had never seen them fired up like that, the ovens were literally filled with flames and there were tongues of fire shooting out the oven doors. They are beautifully done. I have heard they are not indigenous but are based on a Spanish design they learned during the conquest. But they are wonderful, organically-shaped like a half circle doomed igloo, about four feet tall with a half-oval door in the front.

Otto drives us a short way out of town and then down a dirt road that is little more than tire tracks across the desert. Before long we see long plastic sheets stretched along the ground and piles of dirt on one side. We get out and see pottery shards littering the ground. We are on a very slight rise on the desert floor and there are a couple of other similar rises nearby, not very tall just slight swells that roll up on the otherwise flat lands covered with thin sage and a few scraggly bushes in a sandy white desert. They have run a few trenches across the rise and have concentrated their attention on a couple of places where they uncovered walls. In one spot they excavated a room with a very nice fire box. The walls are laid up stone with the mortar still intact and in a couple of places there are other exposed walls covered in white clay. Otto points these out and talks about how the people in the old pueblo, even up to modern times, would use white clay to plaster their interior walls. I called it Zuni sheetrock. Everywhere we looked there were pottery shards with delightful designs painted or incised on them. The shards were very thin, very nice pottery, all of it painted or decorated. I mentioned to Otto that in Tennessee when you visit an ancient site it is very rare to find pottery shards but common to find flint chips and arrowheads. He says it is just the opposite at Zuni and when anyone finds a flint arrowhead it is a treasured find.

It was strange roaming around the site. There was surface debris lying about, old beer bottles broken into shards, the glass suncured, shining in the blazing sun, reflecting orange and gold corollas. There were bits of wood, old tree branches mummified like rigid viscera leaching out of the trenches, like arboreal bones mingling with the bones of the villagers. The trenches were fluted gullies exposing the muted freight of times long passed, their chattel and their dead now unearthed, coming down to us with a message from the past.

I wondered how they recognized it as a village since there is nothing distinguishing this spot from the rest of the desert floor. Maybe the shards or perhaps the little rise was a giveaway that this could be an ancient ruin. I wondered if the other rise I could see nearby was another set of buildings and thought there had to be a graveyard close by. Otto agreed and mentioned that witches would often dig up graves to get the possessions and they didn't limit themselves to ancient graves. Everyone in Zuni was buried with their best possessions and that it was a problem that the witches would go after a burial site at the first opportunity. I said I suppose in some ways there isn't much distinction between archaeologists and witches. Otto wasn't willing to go that far. Otto asked what I thought about cremation and I told him that I supposed that would be what happened to my body. He remarked that he had considered being cremated so that no one would dig up his grave, but that some of the elders advised against it saying that it could have an effect on what happens in the afterlife, that you might not get to Zuni heaven if your body has turned to ashes. That gave him second thoughts about that idea.

Otto told us that when Coronado came the Zuni had six villages along the river and that the ruins are mostly still known. I asked if this was one of the six and he said it was difficult to know. I already knew about the ruins on the top of the mesa at El Morro, the ruins at Hawikku and now these. The Zuni have been living in this land for a long time and have moved about, living at one spot for a while, then building a new village somewhere else in the long river valley. I have seen archaeological maps of the area that show many more ruins along the river and in the cliffs that line the buttes and mesas.

We gathered at the truck and headed back into town. On the way back Otto pointed out a little knoll on the right and said that is where the kachina procession begins. It is a small rise and there are a number of trucks parked around it. He says they are out there getting ready to put on their masks and that involves a lot of ritual and ceremony and they have to do prayers and plant prayer sticks in order to be ready. Once we get to town, we stopped at the grocery store at the Halona Plaza. We went in the store to get some blue corn meal but they were sold out. The store hadn't changed much, jewelry supplies on one side with boxes of turquoise and red coral. I did notice a sign by the main door about tofu and I pointed it out to Otto. It is ironic to be in the only grocery store in town and watch the Indians buying high-sugar, high-salt processed foods with exorbitant fat content and, then walk out the door and see the diabetes clinic right across the street. Unfortunately, Zuni is a true food desert where the choices you are offered in the store create the health problems, especially the diabetes and heart problems.

It is late in the afternoon and I am getting excited about seeing the kachinas. Otto has his cell phone and has family members who will warn him when the time is getting close. He invites us over to his place and we drive to his family compound. The place is on the western perimeter of the village. The main house is a big red adobe house that stretches out under a grove of cottonwoods. The line of ovens is in the side yard and past that is a newer two-story house and then a series of trailers arranged so that the front doors all open into the courtyard. Each of the houses is for the family of the daughters of the matriarch who lives in the red adobe house. Otto remarks that the women own all the property and it is owned in common between them.

Otto invited us to come see the women cooking bread for the big feasts they were planning tomorrow. There were ten or twelve woman in the yard. One of them had a fryer set up with a propane tank and a big pot of oil boiling and trays of chicken she is frying. But the main focus was on the ovens. Francine, Otto's wife, was there along with her sisters and her mother and her mother's aunts and they were sweating and working around the ovens. They were raking the red-hot coals out of the ovens. They would pull them out toward the door with the rake and then scoop them up with a shovel and put them in piles in the yard. Once all the red embers were out of the ovens they came along with buckets of water and long sticks that had cedar boughs tied on the end. They dipped these in the bucket of water and used them to mop up the floor of the oven and get the rest of the ashes out. I looked in one of the ovens and the floor was a big slab of flat stone, smooth and nice as could be. The older ladies were obviously in charge and were overseeing the whole operation. Francine came out with a big bowl of green chilies and started putting the chilies right on the glowing embers. She had some pinchers she used to turn them and once both sides were blistered she put them in a plastic bag. She wanted them to sweat in the bag so the skin would peel off for the finished product.

Once all the ovens were suitably washed out it was time to bring out the bread. Susan and Otto and I had been standing around so I asked if we could help. Otto took one of the old ladies aside and said we wanted to help so they put us to work carrying out loaves of bread dough, which were in two different houses. They used one hundred and sixty pounds of flour and had hundreds of loaves of bread dough lined up on long wooden planks and covered with clean white cotton cloth. I started carrying the planks out to the ovens very carefully. At the oven the woman in charge of that oven would uncover the bread and sprinkle it with white flour. Then she would put it on a big wooden paddle like they use in pizza ovens and place it in the back of the oven. She did one loaf after another until it was time to go get another plank. One older woman supervising the operations was named Ester and the other women wouldn't let her put any of the bread in the oven. They told us that when Ester was a little girl she had a problem with her leg and they got a medicine woman to come and she put ashes on her leg and it healed right up but ever since then anytime she puts food in the oven it won't cook. If she puts bread in the oven it will come out doughy in the middle and meat won't cook if she puts it in. So at home she prepares all the food but if anything needs to go in the oven she makes her husband put it in, even though he isn't very happy about it. So now Ester sat down beside one of the ovens and watched as the rest of the women slide the loaves into the ovens. There were several of us designated to carry out the bread, mostly the younger teenage girls, along with Susan and me. Otto carried out one but that was enough for him; it isn't considered man's work in Zuni, but I was delighted to help and enjoyed watching the women line the bread up in the ovens until they were all totally filled. Then they put a piece of plywood, covered with an Indian blanket, over the oven door. Once the loaves were all in the ovens we were done. They had killed a sheep the night before and prepared the meat. They were going to be cooking it tonight and making a traditional mutton stew. Otto goes off to check with the family who are all in the main house getting ready for the procession. In a few minutes he reappears and says we still have another hour to wait.

ZUNI CEREMONIALISM

Zuni ceremonialism is built on ritual and ceremony done for the ancestors. They make offerings for the dead in the form of food, which is fed to the fire or tossed into the water along with quantities of cornmeal and the planting of prayer sticks. According to Bunzel these offerings are made in all the various ceremonies not strictly during those consecrated for the dead. She contends that all the supernatural beings in the Zuni tradition are tied to the ancestors. These ancestors are referred to as "keepers of the roads" meaning that they are the guides and protectors who provide sustenance to the current generations. They are associated with the clouds and rain and are called "those who have attained the blessed place of waters". It is thought they return to the earth "clothed in the rain" so every time it rains it is both a blessing from the ancestors and a physical manifestation of their continuing presence. But the picture is even bigger in that, according to Bunzel, the rain is associated with the supernatural realm and there are "rain makers" as well as the masked gods who are highly involved in rain making. For the Zuni the divine realm is amorphous and mysterious. All the supernaturals, as well as the dead who have gone to this realm, are absorbed into this divine force and can arise from it in various manifestations. Each of these manifestations can take a distinct form but they all partake of the power manifesting from the ancestors who are shared by all the people. The worship of the ancients is done by all without the mediation of priests or shamans.

The most distinctive representation of the divine realm is the sun, which they consider the source of all life. During all the rituals the priest greets the sun each morning as it rises with an offering of cornmeal and the recitation of a hymn. It is the sun priest, known as pekwin, who is the most revered and has the greatest responsibilities in the community. It is his job to observe the movement of the sun and recognize the solstices where the sun sets in the same spot for four days. He then sets the calendar for the fasts and retreats as well as for the ritual ceremonies and dances that take place at the summer and winter solstice.

Second in importance to the sun rituals are those associated with rain. The rainmakers are the spirits of the springs and rivers and lakes. They live in the great clouds, which are formed from the mists. There are rain priests who are responsible for the summer solstice dances. Their preparation includes a series of four-day and eight-day retreats. These include fasting from meat and sex and staying secluded with no commerce of any kind, and planting prayer sticks. They are expected to expel any negativity and to think only good thoughts for the rain and the fertility of the village. They are expected

to be gentle, humble and kind and to never provoke or be involved in alter-
cations. There are long prayers that they repeat daily, including a recitation of
the names of all the previous rain priests and other ancestors. Everyone in
the village is expected to do a four-day retreat during this time.

There are a long series of recitations at the heart of each ceremony.
These prayers or hymns or chants are sacred and have great power, but only
if they are correctly recited. Those who know them by heart are considered
wealthy and the more of them you have in memory the greater your wealth
in the village. There is a process of learning where a person wishing to learn
them must request someone to teach them. Then they must appear in certain
dress and repeat after their teacher until they have committed it to memory
and can repeat it back without error. When they are successful their mentor
inhales deeply and takes from them the essence of the prayer, acknowledging
that they have mastered it. Each kiva has a member who has the responsibility of holding all the chants associated with the rituals that take place in
that kiva in memory. Each ritual has chants that accompany it. There are
specific chants that go along with planting prayer sticks, with making offerings and with acquiring and wearing a mask. These hymns have three basic
characteristics; first, they announce what type of prayer or what ceremony is
taking place; second, they give a vivid verbal rundown of the offerings they
are making at this time; and, finally, they state their requests and why they are
making the offering. This expresses exactly what they wish to get out of it,
typically rain and fertility for the crops and the people, safety in battle, good
health or long life. The offerings and the accompanying prayers are to strike
a bargain; it is quid quo pro, this for that, with the hope and expectation that
the gods who accept the offering will follow through on their part of the
bargain and bestow good weather, the rain, the victory in battle, etc.

THE PROCESSION OF THE GODS

Finally Otto announces it is time to go out to watch for the procession.
Apparently they have left the hill and are heading toward town. Francine and
Susan get in the back and Otto and I in the front and we ride down to where
their lane comes into the main road, Otto parks and we all get out. There is
yellow crime scene tape up along the other side of the road and they want all
the people to stand on this side. Otto and Francine and all the family go up
right by the road but we don't see any other white people in this crowd and
Otto advises us to stay by the truck and watch from here, which is only about
thirty feet from the road. There are several hundred Zuni lining the road and
soon we hear distant drums and see banners in the distance, then the faint
sound of chanting and the first of them comes into view. There are a line of
men all dressed in white with headbands carrying yucca leaves; a drummer is
with them with a big bass drum that makes a deep hollow booming sound.
The men dressed all in white are the priests and there are ten of them leading the procession. I imagine the guy in the very front is the pekwin but I
am guessing. After the priests come a long line of kachinas, some of them

barefoot, most wearing moccasins. Many have similar masks but I see the fire god go by and others with elaborate painted masks. The bulk of them have a mask that has shaggy hair on the head and a straight beard that hangs from the middle of the face down over their chests. Then at the end of the procession comes the mudheads, ten of them. The people lining the roadway have cornmeal and as the dancers come by they reach out and sprinkle corn meal on them. When they have passed by Otto and Francine come back and we all get in the truck.

"What did you think?" Otto wants to know.

"Adventures in dream time; it is like a dislocation in time being able to see something that has so much tradition. To know this has been going on as part of the Zuni tradition for centuries and to see it still happening is an incredible event. This makes the Pow-wows they hold back East look like watered down versions that have lost their roots and have become fund- raising events with no religious significance at all."

Susan said, "It is a privilege to be here; it is a beautiful event, very moving."

One of the big controversies in current Southwestern archaeology is trying to figure out when the kachina cult got started, where it started and how it spread. They are slowly putting together the pieces using excavations of kivas that have murals depicting kachinas painted on the walls where they can date the paint. There are also images of kachinas found on pottery designs and petroglyphs that they use to trace the introduction of the kachinas. It is assumed that there was a major population shift around the twelfth century C.E., ascribed mostly to severe drought, that forced the population to move from the Chaco Canyon, Mesa Verde area down to the Rio Grande valley. They believe the kachina cult began sometime soon after that great migration and probably in the borderlands between New Mexico and northern Mexico in the area of the Mimbres Indians. They find few representations of masks of any kind prior to 1050 C.E. but by 1300 C.E. masks have spread through the pueblo culture along the Rio Grande. This period marked a remarkable cultural transformation from a tradition of Great Houses with elites living in special palaces and the bulk of the people living in smaller farming communities. By 1300, the people had congregated into large multistoried plaza-oriented villages.

Otto starts the truck and heads over to the village in a long line of traffic that is working its way into town where the plazas are located. There are police cars at the main intersection in town and they have closed the north/south streets to traffic, so Otto works his way around and gets a parking place and we head for the centermost plaza in the village. The inner plaza is the center of the world and as we walk up a set of steps Otto points to the west and there is the great massif of Corn Mountain with the last rays of the sun illuminating it, making it glow a vibrant shade of red. Then we are at the top of the steps and walk out onto a flat roof looking down into the plaza. We are on the south side of the plaza, on the first roof of a two story pueblo building with flat roofs. We hear the sound of the kachinas in another plaza, the sound of the drum, the low hum of the chants like a deep vibration reaching us from a distance. There are buildings enclosing all four sides of the plaza with two narrow alleys that lead into it; this plaza is the most revered sacramental space in the village. It is a spot where the people have gathered for untold generations, a place where the kachinas come to dance. It has been this way since the founding of the village. There have been kachinas coming to this plaza and the people have gathered on the roofs to watch for countless generations. There are only a few white people in attendance. On the roof across from us are four whites, an older couple who are there with their family of Zuni grandchildren or nephews and nieces, and a young couple who stay more in the back. Susan and I also stay in the back as the Zuni sit in folding chairs or on the roofs with their feet hanging over.

Then the sounds grow louder and we feel the excitement as the procession starts up the alleyway. There are Zuni lining the way and they are sprinkling cornmeal on the shoulders and backs of the kachinas. The priests lead the procession and form a circle on one side of the plaza, then all the dancers make their way into the plaza, filling it with nearly a hundred participants. Three of the priests form a line across the center of the plaza and twirl bullroarers that make a whirling sound like the wind whipping the branches of a tree. Then other instruments enter so that the whirling bullroarers create the auditory background for the songs the priests are singing, marked by the drums reverberating off the walls of the plaza, along with the ringing of dance bells and the staccato resonance of turtle shell rattles the dancers have on their legs, sounding out in time with the drum. The priests are all chanting and it all combines to make an unearthly soundscape unlike anything that I ever experienced.

I look around at the faces of the Zuni on the rooftops; they are transfixed. It is a theophany, the gods are in the village, it is an appearance of the supernatural, a divine presence, and the energy level of the place is accelerated as if an invisible wind is moving through us, produced by this theurgical drama enacted below. To the uninitiated it is a dance performance, but to the Zuni these are the gods and they are in the village with the people for this night. In preparation, everyone is expected to purify themselves with retreats from commerce and sex and meat, and to prepare themselves for an encounter with the elemental numinous forces of nature, with their ancestors, not only their human ancestors who have returned in this form but with the primordial ancestors, with the earth mother and sky father, with the forces that created this earth and all living things. It is as if the divine realm is a polymorphus undifferentiated supernatural energy that includes all these things and when we die we become one with this force and with all living things. All things organic and inorganic have sprung from this source and the kachinas are aspects of this and represent all the dead who have gone on before and all the various manifestations this energy can assume, from awesome dreadful destructive forces like lightning, to the gentle rain that nourishes the corn.

Standing here watching the movement of the masked gods is a revelation, an epiphany of original nature. In this emblem of temporality the gods participate in the life of the village and commune with the people of this generation like they have with all the generations before them. It is a gift from the gods, a divinization of the village, a visitation that gives the people the opportunity to propitiate the divine and access the sacred energy of creation to bring the rain and the fertility to sustain the life they now carry forward. It is a bucket that comes up from deep in the well. It is a reenactment of the moment that light appears; it is what burns in the fire of the sun, in the fire that cooks the food, it is all the possibilities of being, the numinous incandescence of the lifeforce, and it is there in the plaza in front of us as we look upon it as so many generations before us have looked from this very same spot upon this same enactment.

There were about sixty rain gods, all in the same basic mask, and then the mudheads. I counted them since in the legends there are ten. They are all present and accounted for. Then there were another half dozen or so different kachinas with full masks but the only one I could name for sure was the fire god since I had a kachina of him and knew what he looked like. They were all inside the plaza and the rain gods and the other kachinas were all dancing. The mudheads were just standing around all bunched up in a group. The rain gods were doing a dance step in place and it created the sound of bells and rattles that accompanied the drumming and chanting and the low roar of the bullroarer. It was fascinating standing there looking down into the plaza. The dance went on about a half hour. Then they filed out of the plaza and we all started down from the roof. I wondered where we would go next. I assumed we would follow them from plaza to plaza but when we got to the truck Otto took us to one of the kivas. Now it was getting dark and the street lights of the village were coming on. We stood on the street looking over at the kiva which was for all practical purposes another of the houses along the street in this section of the village. There is a big bonfire burning in a lot across from the kiva. We moved across and stood in front of the building and in a few minutes we could hear the sounds of them coming and sense the anticipation of the small crowd that stood around the kiva. There are six kivas and the priests and the mudheads are all at this kiva. The remainder of the kachinas were scattered about the village in the other kivas. I was very surprised that this kiva had two windows and we were standing right in front of the windows and I could easily see into the main room. It was a large room and had a bench around the wall which was the only furniture in the room. Otherwise there was a Zuni altar made of decorated planks all standing up about two feet tall, painted white with green designs. I couldn't make out the designs but there were some pots of what I assumed must be corn meal on the floor in front of the altar.

Then they all lined up with the priests in the front of the line and the mudheads in the back. This was the closest look I had at them. The priests were all dressed in white shirts and loose white pants and had white headbands, I looked at the one in the front who I thought might be the sun priest, an older man with white hair. Some of the others were younger. Then a really old man in a wheelchair was brought up to the door and was the first to enter and the rest trailed in behind him and went in the room and circled the wall all facing the interior. At this point someone closed the blinds so we could no longer see into the room. They would spend the night dancing and chanting and reciting prayers and hymns and stories in Zuni. I had read that each person was responsible for memorizing certain parts of the liturgy and would have to recite their portion as part of the ceremony.

We went back to the truck and Otto drove us back to the family compound. I had heard Francine saying earlier that she was responsible for part of the cleanup so I assumed she still had work to do. Susan and I said goodnight and Otto told us to be back about nine tomorrow morning and warned me about elk wandering across the road at this time of the night and away we went. As we drove across the village we could see fires burning here and there all over each neighborhood. I remember reading that as the kachinas come into the village the people make fires and create all the smoke they can make. They believe the smoke rises and forms into clouds in the sky to encourage the rain.

It is about forty-five miles back to the bed and breakfast where we are staying and sure enough about half way back I am whizzing along sixty miles per hour on an unlit two lane road and all at once there is an elk in the headlights. It is standing beside the road and looking like it might be starting to cross. I hit the brakes hard but before I know it I am by it as a wave of shock and relief floods over me. It could have easily jumped into the road and a collision with the elk could have been fatal for all of us. That slowed me down and then in about ten minutes there was another elk. This time I was going considerably slower so it wasn't nearly as frightening.

KACHINAS – THE DANCING GODS

In another version of the great myth about the Zuni's journey to find the middle place as they were fording a river the young children in their mother's arms began to turn into snakes and frogs and were wriggling to get loose from their mothers and some escaped into the water and swam away and became the first kachinas. The kachinas made their way to a lake called The Lake of Whispering Waters and established a village where they could sing and dance to express their joy. After that when anyone died at Zuni they would go to the village at the bottom of the The Lake of Whispering Waters where they would join in as kachinas to dance and sing. Some believe that only those people who have a mask can live in the kachina village in the afterlife.

The kachina societies of the Zuni nation present elaborately costumed dances throughout the year. Each dancer wears a mask representing a spirit which has power to benefit the nation. The six kivas present three dances each year; and each dance follows a certain order but has no fixed dates. The summer dances includes the Kokokshi dance which attracts the "breath of the dead" in the form of rain. Kokokshi is the most ancient of the kachinas, being the spirit of the children lost in the lake during the migration. Kokokshi is kind and gentle and brings a soaking rain. He is accompanied by the Kokwele, who are the Kachina Girls, dancing in parallel lines, singing melodic songs. They are much loved by the people and are considered the most beautiful kachinas. They wear white kilts and blue face masks with long hair cascading down their backs like rain curtains over the mesas. The feathers falling down their back are the clouds moving across the sky, ready to bring the rain.

When a Zuni dies they go to live in the dance village of the kachinas where the council of the gods directs them to collect water from the springs, which they carry to the upper world with the aid of painted feathered sticks called breath plumes which are offered at each moon. These shadow people are the rain makers who hide behind the cloud masks which are formed from the breath of the gods and the smoke from offerings which the people make during the rituals. If the smoke from the offerings has been sufficient and the daily lives of the rain priests has not offended the gods, then the council will order the shadow people to pour the water from the vases to rain down upon the earth.

The Zuni kachina are called koko, which has multiple meanings such as; a spiritual being, a mask, a cult,   a carved image, a visible language, and a way of life. When the Zuni found the middle place at Halona the kachinas would come to the village to dance with the people to bring rain and fertility but each time one of the mothers would return to the lake with them. So the kachinas told the people they would not come any more but showed them how to make masks and invested the masks with their spirits. After this, if the people make offerings of prayer sticks and cornmeal and live lives of purity, when they wear the masks they transubstantiate and become the kachinas. Then, when the person dies the mask is buried with them and they go to live at the village at the bottom of the lake.

Kachinas are spirits of all that lives, not only of the shadow people who have passed away but also of the minerals, the plants, the animals, the planets, the stars, the clouds, the lightning, the colors, and even the directions. The kachinas are the inner spiritual form of the outer manifestation of the forces of life. These forces can be invoked to help the people on their path especially as rainmakers, but also to insure fertility and abundance of life. The masks are animistic anthromorphs invested with powers such that those who wear the masks must be above reproach and fast from meat and sex. They must not provoke fights and think only good thoughts, and if they fall during the ceremonies they are whipped as mistakes are signs of immoderation and could ruin the ceremony and bring on drought.

According to the early accounts, the sun priest goes into a four-day retreat before the summer solstice. He must be pure in heart and during this retreat he "tries himself" sitting before an altar where he makes a painting on the floor with cornmeal. Before starting the retreat he makes and plants prayer sticks at his corn fields. These are offered to the sun, the moon and the rain makers. When he plants the plumes he must eat no animal flesh. The sticks are made with the downy feathers of an eagle. The eagle feathers are used at summer solstice and only when there is an urgent need for rain. Otherwise, the prayer sticks are made with turkey feathers. The prayer sticks convey their prayers. The sun priest spends his time praying for rain. His altar is ornamented with corn fetishes, thunder stones and his sacred bundle. When he is ready to announce the summer solstice, once all the prayer sticks are appropriately planted, he climbs to the highest rooftop in the village and makes the announcement.

THE FEAST

Next morning we return to the village and find our way to Otto's house. He says he has been up early, that he wanted to get up and go hear the kachinas chanting. He had already been to one of the kivas. Otto is a member of a kiva group and I wondered if he was allowed inside but didn't ask. Today is the big feast day and all the woman have been cooking for the past two days, making the bread and the mutton stew, and today they deliver the food to the kivas. Otto makes some tea which he says is Zuni tea. We saw an ad for it at the visitor's center but had never heard of it before. He says it grows all over the reservation and this area around Zuni is the only place you can find it. He says there is a guy who sells it at the visitor's center but Otto is a bit incredulous about it since this is a common plant and you can pick it anywhere. He had a plastic bag with a dozen or so bundles of it, each one wrapped in string and he has one of the bundles in a boiler with some water. He serves us the tea, and it is delicious. I ask about picking some and Otto gives us most of what he has in the bag, and when we step outside he points to the plants that are used for the tea. They are everywhere, stocky little plants about a foot tall with small yellow flowers that are in bloom at the top of every stalk. We quickly pick a bunch of it and put it in the car to bring home.

Francine is busy next door helping with all the food and Susan wants to go see if she can help. Otto and I go next door to see Gabriel Paloma, the potter I had met the year before. Turns out he is married to one of the women in the compound. He is sitting at his kitchen table working on a large pot. He has a big book called *The Pottery of the Zuni People* by Dwight Lanmon and Francis Harlow laying open on the table and he is using the pictures in the book as the template for his design. I look at the book, an oversized coffee-table book with large beautiful illustrations of the different types of Zuni pottery. I am delighted to see the book and study it while we talk. I want to commission a nice pot so we discuss that. I show him a picture of a type of pot that was part of the altar that I reproduced out of the Bunzel book. He took the big book and paged around in it until he finds that same pot, It has a different design with the sides raising up into a stair-step, like the shape of a butte silhouetted against the sky. We pick out the types of design that would be appropriate and he suggests making an eight-inch pot and I agree. He says it is a pot used to make offerings of corn meal. Gabe takes his time and shows me the various tools he has laying on the table. He has a glass vial with a bunch of dark green lozenges in it; he takes some of them out and says they are wild spinach and that he uses them as part of the coloring process and grinds them to a powder and mixes them with liquids to make his paint. I want to buy some fetishes and Otto takes me to a different house in the compound and we meet a family who have a big display of fetishes on a table in one of the rooms. We look them over and I pick out a half-dozen and the deal was done.

Next we go to the house where the women are preparing the food. Susan is having a great time, sitting at a big table eating mutton stew with large kernals of hominy and the wonderful bread baked the day before. I am invited to join and we sit with about a dozen Zunis and eat. Then Otto takes us back to his place and asks if I have a camera. I said yes but I thought there were no pictures today. He says the women are all getting dressed and are going to deliver the food and would like me to take some pictures. I am surprised and delighted and go out and get the camera. In a few minutes we are back to the main house where we had eaten and all the women are dressed in their finest Zuni clothing. They have on an array of silver and turquoise jewelry, plus they all have big bowls of the food to deliver to the kivas. While I get the camera ready they put the bowls on their heads and lineup, from oldest to youngest, and I start taking pictures. I take several shots of them lined up and then portraits of each of them. When all the pictures have been taken, the women take off walking down the road with the food balanced on their heads.

Otto and Susan and I jump in the truck and head for the kiva to watch as they deliver the food. We get to the kiva where we had been the night before and watch as women from all over the village walk in single file with the food on their heads, delivering it to the kiva. It looks like the men in the kivas are going to have a huge feast. They have been fasting since yesterday so they didn't have dinner or breakfast this morning. We move to a second kiva, this one in the main plaza behind the old mission, and see more lines of women coming and this time someone pulls up with a truck full of food and some men jump out and deliver food from the back of the truck. I say to Otto that being a kachina dancer must be a big commitment, that it seems like it would be difficult to hold down a regular job and to set aside the time needed for this kind of ceremony several times a year. He said yes that you just can't do it and they all have to have alternative means of making a living and many are carvers or make jewelry so they can do their work at their own schedule. He says it costs a lot to be a kachina dancer and means making a big outlay of money in order to take care of everything thatis involved. I ask how it is possible to do all that and he says some people care enough to do it. He says that for the Zuni a "poor person" is one who has little or no ceremonial knowledge or one who doesn't participate in the ritual recitations of the prayers; whereas a "valuable" person has this knowledge which brings with it great prestige. In Zuni the word for knowledge is also the word for power and your wealth is not measured by the accumulation of material goods or money but rather by your ability to recite the appropriate prayers and take part in the ceremonies.

I ask what they do to bring the ceremony to its conclusion. He says they break their fasts and enjoy the feast and then take the food and go to their homes and when they get home their wives or other female family members wash their hair with suds from the yucca plant. He says before that they are still empowered as kachinas and once they get their hair washed they are able to reenter the family and go on with life as usual.

Francine and the women have to walk back to the family compound and Otto thought they were due back soon so we get in his truck and head back. Francine has changed out of her fancy clothes when we get back. I ask Otto if there is anything else we should stay to see but he says there really isn't anything else. He then pulls out a little fetish of a bear and gives it to me and says I should carry it with me. I put it in my pocket and we head out of Zuni telling Otto and Francine that we will come back for the winter ceremonies next year when a different group of kachinas come to the village.

ZUNI POETICS

Bunzel recorded and transcribed many of the songs that are recited at summer solstice. When the sun priest has determined the date for the solstice dances to begin, he must do a public recitation of one of the hymns as an announcement. The sun priest has a gnomon where he stands to watch the first rays of the sun as they strike Corn Mountain. This allows him to track the movement of the sun as it goes north in the summer seasons and south in the winter. When the movement of the sun along the north south axis of the horizon stops for four days for each of the solstices, the sun has reached what they called his summer and winter homes.

The sun priest then distributes prayer sticks and designates the dates for the various four-day and eight-day retreats and for the dances and feasts. In order to make this information public he climbs to the roof of the pueblo at a certain spot and repeats this prayer.

The ancients who hold our roads
and mark the sacred places
have raised their curtains
Here on the corn priest's housetop
I stand
We remember our fathers
our sun father

during these days

these Divine days

When eight days have passed

we will, all together,

reach the sacred time

anxiously awaiting

as the time passes

on the ninth morning

grant that we finish our road [11]

Once this announcement has been made all the priests in the village go on retreat for at least four days. They go to the house where their sacred bundle is kept and spend their time in an inner room set up with an altar with a design of cornmeal sprinkled on the floor along with their fetishes, their paints, thunder stones and their bundle. When he places his bundle on the altar he recites this prayer,

This many days

since our fathers

    since our mothers

        since the ones who first had being

have kept

this many days

at their appointed times

you stayed quietly

in your inner chambers

now we have reached this time

Our fathers

    our mothers

        our ancestors

            our former priests

when you were alive

on this appointed time

you kept your way

and for four days

I will hold you fast

with the flesh of the white corn

offered to you

with the mist blanket

of clouds painted on the altar

in the house of massed clouds

on the road that gives us life…

all our corn

all over our land

stands poor

their hands burnt

their heads are brown

may they be watered

we keep your days

that all our children

will be nourished

will have water

and can rear their own young

and we shall be happy

all our days

thus it is

I set down quietly [12]

The Zuni understand all natural phenomena by analogy and by symbol-ism. They believe every object is alive, including the earth itself which is the Great Mother to whom we are all indebted for life and nourishment. The supreme life giver for the Zuni pervades all space and time and is referred to as HeShe, the bi-sexual initiator of all life, who was at work before sexual differentiation began. In the realm of the gods the celestial powers are per-sonified as the anthropic beings depicted by the masks with the father sun as the supreme power who was and is and will always be, the giver of light and warmth, above the anthropic and zoic beings. The moon mother lights the nights and divides the years into months with the aid of the fixed stars and the planets. The subterranean anthromorphs are the great war gods and the cultural heroes including: the corn mother, the salt mother, the corn father, the turquoise man, the plumed serpent and a host of others. The terrestrial zoomorphs are the great earth mother and all vegetative life, who act as intermediaries to intercede between the sun father and moon mother on behalf of the esoteric fraternities.

These dance dramas are built on the ideal that the earth and the forces of nature can be propitiated to influence their behavior. This takes place in the form of elaborate dramaturgical ceremony and ritual. The means for creating this beneficence on the part of the elements has to do with a reenactment of the events that occurred when the forces of nature first came into being. So, a theater was born to act out this drama with fantastical costumes to represent all the players and long recitations that retell the story and make the pleas for restitution and forgiveness. If done successfully the rains will come and the forces of nature will grant fertility and fecundity for the crops, the animals and the people. This revivification of the creation myth reorients the powers of nature, takes them back to square one, resetting them so that they perform their functions in harmony with the humans who depend on them. This is based on the principle of analogy and on symbolic identification. In this dramatic enactment the weather and the earth and sky and sun and wind and rain and all the other forces needed for survival resonate with the reenactment and become what is being re-enacted in the plazas. In this way, all the forces of nature realign themselves with the ancient pattern established at creation.

ZUNI
SHALAKO - 2017

INTRODUCTION

Otto had told me repeatedly that I should come to Shalako. He said that it is one of the most important events in the annual Zuni calendar of ceremonies and dances. I have been determined to attend for many years. However, Shalako is held in early December and to make a trip to New Mexico between Thanksgiving and Christmas has been an obstacle. It is not a tourist event and is not advertised and the date is not announced to the public until a few weeks before it happens. As a result, getting plane tickets and room reservations can be challenging and expensive. But this year I determined that no matter what I would go. Now I understand why I was urged to attend. I have never experienced anything comparable to Shalako. Getting to visit the Shalako houses is unlike anything anywhere in the world. The Shalako houses are temporary temples decorated with ornamentation as colorful and beautiful as any ceremonial space I have ever witnessed. The only thing similar in my experience is the great monasteries of Tibet. The overwhelming aesthetics of the event, the color, the song, the music, the dance all combine to make Shalako an incomparable experience.

Any story about Zuni starts with the creation story. An interesting rendition of the Zuni creation myth was given to an early ethnologist named Matilda Stevenson. She records the story that, "Sun Father created two sons and sent them down into the dark sunless Fourth World to lead the A'shiwi, the ancestors of the Zuni, into this world. They traveled quickly by way of Rainbows and with Lightning Arrows and Cloud Shields. Interestingly, the homes of the A'shiwi were holes in the ground and their food was grass seeds. The two young gods threw out a line of meal which guided them to the north and here they planted a pine tree so that the A'shiwi could climb up to the Third World. Another line of meal guided the people to the west where a spruce tree gave access to the Second World. Following a line of meal to the south, an aspen tree carried them to the First World where there was a little light reflected from the Sun's rays. A last meal line, this to the east, led to a silver spruce. Climbing this brought the A'shiwi to the 'light of day place' just as the Morning Star rose above the horizon." [13] After this the Zuni went on a long migration, searching for the middle of the world where they could settle. After many struggles they found the middle place and built a village where they still live to this day.

The poverty level at Zuni is as high as forty percent but at Zuni a person's wealth is measured by how many prayers and chants they have memorized, not by the amount of money in their bank account. We are dealing with a completely different kind of economy. In the past Zuni was largely agricultural but these days many of the people make their income from carving fetishes and making jewelry. At Zuni the people manage to get by in ways that allow them to keep the ceremonial calendar in effect. All the men have gone through initiation as boys that comes in two parts. Up until they go through the first initiation the children don't know there are people wearing the kachina masks. The first initiation is about age nine and the second a few years later. At both initiations they are whipped by a kachina with yucca whips, which are several spikes of a large yucca plant tied together in a bundle with a wrapped handle.

Zuni has three head priests. These are lifetime positions and include observing a complex religious calendar that involves fasting and praying. The priest of the above is called pekwin and he is responsible for determining the dates of the ceremonies by observing the rising and setting of the sun. Then there are twelve different priesthoods with two to six members each. Plus there are six religious societies each with its kiva. The curing societies are for those who have been cured of an illness and are responsible for ridding the village of disease, pests and witches. They are each associated with a Beast God which helps provide them medicine. Sickness can be cured by chants, by medicinal plants, typically associated with the Bear, and by sucking to extricate objects implanted by witches.

Until recently, the political power in the village was in the hands of a council of six priests who represent the various priesthood groups. The head was the pekwin who was responsible for watching the sun and maintaining the calendar. This group would appoint all the dancers and the people who served as civil authorities. They would not settle secular affairs but only dealt with the sacred business of the tribe, making sure all the ceremonies and dances follow in the right order at the right time. The Spanish organized a separate system of government with a governor, a lieutenant governor and eight assistants who help with enforcement. Before civil standards of law were imposed, witchcraft was a crime punished by public torture and execution. Revealing any information about the kachina dances or other sacred information also merited the death penalty by decapitation. Acts of violence were handled within the households based on a system of revenge and retribution. Adultery was not considered a crime. Most deaths were attributed to witchcraft, typically as the result of having some small foreign object shot into the body by a witch. The dead person's soul, which was identified with the ability to think, to feel and to breathe, would stay in the village for four days before moving to the kachina village at the bottom of the lake. Some priests could have an afterlife in the place of emergence or by the shores of the ocean. The dead were then responsible for helping bring rain to the village and assuring that the people are happy.

When it comes to getting information about Zuni beliefs and the symbolism or religious significance of the dances and chants it is often the case that those who know won't talk and those who talk don't know. In light of this, all the information from the various ethnological sources has to be examined very carefully. It is, however, interesting to see the points where they agree and where they disagree. However, even then different informants might have very different takes on the religious significance of some events and, in fact, there is no orthodoxy that determines who is right and who is wrong.

THE PROCESSION OF THE GODS

My friend Sifu and I were standing by the river with a group of Zuni when we heard bells, then drums. Everyone was looking up the road where we saw a procession of the gods coming toward us. The Zuni people quickly formed two lines down the middle of the road. Our Zuni friends pull out bags of corn meal and run out in the road to join the crowd. We watch respectfully from a distance. The first in line as the procession approaches is a man wrapped in a blanket, wearing a headband. He is carrying a large offering bowl full of cornmeal with a Corn Mother propped up in the bowl. He is scattering cornmeal on the road so the kachinas will have a sanctified pathway. Behind him are two priests, also wrapped in blankets but with red headbands. Behind them is the Little Fire God's ceremonial father, then the Little Fire God, painted all in black with multicolored dots all over his mask and his body. Next is Long Horn and Hututu, followed by a line that alternates between Wood Carriers and Warrior kachinas; all masked and moving slowly in the procession. There is cornmeal all along the road where they walk and the people are sprinkling cornmeal on them as they pass. Long Horn moves slowly and with a sense of dignity and detached nobility, whereas the Warrior kachinas are in constant motion and dart around, with every movement done quickly. They have a loud quick call they make as well and they shake their heads, which appears especially dramatic with their ruff of raven feathers around their necks. Then they are followed by the usual cadre of drummers, all wrapped in blankets wearing headbands. The music of the drums and rattles measures their cadence down the road. We watch, mesmerized, as they pass. They go to the little bridge and gather on this side of the river.

There are twenty-seven kachinas that make up the assembly of the gods for this ceremony. They include: six Shalakos, each with an alternate; one Long Horn kachina (Saiyatasha); one Rain Priest kachina (Hututu); two Log Carriers (Yamuhakto); six Warrior kachinas (Salimopia); the Little Fire God (Shulawitsi); the Little Fire God's ceremonial father, (Shulawitse An Tatchu); and ten mudheads (Koyemshi). The Little Fire Gods ceremonial father is not masked.

Each Shalako is the ten-foot-tall messenger of the Rain God. His alternate is called Anuthlona. Since it is a strenuous job controlling the ten-foot-tall mask, the person personifying Shalako can take a break and the Anuthlona takes their place. Consequently there are two people for each mask alternating through the night. Shalako has a turquoise-colored mask with a crest of eagle and macaw feathers. The crest is made of the tail feathers of an eagle. He has two blue horns that are decorated with a red feather on one horn and a white feather on the other. He has round eyeballs with a movable black iris and a blue snout with teeth represented by four black streaks at the tip. This snout can open and close, making a great clattering sound.

He has hair hanging down in the back that is at least five-feet long and a collar of black raven feathers; two fox skins hang down from his shoulders like arms for the costume. He also has a dance kilt over his shoulders. Below the kilt he is wrapped with two long white blankets with an eagle feather sewn on them. The mask is held in place with willow hoops that makes the skirt stand out about four feet at the bottom. Inside the outfit the impersonator has a stick supported on a leather pouch attached to his belt. This holds up the whole mask. A second stick controls the beak and makes it click. He has a stone axe in his belt to show he is a warrior and has colored yarn wrapped around the bottom of his legs, the only part of his body that shows, and bells tied to his ankles.

It is a year-long commitment to enact the role of Shalako. Each person chosen must memorize long prayers and chants and rehearse regularly for the year. He must go on monthly visits to the springs and shrines to plant prayer sticks. Then he goes on a four-day retreat before the main event. Both the Shalako and alternate are required to memorize the chants and make the long journeys to offer prayer sticks. On the day of the ceremony, when they see the fires started by the Little Fire God they don their masks and begin the journey into the village for a night of feasting and dancing.

The Shalakos come down the slope from Greasy Hill, approaching from the south. They cross the bridge into the village and leave their masks by the river and go to eat and paint their faces before returning to put on the masks. Then they disperse to six houses that are hosting one of the Shalakos. In the house they do a long recitation of the mythic history of the people's migration. Once this is complete, the women bring a feast for everyone. After the feast the dancing begins. Shalako dances to the beat of the drum while clacking his beak. This goes on until Venus appears on the horizon. The next day they have a race across a field between six pits where prayer sticks are planted. This ends the event and they leave town in another procession.

Shalako impersonators (Anuthlona) have a distinctive dress of their own. There are two dancers for each Shalako mask and they are called the elder brother and the younger brother. The impersonator who is not under the mask dances at the same time the person in the mask is dancing. Both persons spend the entire night after the feast dancing. They have a distinctive white buckskin skullcap with pendants on the sides and cut short in the back. On the crown of their heads they have an upright tuft of cloth and buttons on the front of the headpiece. Their hair is in a bang in the front and a ponytail in the back which is wrapped in red and yellow yarn. They wear a short black kilt with a white sash and a woven belt andh a fancy shirt with red, yellow and white ribbons that pass over the shoulders and drape across their backs. They paint their face with a horizontal back line under the eyes and a red spot on their cheeks. They carry a stone axe with a horsetail pendant in their belt. They have bells wrapped around their calves tied on with black yarn; their legs are painted white. They hold a yucca whip and prayer sticks when they are not in the mask. Their face paint is called a warrior's stripe, being a bold black line running from cheek to cheek across their nose. They wear short pants along with a blue breechcloth with embroidered belt. Their moccasins are blue with red-and-yellow turn-back cuffs and quill-worked heels.

The Long Horn Kachina (Saiyatasha) is the leader of the gods. The Shalako requires the presence of Long Horn along with the Little Fire God, Hututu, the Wood Carrier and the Warrior Kachina. The Long Horn is the Rain Priest of the North and is the most important kachina, second only to Pautiwa, who is considered the Chief of the kachinas. The Shalako is the only time that the Long Horn Kachina appears. He is in charge of the calendar that shows people when to start planting and when ceremonies are to be held. He controls weather and the length of a person's life. The one long horn of the mask is believed to bring long life to all the people. The small right eye is a warning to the witches that their life will be short and the long left eye is for a long life for the people who have good hearts. There is black goat's hair hanging from the long horn and over the eyes. He has a quiver made of mountain lion skin and carries a bow and arrow in the left hand and a deer scapula rattle in the right. He wears numerous necklaces and bracelets to show that he is a valuable kachina. He also has a white down feather that indicates he is a priest. He wears a white shirt and white kilt with fringed white leggings, a fox skin, and colorful moccasins. His job is to make the days warm which is accomplished with twice daily prayers, morning and evening to the sun. This is done with special emphasis in the spring and fall when there is danger of frost harming the crops. He also influences the deer hunt. All during the year the impersonator is called by his title rather than by name and must not leave the village or engage in any bad behavior. It is a high-prestige position and includes observation of the moon to determine the day of the full moon when prayer sticks are planted in various locations. He represents the northern kiva.

Hututu is the Rain Priest of the South from the southern kiva and is the deputy of Long Horn. Hututu also only appears at Shalako. He makes a deep sound calling his name Hu-tu-tu. He is a Bow Priest (Master of Arms for the Long Horn). He attends to the secular issues while the Fire God takes care of sacred affairs. His apparel is identical to Long Horn except that his ears are equal sized with no horns.

The Wood Carrier (Yamuhakto) is the assistant of Hututu and Long Horn. Two Wood Carriers are required at Shalako and they have a piece of cottonwood on their masks with a tassel of colored string at each end and a deer antler in one hand. They are warriors of the east and west. Their mask is blue with a black collar stuffed with hair. The mask has a ruff of spruce boughs dotted with white popcorn. Their upper body is painted reddish with dots of yellow. They have necklaces and bracelets on both wrists and wear blue moccasins. They wear a white kilt with embroidery fastened with a sash. They have a fox skin pendant in the back. This is the only time of the year that they appear. Their job is to bring firewood and timbers for building, which is symbolized by the piece of wood on the crown of their head. The antler they carry symbolizes the deer. They have the responsibility to pray for the trees so that the people will have all the wood they need for building and to burn to stay warm and cook. His name means "carrying wood" and as a kachina he is considered the father of the trees and has authority over the forests. As a representative of the trees he provides a place where the deer come to lay down; and thus, the deer antler he carries.

The Little Fire God (Shulawitsi) represents the sun and is accompanied by his ceremonial father Shulawitsi An Tachu. It is their job to make fire using a wooden drill stick. This fire is used to light the torch of Little Fire God. He is known as the Speaker of the Sun and controls fire and warmth. In the old days he appeared completely nude but now wears a breechcloth. He is painted black from head to toe with dots of yellow, blue, red, white and green. He is adorned with numerous turquoise necklaces. He has a fawn skin pouch filled with seeds and has two rabbit skins with a fringe of rat skins hanging on his back. He carries a fire drill and board in his left hand. His mask is topped with a turkey feather and two heavy strings. He has two cedar bark torches and lights fires along the way. The smoke from these fires is considered to be filled with water since the smoke looks like clouds and they believe the smoke feeds the clouds and brings the rain. All things related to fire are his province . He is from the Badger clan, which is the fire-making clan.

His ceremonial father has white cotton pants and shirt with a white sash. He wears a buckskin cape and has a black line across his face below the eyes. He carries a bowl of cornmeal, a number of prayer sticks and a ceremonial ear of corn wrapped in feathers called a mili or Corn Mother.

There are six Warrior kachinas (Salimopia) whose job is to guard the procession. The six Warriors represent each of the six directions and the six kivas which are identified by the colors on their masks. Only two of the warriors are required at the Shalako ceremony. They reside in the sacred village of Kothluwala, waiting for this ceremony. They bring a cold wind with them so they can only appear in winter when it won't damage the crops. They have a dome-shaped mask topped with a few feathers that stick out toward the back and a stick-like nose about six inches long. The mask has a round graphic design with two small round eyes that can have a bar connecting them. They wear a breechcloth and are painted with the colors that designate the direction they represent. They have wreaths of spruce boughs around their ankles and wrists. They have a pouch filled with seeds and necklaces made of grains of corn and carry yucca whips. They are typically young men who are chosen for their beauty and grace of movement. At almost any time they can rush out and strike a bystander with their yucca whips; this is actually considered a good thing that will bring luck to the person who is struck. They act with exuberance and vitality. Their main role comes after the all-night dances when the Shalako have their race in the field. If the Shalako should fall it is their job to whip everyone present, which they believe will take away the bad luck that is indicated when the Shalako falls down. They do not whip the Shalako but only the bystanders who are unlucky enough to be nearby at the time.

The mudheads (Koyemshi) are the most sacred of the kachinas and the most dangerous. They appear in a group of ten, representing one parent who appears normal with nine grotesque children. Their job is to provide comic relief and to help the kachinas if anything goes wrong with their costumes. Their masks are made of cotton with knobs of wadded cotton stuffed with seeds and dirt from the footpaths of the town. Cushing describes mudheads as having, "warty, wen-eyed, pucker-mouthed pink masks and mud-bedaubed equally pink bodies." [14] The Zuni consider the mudheads the most dangerous of all the kachinas. They say that if anyone touches a mudhead they will go crazy. They consider them innocent and sexually immature, like small children. They can go naked with no shame and they have a drum which has butterfly wings inside the drumhead that causes women to be sexually uninhibited. When they arrive at the village they are sprinkled with corn meal and go to the house of the "Father" of the mudheads where they enter an eight-day retreat.

Mails reports that upon the birth of the mudheads, "The first was normal in all respects, but the others did not have their seeds of generation within them, and accordingly were not fertile. Their seeds were 'outside', contained within great wart-like knobs that began to grow on their heads. They had puckered mouths that garbled their speech, so they spoke unintelligibly and became silly, even though they were as wise as the gods and the high priests." [15] They have many responsibilities during the year and have to forego regular employment due to the work required as part of their duties. They help with the home-building at the houses that are hosting the Shalakos and have regular religious duties all during the year. They go on retreat eight days prior to the arrival of the procession and continue on retreat for another six days after the procession leaves town.

Baron Wright reports that, "each one has his own name and characteristics. Invariably, these are the reverse of what their name implies. Thus, Koyemshi Apithlashiwanni, the redoubtable Bow Priest of the group, is an utter coward frightened of everything, while Awan Pekwin, the all-important speaker for the Sun, is a day-dreamer who rarely speaks but when he does is witlessly irrelevant. Eshotsi, the Bat, is deathly afraid of the dark, avoiding every shadow regardless of its size and is able to see marvelously well in the daylight. Awan Tatchu, the Koyemshi Father, stands helplessly about with arms hanging and does nothing, while unbearably vain Muyapona believes himself hidden behind the smallest feather or straw held before his face. Posuki, the Pouter, laughs hilariously at everything, as does Itsepasha, the Glum One, who is forever cheerful and obliging. Nalashi, the Aged, is the biggest of them all with an ancient wrinkled face and acts like an ingenuous child, while Kalutse, the Infant, who would presumably know nothing, tells everyone what to do. Tsathlashi, the Old Youth, is a self-centered, self-important, thoughtless, posturing individual." [16] They are the first to appear, coming into the village eight days prior to the main event. They go to each of the plazas and announce the upcoming event. The mudhead father calls on each of them in turn to give the news but each of them ends up saying something ridiculous or outrageous, even obscene, until finally the father makes the announcement.

Then, after the main dances when the procession has left town, they stay behind and do a Mountain Sheep dance all around the village. In the old days they would dance on the roofs of the houses. Then they go back into retreat for another six days, during which they dance every night, either alone or with other kachinas who are visiting the village, or they go out to the houses that hosted the Shalako and dance there. They have a choir that goes with them to provide the chanting and music. One morning during this time they appear in the plaza and pass out presents and play guessing games with the people. On the sixth night they are fed stew and pili bread by the women of the mudhead house. Then, they fast until the end of the retreat two days later. On the final day they go to the plaza and receive presents from the people. They get slaughtered sheep and watermelons, even new clothes. Then their paternal aunt gives each of them a ritual bath and they go back to the plaza to pick up their gifts. They finally go around one more time to all the hosting houses and gather up prayer sticks. Other kachinas come to town that day and they dance in the plazas and once all the dancing is done they go house to house, thanking all the women of the household and go back to their residence where they unmask, break their fast with a feast and return home. The masks are all gathered up and put in blankets into storage at a common location.

LITERARY ETHNOLOGY

In the 1870s ethnology was a new discipline and the Smithsonian Institution in Washington D.C. started a new branch to explore its possibilities. In 1876 the Smithsonian sent an expedition to the Southwest to study and explore the pueblos. Frank Hamilton Cushing was one of the first ethnologists and was on that expedition, as was Matilda Coxe Stephenson, whose husband was the leader. Zuni was the first stop on their itinerary and Cushing immediately fell in love with Zuni and when the expedition returned to Washington he stayed at Zuni. He wrote the first account of the Shalako ceremony, which was soon followed by a more detailed account written by Matilda Stevenson. Since that time there has been an unending tide of ethnologists, anthropologists and archaeologists who have come to Zuni to study their culture and traditions, past and present. Seven of the more prominent scholars who have attended the Shalako and have written a brief synopsis of their experience at the Shalako events are:

Frank Hamilton Cushing 1876
Matilda Coxe Stevenson 1891

Ruth Bunzel	1926
Elsie Clews Parson	1930
Erma Fergusson	1931
Barbara Tedlock	1974
Thomas Mails	1977
Frank Hamilton Cushing	1876

Cushing gives the earliest recorded account of the Shalako festivities. He reports that the mudheads showed up in the village and went from plaza to plaza repeating at each one a chant telling the people to prepare for the Shalako in four days. But each mudhead would start off the recitation and then bungle it in a different way. They started with one mudhead and he would start the recitation very somberly but then go off on some nonsense, then the rest would ridicule him and another would take over and he would do the same, ending up with some absurd tale that brought laughter from the crowd and this would go on through all the mudheads until they came to the "father" who solemnly went through the chant. All the mudheads then retreated to one of the houses. Cushing learned they had been in retreat for the past four days and had four more days to go. He asked permission to visit them and take them some tobacco and was given instruction telling him to be sure not to touch any of the mudheads because it was a fearful situation to be in the presence of the gods and potentially dangerous. He was instructed not to speak in either Spanish or English and warned that he would be whipped with a yucca whip if he disobeyed.

At this point Cushing had only been at Zuni for a few weeks and it took him nearly nine months to become fluent in the language, so he was still struggling with conversing in Zuni. He goes into the house with the mudheads and sure enough when he tries to repeat the opening lines he is supposed to recite he blows it and reverts to Spanish and promptly gets whipped. He was struck once on each wrist and ankle and reports that the pain was excruciating. He was quickly escorted out of the room before he had a chance to make any other mistakes. However, he got a good look at the room and reported, "At the western end stood an altar, composed of tablets of various heights and widths, strangely carved and painted in representations of gods, and set up in the form of a square. At the back were larger tablets, on which figures of the sun, moon and stars were painted and cut. Within the square stood a number of sacred wands of long macaw feathers inserted into beautiful wicker-work handles." This was an ear of corn, called the mili or the Corn Mother, which is an ear of corn carefully and beautifully wrapped in feathers. He also reported, "All along the walls of the great room, now vivid in the fire-light, now indistinct in the flickering shadows, were painted in red, green, blue and yellow the figures of animals, birds, human monsters, demons and significant pictographs." [17]

That night he could see fires in the distance and hear the faint sounds of drumming and chanting. Then the next day the pueblo filled with Hopi and Navaho visitors come for the festivities. Cushing reported that once he agreed not to sketch the event he was allowed to attend and was the first white person on record to witness the Shalako dance. The next day he watched as the gods came to the village and saw for the first time the Long Horn, the Wood Carriers and the rest of the kachinas who participate in the dances. He says the Little Fire God was completely nude except for his black and spotted body paint and his mask and his fawn skin pouch. Also, he had a smoking torch in one hand. The Little Fire God proceeded to the plazas where he deposited prayersticks in holes that had been dug for this purpose and then did the same thing at all the houses that were hosting the dances. When the Shalakos came in the procession they parked their masks by the river and about dusk they went back and put on the masks and went to the houses where they were to dance. He says, "To each new house of the pueblo one of these monsters was guided by two priests. The latter were clad in closely fitting buckskin armor and round, helmet-like skull-caps of the same material. Several elaborately costumed flute-players, together with a mudhead or two, attended." [18] These two priests were then seated in each house next to the altar. These priests than recited a long rhythmic chant and once that was complete the hosts brought out a huge feast. This was blessed by a priest and then the Little Fire God waved his fire wand over all the food and the meal commenced.

He describes the group of chanters whose, "nearly nude bodies were grotesquely painted with streaks and daubs of white." [19] After the feast the chanters gathered around a large drum and filled the room with the sounds of drums and rattles and chanting at which time the dancers began their dance, which went on non-stop until the morning star appeared on the horizon. The Sun Priest then went up on the roof and recited another long chant to the rising sun. Once they finished the final chants and the sun appeared in the sky, everyone dispersed to their homes.

Later that day he reports that all the dancers came to the field by the river accompanied by flute players. All the dancers plus all the priests then assembled in the field and the rest of the people had to watch from afar. The dancers raced back and forth across the field planting prayersticks and then marched away in a procession out of the village. He says the ceremonies continued for three more nights in the houses and kivas and then the visitors all left. Cushing says that on the last day of festival, "Colonel and Mrs. Stevenson came in to bid me good-bye." Ms. Stevenson returned to Zuni many times and wrote a lengthy report published by the Bureau of Ethnology and gave other extended descriptions of the Shalako events in later years.

He reports that the mudheads appear eight days prior to the Shalako festival and announce that the men should make new clothing for the women and the women should renew the whitewash on the walls of the houses and start preparing the food for the feast. He reports that hundreds of sheep and dozens of cattle were slaughtered for the feasts. Fires could be seen burning on the hills in the distance where the kachinas were preparing. The procession came to town and then dispersed to the various houses that were to be consecrated. When it was time for the feast the Sun-Priest, the hereditary priest of the house, and the chief priest of the bow all provide ritual chants over the food. They are followed by the Little Fire God who waves his burning torch of cedar over the food. Then bits of each dish are taken to the river as sacrifices to the gods with the prayer,

> "Thus many have the days been numbered,
>
> The days of our anxious awaiting,
>
> That we might eat with the beloved!" [20]

After which the feast begins.

Matilda Coxe Stevenson 1879 - 1891 - 1896

Matilda Coxe Stevenson presents the most comprehensive description of the Shalako ceremony in print. She attended the event in 1879, 1891 and 1896. She reports, "The Sha'lako festival is the great autumn celebration, and is of more general interest to the Zunis, and also to the Indians of the surrounding country, than all the others. At no other time is there such feasting among them." [21] She uses the terminology "the Council of the Gods" and refers to the people who wear the masks as "personators". I heard a number of Zuni ridicule the phrase "Council of the Gods" but didn't figure out what terminology they use to refer to the processions of kachinas that come to town for the ceremonies.

In her account the Sun Priest has authority to assign people to help with the house building in preparation of Shalako. Those who don't comply or appear lazy on the job could get a beating with a yucca whip given by a masked kachina. Men can also be commandeered to work in the fields of the families hosting the event. However, the family has to feed the work crew two meals a day when they are on the job. The personators meet twice a month for rehearsals and once a month make a pilgrimage to a shrine to plant prayer sticks. Forty-nine days prior to the ceremony the priests meet at a special shrine and tie forty-nine knots in a cotton cord. These are presented to Long Horn and the mudhead father; from then on the personators meet regularly to rehearse their chants and dances. Then every ten days all the personators make pilgrimages to various shrines to plant prayer sticks. When the time is right the mudheads come to town and announce the coming of the gods in four days and the advent of the Shalako in eight. The people all build big fires in their houses and in all the outdoor ovens to mark this occasion. The mudheads make fun of each other, the people, and the coming event. The head priest then tells the people to complete their preparations for the big event. Then the mudheads go to a specific house and do not leave (except to gather wood or to make announcements) for eight days. Great piles of wood are placed along the route where the procession of the gods will make their way into town. When the procession comes into the village the Little Fire God lights all the fires along the way. Then all the gods in the procession go to the house hosting the Long Horn and stay there in retreat for the next four days. During these days the women in the host houses are busy grinding corn, there are chants that accompany this task and a group of young men provide accompaniment on drums and rattles. The women who are not grinding corn dance to the chants. At the end of the day they all gather and recite prayers to the setting sun.

1879

On the day of the arrival of Shalako the streets are all swept. Holes are dug at each hosting house where prayer sticks are to be deposited. People gather on the housetops to watch. The personators had to leave the village when Venus appeared in the sky and are spending the day rehearsing chants and preparing their masks with a new coat of paint. The Little Fire God and his father are the first to come to the village. They visit the houses that are hosting for that night and deposit corn meal. Then they leave town to join the rest of the procession who are meeting at a shrine just outside the village at the foot of Corn Mountain. Then the Little Fire God and his father come back to town and are greeted by the Hehea kachinas (the blunderers).

On my visit to see Shalako I didn't get to see this part of the ceremony and have not seen references to this kachina being a part of the ceremony elsewhere. Then the Little Fire God and his father go to each of the houses and plazas and are followed soon after by the entire procession, except for the six Shalakos and the mudheads. The procession plants more prayer sticks at each hole excavated at each site and Long Horn and Hututu dance back and forth crying out Hu tu tu tu, hu tu tu tu. Then after visiting all the sites they disperse to the houses where they will spend the night. A group of priests remain outside town at the Corn Mountain shrine and greets the Shalakos as they make their way toward the village. As the procession enters the town they are sprinkled with cornmeal. Then the Shalakos split up and each one goes to a separate house which will host them for the night.

When they arrive at the house the dance floor has a line of cornmeal down the middle, with cross marks every three feet. The choir takes their place by the altar. The Shalakos present the host with seeds of six colors of corn along with squash, watermelon and muskmelon seeds from their pouches. Then they mark each wall with four lines of cornmeal and strike the wall with a yucca whip. Then prayer sticks are deposited in the cloud shrine that hangs from the ceiling. All this is accompanied by chants, drums, rattles, flutes and a rhombus. Prayers are made for rain and long life and all the good that can come. The music stops and there is another prayer to overcome all enemies. The procession is seated at the front part of the room where they smoke reed cigarettes. Then a litany is chanted that lasts up to two hours and is accompanied by whirling rombi and occasional responses from the people saying "Athlu". When this is complete the feast begins. Samples of the food are taken as offerings to the other kachinas. When the feast concludes the gods don their masks and dance until the rising of the morning star. Then Long Horn and the Sun priest go to the roof and chant a greeting to the sun. They return to the altar and do more chants, which concludes the ceremony for the night. They are fed a breakfast feast and rest for a few hours.

1891

Stevenson's account from 1891 is by far the most detailed and provides more information than her other accounts. This account skips over what transpired leading up to the main event and begins with the Shalakos coming into the village.

At the beginning of the evening the six Shalakos and their managers come to the village where they are sprinkled with cornmeal. The Shalakos then disperse to the respective houses that are hosting them for the night. Here they deposit prayer sticks before coming into the house. Once in the house the Shalako take seeds from their belts and deposits them at the altar. They then mark each wall with four marks and strike it with their yucca whip and deposit a prayer stick in the "house of the clouds" that is suspended from the rafters. This is accompanied by rattles and drums and flutes and a rhombus. The personators then repeat chants and dance with four members of the Hunter society who are dressed in breechcloths.

After all the chanting and the feast the Shalako puts on the mask and the dance begins. People coming to watch sprinkle cornmeal on the altar before finding their seats. The house is like a primitive theater with side rooms where people can sit and observe the dances through large windows. She reports that, "as the night advances drinking is indulged in until the scene becomes disgusting in the extreme. No whisky is served in the ceremonial chamber, and great care is observed that none but Indians know the source of the intoxication." [22]

The next morning the streets are full of people milling around and the roof ops are crowded with spectators. Nearly all the pueblos are represented with large numbers of Navahos. She again reports, "The scene of debauchery in the morning is shocking, but as the day wanes it becomes disgusting in the extreme. The mad desire for drink among many of the Zunis is too great for them to remain sober enough to observe the ceremonial of their gods, to which they have looked forward for many days. Many of these staggering Indians are not over 14 or 15 years of age. Numbers of Navahos are fighting with one another or with the Pueblos, drawing knives and pistols. Many fall from their saddles during their quarrels, others lie motionless in the streets, too drunk to move away." [23]

Before noon the first procession moves through town with one of the Shalako heading to the bridge over the river. The procession includes ten men who are playing flutes which are as long as the barrel of a rifle. They are followed by an officer of the kiva carrying his mili and sprinkling meal. Then the alternate and the Shalako followed by a thirty-person choir who are chanting. As they go through the streets of the village the people on the roofs rain cornmeal down on the whole procession.

Then one Shalako after another crosses the bridge to the ceremonial field. A series of square holes have been dug in the field and each hole is watched over by an attendant while the Shalako and their alternates line up to much chanting and music. Again the Little Fire God goes first depositing prayer-sticks in each hole. Then Long Horn and other of the gods follow suit. A line of priests sprinkle each of the kachinas with cornmeal as they pass. The Warrior kachinas run back and forth across the field. Finally, the Shalako begin running from their resting place each to a designated hole to deposit more prayer sticks. Then the alternates change places with the runners who are in the masks and repeat the pattern of running to the holes. Then all six Shalako run as rapidly as possible across the field and gather in a group and leave the field. Once they are out of the village they are pursued by a number of young men who chase them and try to throw them on the ground. If they succeed they call out, "I have killed the deer." They sprinkle it with corn meal praying for success in the coming year in the hunt. The Shalako then go to the cabin outside of town where the masks are taken off and returned to the village, covered with blankets. She says, "The rapid running from one excava-tion to another is a dramatization of the services performed by the Shalako, the couriers of the rain-maker priests of the six regions, who when wishing to communicate with one another, employ couriers for the purpose." [24]

Once the Shalako leave the field the people race across the river and there are foot races between the Navaho and Zuni with great betting. Lastly, the mudheads emerge from their house for the first time in daylight and travel around the village blessing each house with cornmeal sprinkled on the roofs. The dancing then continues for another five nights. At about nine o'clock on the first night a line of dancers enters the dance room of one of the host houses. The dancers are lead by a woman with a fluffy eagle plume attached to a forelock of hair, followed by a male dance leader who has a correspond-ing eagle plume. The host prepares the ground with a line of cornmeal. The dancers are painted purple on their chests and limbs and wear a white kilt with a fox skin hanging down in the back. They have tortoise shell rattles on their right leg and bells on their knees. No masks are worn for this dance. Each dancer has a spruce twig in one hand and a rattle in the other. Four musicians in masks are seated and play notched sticks. When they finish, another dance troupe enters with seventeen tall thin gods who are similarly dressed. They include a boy wearing a bear skin who growls animal-like. A third troupe fol-lows them led by a young boy who carries a mili and a cornmeal basket. The arms and legs of this troupe are painted white with zigzagged lines. They are wearing white deerskin kilts and fox skin pendants in the back. They carry a quiver full of arrows and a yucca whip. One of them has a duck skin hat that looks like a duck sitting on his head. This troupe includes two masked kachinas. The person in the bear skin leads the line of dancers. When all the dancing is done the mudheads arrive, led by sixteen men and a woman. The men are dressed in black breech-cloths with their chests painted white and an eagle plume attached to the front of their forehead.

The dance director carries an eagle plume in each hand and a basket with six wooden disks painted blue-green edged with black and white representing the house of the clouds. These discs are called small suns and are placed on the chests of the dancers. Whether the disc remains in place or falls to the ground is taken as a sign of the faithfulness of the wife of the dancer. If it stays it is a good omen; if it falls it means his wife has been unfaithful.

There are separate dances that take place in the house where the mudheads are hosted. Here twenty-four dancers painted white appear decorated with lightning. The dance director is the last in the line and he carries a mili and a basket of cornmeal and has an eagle feather thrust through the septum of his nose. All the dancers have gourd rattles. The mudheads dance after the other dancers and then leave to visit the other houses. When the mudheads arrive at the other houses they do sleights of hand which appear like magic. In the first house one of the mudheads takes two eagle feathers and dances like a wild animal as everyone cries out. He takes the feathers to the fireplace and passes them through the flames, which reduces them to charred embers; he then waves them about and rubs them across his chest and restores them to full plumage before the eyes of the spectators. At the second house, a different trick is performed with a gourd which is lifted out of a basket using only a feather to the astonishment of the crowd. Another trick is done at yet another house, this time producing grains of wheat from the end of an eagle plume until they fill a quart jar, much to the amusement of the crowd.

On the final day more prayer sticks are prepared and women from all over the village come to the mudhead house with baskets of meal on their heads. At about nine in the morning the mudheads line up each wrapped in a blanket carrying a large roll of canvas and his prayer sticks. They have their fawn skin pouches which have been refilled with seed. They proceed to the sacred plaza, circle the plaza four times and line up sitting against one wall. They leave the canvas unrolled on the ground and plant a prayerstick in the plaza and are sprinkled again with cornmeal. The mudheads then retire into the kiva at the plaza. People congregate in the plaza from all over the village, bringing gifts for the mudheads. They place the gifts on the canvases one after the other. Gifts include loaves of bread, dressed sheep, watermelons and food of all kinds. After all the food is placed on the canvases, the mudheads re-emerge and other dancers appear in the plaza in masks. The dancing continues for several hours and the rooftops are crowded with spectators. The dancers all bring ears of corn which are added to the bounty of the mudheads. The mudheads frolic with the dancers, making fun of them much to the amusement of the on-lookers. The final dancers bring cooked corn, rabbit and sliced watermelon.

Her account ends here without bringing the event to any further closure.

1896

In this brief account she gives no introductory remarks and leaps right into her description of what she witnessed in 1896. She was visiting the house that hosted the mudheads and her descriptions center on what happens at that house. She notes that ten mudheads follow the Shalakos into the village, wearing white cotton trousers and white deerskin shirts. They each have their fawn skin pouch filled with seeds and pink gourd rattles. They visit each house that is hosting a Shalako and then go to the house where they are being hosted. In the main room of this house there is a choir of Zuni chanting with drums and rattles. The father of the mudheads deposits prayersticks and sprinkles corn meal at the altar. The mudheads each come forward to the altar to give seeds to the host. Then the father marks the walls with cornmeal. A priest comes behind him and strikes the wall with a yucca whip. They place prayersticks in the sky shrine, also called the house of the clouds, which is suspended in the middle of the room. Then the mudheads are seated in relation to other members of the household and the clans. They remove their masks and all smoke reed cigarettes of native tobacco.

After they demask the father recites the myth of the people, which takes up to two hours. Those present respond saying "Athlu" at the end of certain lines. In the course of the recitation he says, "I leave my children with you for five days: they will dance in your house: they will then go to the home of the gods in the east... Give us food that we may eat, and next year we will bring you all kinds of seeds." [25] When he completes the recitation the feast begins. After the feast and more smoking, the dancing begins. The mudheads all dance to the accompaniment of the chanting and music. During the course of the night, the mudheads go around to the other houses that are hosting the Shalakos. While the mudheads are gone the members of "fraternity" in the house hosting the mudheads continue the dance with dancers who are elaborately decorated with white paint. The dance goes on until dawn.

Stevenson's account, published in 1901 – 1902 in the *Twenty-third Annual Report of the Bureau of American Ethnology*, is among the most detailed ethnographic reports about the Zuni. It is a voluminous report and includes some of the best depictions of the kachina masks that exist to this day. It is titled, *The Zuni Indians: Their Mythology, Esoteric Fraternities and Ceremonies*. The Zuni priests were very dismayed at the amount of information she revealed about their ceremonies and attempted to clamp down on any future informants.

Ruth Bunzel 1926

Ruth Bunzel's book, *Zuni Katcinas: An Analytic Study* was published in *the Forty-Seventh Annual Report of the Bureau of American Ethnology, 1929-1930*. She references all the kachina dances in the ceremonial calendar, with special attention to Shalako. She reports that, "Katcina dances are performed in all the pueblos except Taos, where, up to the present, no trace of the cult has been found. It has developed luxuriantly at Zuni and among the Hopi...At

Zuni the winter solstice ceremonies form the keystone of the ceremonial system, the point of greatest intensity is unquestionably the Ca'lako ceremony, the culminating ceremony of the katchina society. Katchina ceremonies are public, spectacular and popular." [26] The Zuni word for the Shalako is kok'wawia which means literally "the coming of the gods". All together it lasts for fourteen days and is the culmination of a full year of preparation from the time of the appointment of the roles at the winter solstice until the performance in late November or early December. When it is close to time for a dance the manager goes around and collects the masks, he goes to each house and calls out, "I have come to get a pumpkin." Everyone understands what he is talking about and they bring out the mask from its place of storage and he takes it in a blanket and takes it to the kiva. They strip the mask of its feathers and the old paint and redo the mask. There are prayers they repeat while painting the masks saying, "I am making you into a person." [27] She reports that, "As a rule the importance of a katcina can be judged by the variety and quantity of his feathers. A katcina without feathers is an anomaly. All use the downy feather from the breast of the eagle. This is preeminently the feather of the katcinas, these feathers represent the breath of the rain. Even those katcinas who wear no other feathers have downy feathers in their ears. Eagle tail feather, feathers from the breast and tail of the turkey, owl feathers and the breast feathers of the yellow macaw are all worn by many different katcinas." [28]

The person impersonating Long Horn (Saiyataca) is a priest and is one of the most honored roles. He is expected to live for this year in a solemn manner, not being involved in worldly affairs and is expected to be kind and good in all ways and to all people and to stay in the pueblo. "His heart must be good." [29] He is at least middle-aged and is chosen because he will take on the responsibilities of this office with deep respect and honor the importance of all that is expected of him. It is part of his performance to give a long recitation that lasts for several hours and is done in a loud slow voice. He has three main chants other than the long recitation at the house. These are in the morning, one on a housetop at dawn, then another to the congregation of the gods, and a farewell when everything is completed. Any time he speaks it is done in a solemn manner. He is considered a leader and is responsible for overseeing the monthly ritual of going to the springs and shrines to plant the prayer sticks. He must pray daily and go to the corn fields before the sun rises and sprinkle cornmeal on the crops. During the summer he must stand before the corn field each morning and recite a prayer saying, "Now you will go on and produce for my people. They need you. Please hurry and make my people happier." [30] As part of this daily routine it is his responsibility to bring the warmth and pray that there is no frost that kills the crops. This is especially important in the spring and fall when the likelihood of frost is increased. During this time he takes a special cornmeal made from baked sweet corn and goes to the field before sunrise and as the first rays of the sun illuminate the fields he puts the cornmeal in his mouth and sprays it out over the field and addresses the sun saying, "Our father, sun, let your rays make the days warm so that the crops may grow quickly, and send us your rains, too." [31]

All of the kachinas in this ceremony are expected to live exemplary lives for this year and those who are found to be in violation are publically rebuked. It is Long Horn's role to be sure that everyone acts appropriately and Long Horn reports these acts to the Hututu, who then rebukes any wrong-doers at the monthly ceremony where they plant the prayer sticks.

On the day of the main ceremony when Shalako comes to town he must recite the prayer, "I have been praying for my people that they may have much rain and good crops and that they may be fortunate with their babies and that they may have no misfortunes and sickness. I have been praying that my people may have no sickness to make them unhappy, I want them all to be happy, and to wait for me when my time comes. I am here that my people may have good luck in everything. I am here to throw out the people with double hearts. I have come that my people may have good luck and be happy. I have been planting feathers in all the springs that they may be happy and that they may have plenty of seeds in their back rooms, that their houses may be so full that they have no place to walk in their back rooms. And if anyone tries to injure my people I want them to watch for whoever is doing this, so that he may stand up in the daylight and the daylight people may know who is trying to injure them. I want my people to reach old age and to come to the ends of their roads, and not to be cut off while they are still young. I want my mothers to have many children, so that each may have one on her back and one in her arms and one walking behind while she is with child. I want my people to have large families." [32]

The Shalako go to a place called White Rocks just outside the village to put on their masks on the day of the main events and proceed to the field on the south side of the river. They leave their masks by the side of the field and go for dinner in the village. They return after dark, put the masks back on, and head into the village. Each Shalako is surrounded by a group of singers from their kiva and walk into town accompanied by songs from the singers. Once in the village they go to separate houses to make special blessings. When a Shalako comes to a house he offers the following prayer:

"I have come to see my people.

For many years I have heard of my people living here at Itiwan'a

and for long I have wanted to come.

I want them to be happy,

I have been praying for them;

especially I want the women to be fortunate with their babies.

I bring my people all kinds of seeds,

all the different kinds of corn

all different kinds of fruit

and wild green things.

I have been praying for my people to have long life;

and whoever has an evil heart should stand up in the daylight.

I have been praying for my people

may they have all different kinds of seeds

and their rooms be full of corn of all colors

and beans of all colors

and pumpkins

and water gourds,

and that they may have plenty of fresh water,

so that they may look well

and be healthy

because of the pumpkins

and the beans

and the corn.

I want to see them healthy." [33]

Once the dancing starts a dancers without a mask carries a yucca whip and uses it to awaken anyone who starts to nap during the dance. All the personators have to learn elaborate prayers and chants. They pray for all the people and for all good things. The chants that accompany the dance, "always refer to the rain and the clouds and all the beautiful things that grow on the earth, and the painting on the mask means the same as the song. They paint something on the mask to please the earth and something to please the sky." [34]

In the morning, at sunrise, the Long Horn goes to the roof and recites the following,

"I have fulfilled

The breath of my father,

His life-giving breath

His breath of old age

His breath of waters,

His breath of fecundity,

His breath of seeds,

His breath of riches,

His breath of power,

His breath of strong spirit,

His breath of all good fortune,

Asking for his breath,

And into my body

Drawing his breath.
I add to your breath now…

To this end, my children;

May you be blessed with light;

May your roads be fulfilled;

May you grow old;

Yonder to where the road of your sun father comes out,

May your roads reach

Together may your roads be fulfilled." [35]

Elsie Clews Parson   1930

Elsie Parson wrote a classic two-volume work on pueblo religion and tried to cover all the pueblos. She attended Shalako and wrote an account. She is known to have paid her informants, a practice that cast suspicion on her findings to her critics.

She reports that the impersonators for the next year's annual event are chosen at the winter solstice and are designated with a "crook of appointment". Two persons from each kiva are chosen. Meetings to practice and learn the chants are held all year long. The impersonators get up before sunrise to greet the sun and make offerings of cornmeal and each evening they take a portion of their dinner and offer it to the dead by putting it in the river and sending it downstream. On each full moon they visit particular shrines and springs and plant prayer sticks. The prayer sticks are made the day of the full moon and long chants are recited at each stage of the process. The impersonators and the mudheads are expected to work for the households who host the Shalako. After planting ten prayer sticks the Long Horn and Father Koyemshi get a string with 49 knots representing a day count; one knot is untied each day until the day of the Shalako ceremony. When each tenth knot is untied, more prayer sticks are planted at White Rocks and other shrines to the southwest of the town.

When the 48th knot is untied the Fire God and his father come to the village in mid- afternoon and plant prayer sticks in six predetermined locations with special dances at each spot. They visit the houses where the Shalako will come and plant prayer sticks inside the doorway. The pathway into the house is laid out with cornmeal. They deliver special seeds to each household and bless the house with the following chant,

"With seeds of all kinds,

I consecrated the center of his floor.

This is well;

In order that my father's fourth room

May be bursting with corn,

That even in his doorway,

The shelled corn may be scattered before the door,

The beans may be scattered before the floor,

That his house may be full of little boys

And little girls,

And people grown to maturity:

That in his house

Children may jostle one another in the doorway,

In order that it may be thus,

I have consecrated the rain-filled room

Of my daylight father,

My daylight mother." [36]

Once the kachinas are gathered in the house where the main events take place they de-mask and have a ritual smoke with the owners of the house. They invoke blessing for the house and for the fecundity of the occupants. This takes several hours as the Shalako performs the elaborate chants. Once all this is completed the owners put on a feast. Portions of the food are taken to the river for the "old ones" who are there in the form of the kachinas. Then, after the feast, they dance for the rest of the night, both masked and "naked", i.e. without masks. When dawn breaks the Long Horn unties the last knot in the string and the kachinas unmask and have their hair washed. Then the Shalakos from all the different houses gather by the river where they are sprinkled with more cornmeal and go to a field on the south side of the river where the Fire God and his father have buried prayer sticks. Then the Shalakos have a race, each one running across the field to retrieve one of the prayer sticks that has been buried there. If anyone falls during the race it is considered a sign that they did not honor their commitments to be celibate. The Warriors who are in the field can step out and whip any nearby spectators. Once the races are over, the young men of the village race after the Shalakos and try to touch them and if they manage to touch them they call out, "I have killed a deer". It is considered a very good omen for future hunts.

After all this the mudheads make a round to all the houses. For the next four days the kivas all hold group dances and have a choir who chant for the dances. On the morning after all these dances the mudheads gather at dawn and are sprinkled one more time with corn meal, then the Father tells the Rain Chief that the mudheads have completed their work for this year's crops and the mudheads each get a ritual bath and receive gifts from everyone. They end with the chant about giving long life and good health to all the people and ask the kachinas not to draw them back into their kachina village.

Shalako is a multidimensional ceremony that honors the dead and asks for their help, plus it is a war ceremony, a hunt ceremony, a ritual for longevity and also for fecundity. The war aspect is illustrated by war clubs that are included, sometimes hidden, in the costumes.

Erna Fergusson 1931

Forty-nine days prior to Shalako, Long Horn and the father of the mudheads are both given a string with forty-nine knots along its length and are instructed to untie one knot each day. Then, there are ceremonies every ten days up until eight days prior, when the mudheads go into the village and announce the coming of the gods. Four days before the ceremony all the performers make pilgrimages to six different shrines where the Little Fire God lights a fire with his cedar torch. The next day each household is required to sacrifice some of their meal to the fire to feed the ancestors. She reports that there are six houses for the Shalakos plus a house for the "Council of the Gods" and one for the mudheads. If there aren't six new houses then some families re-plaster their walls and host a Shalako there. Those who host are assisted through the year by various dancers and the entire village helps them at harvest and in the construction effort to prepare the house. Just before the ceremony there is a flurry of activity, slaughtering sheep and cattle and preparing loaves of bread along with paper-thin wafer bread.

On the day of the ceremony all the personators leave the village when the morning star appears on the horizon. All the masks have been repainted and have new feathers. She reports that, "Every ceremonial chamber is hung with bright cloths, blankets, brilliant silk shawls, feathers, and skins. A hole has been dug in front of each house: and a causeway of stones and dirt has been made across the river." [37] In the afternoon the Little Fire God is the first to cross the bridge. His fawn-skin pouch is filled with seeds and he carries a smoldering cedar torch. He and his father visit each of the houses and deposit two prayer sticks which represent the first man and the first woman. Then, the Council of the Gods comes to town led by Long Horn. He is wearing a white buckskin shirt with extravagant jewelry and carries a bow and arrow and a rattle made of deer bones. He and Hututu are escorted by Warrior Gods who act as whippers. This whole party follows the route of the Little Fire God to each of the hosting households. At each house Long Horn and Hututu dance and call out to each other hu-tu-tu. At each house the walls are marked with cornmeal and, once the gods arrive, there is a long recitation followed by the feast. She reports the Zuni use the word KoKo and don't like calling them gods. She says the Zuni have, "no anthropomorphic gods." [38] Rather, they are the forces of nature, especially those that bring the rain. Yet she persists in referring to them as gods in her text.

Finally the Shalako come in their procession. She says the Shalako personator, "manipulates strings which roll the great bulging eyes and clack the wooden beak" [39] She describes the Shalako personators saying they, "Wear only a black-velvet jacket, a close-fitting white buckskin cap, and a string of bells tied under the bare knee." The Shalakos stop before they cross the bridge and do a running ceremony in the field, which marks the last stop in the Zuni migration to find the middle place. About dark they cross the river and come into the village, dispersing to the assigned houses. The mudheads go from house to house at this time. In each Shalako house a long prayer ensues that lasts for two hours and each house fills up with visitors. After this all the guests are invited to eat. Sometime after midnight the dancing begins. There is a high seriousness to the event.

In the Long Horn house he and Hututu dance along with the Little Fire God and the Warriors. In the mudhead house they remove their masks and dance carrying prayer sticks. All the dancing goes on till dawn when all the dancers are sprinkled with cornmeal and are given a rest. After noon, a final ceremony is held back in the field south of the river. The first procession includes the Little Fire God, Long Horn and Hututu. When the Shalakos arrive they put prayer sticks in certain holes and do a race that reenacts how, "couriers of the gods, run back and forth all the year carrying messages, bringing moisture wherever it is needed." Then the whole procession marches out of Zuni between long lines of the people.

There is dancing every night for another six nights after the Shalako leave town. At night they dance in the Shalako houses and during the day they dance in the plazas. The altars are removed from the houses but the dances continue and increase in the number of dancers each night. She reports that, "During these days every man in the village must dance" [40] Each dance group has masks but the masks are not used until the final night. The Bears are first and wear no masks. They have an orange feather over one ear and a white one over the other and carry a yucca whip. There is no chorus during this time and the dancers provide their own chants. The next group includes a variety of different masks. They use the same song each year but make up new words. Each group has a Corn Mother and a bowl of cornmeal. Every group dances in every house. On the last night in the mudhead house the mudheads do clever sleights-of-hand, such as making a bowl disappear and reappear. Another group is the Tadpoles, who carry tall poles with a feather on the top. On the fourth night the dancing goes all night with women and guests escorted out about eleven o'clock. After the fourth night the mudheads have to fast until the dancing ends on the sixth day. On the next day the mudheads receive gifts in return for their year of service. They have a ceremony in the plaza and then go to the home of their maternal aunt, who washes their hair while they chant prayers. Then they return to the plaza in their mask accompanied by their clan and receive dead sheep and other gifts and bowls and baskets of food. Ten big piles of food and gifts are made in the plaza, one for each of the mudheads. All the dance groups come together in the plaza, dance and then go to the river to plant prayer sticks. The mudheads stay in the plaza and maintain their fast until the sunrise of the next morning. Then the mudheads gather up their gifts and return to their ceremonial home, where they break their fast, ending the Zuni ceremonial year.

Barbara Tedlock 1974

She describes the procession coming into town and calls them the "Council of the Gods", and calls the village of the kachinas the "land of the dead".[41] She says the Little Fire God comes first with a fawnskin pouch over one shoulder filled with wild and domestic seeds. He has a rabbit, a duck and a pheasant in one hand and a cedar torch in the other. She remarks that the torch has been "friction-lit in the ancient way". [42] He is followed by Long Horn and his assistant and two of the warrior kachinas. They are coming from the house where they put on the masks called White Rocks. They come to town in single file. The Hututu is hooting accompanied by the sounds of the bone rattles. The entire procession goes to each of the six plazas and deposit prayer sticks in holes at each plaza.

She is visiting a family that is hosting the Shalako. She gets to help decorate the room and prepare the food. She describes the main room as a sacred shrine. The walls are covered with blankets and fringed shawls. They have mounted deer heads all around the walls, each one ornamented with turquoise necklaces. The floor has been prepared and the altar is in place. She gives a detailed description of the Zuni altar at one of the houses: "A turquoise-studded meal painting swells outward before the altar in great white cumulus scallops with a cornmeal road emerging from the center, trailing off toward the front door. Scattered along the cornmeal path are, pottery jars of mossy spring water, tadpoles, water skates, and baby water snakes; there is a crystal ball that snows when shaken; baskets of tinkling all-colored corn kernels; small handled pottery jars containing white cornmeal, ground shell, and gems; and tiny paint pots. On the linoleum floor before the altar stand perfectly ears of unblemished yellow corn clothed in beadwork with olivella-shell, turquoise-nugget, and branch-coral necklaces, the corn is covered with mallard, macaw, parrot, turkey, downy-eagle, blue-jay, and songbird feathers, butt ends nestled in oat-straw basketry. The inside of a cavity in the floor is filled with all-colored corn kernels, wheat, squash, watermelon, muskmelon seeds, and pinon nuts. Stuffed parrots, red-tailed hawks, and golden eagles in stone-fetish necklaces, jet bears and quartz mountain lions with tiny tight turquoise eyes line up one behind another along the meal road facing the front door." [43] She calls the room, "the dance Hall of the Dead". [44] There is a hanging shrine as well and she refers to it as a star-cloud mobile where more prayer sticks will be deposited in the course of the ceremony.

When it is time for the gods to enter the room, the Shalako inpersonators, the elder brother and his alternate, the younger brother, both come in the room unmasked. The elder brother then goes to all four walls and marks them with cornmeal and younger brother follows with a yucca whip and strikes the walls. Then they climb up a ladder and place prayer sticks in the star-cloud mobile and drop seeds into a hole that has been excavated just below the hanging shrine called the Shrine of Emergence. They go outside and elder brother dons the masks and takes up the seven-foot pole that holds it up and is prepared to enter the house. The head of the mask is crowned with twenty-four tail feathers from an adolescent golden eagle. Behind the eagle feathers are the bright red feathers of scarlet macaw and hanging down in the back is a string with a garland of downy eagle feathers ending in a shiny abalone shell. The beak on the front of the mask is about a foot long with black and white teeth painted on the sides and across the front.

Shalako enters the room and goes to his spot by the side of the shrine and quickly removes the mask. The dance room is filled with people and when some whites try to enter the room they are politely informed that the room has been consecrated and that, while they are welcome to watch, they must do so from the side rooms and are not to enter the consecrated space. She then reports something that I have not seen in any of the other reports. She says an elderly man walked up the cornmeal path and in front of the shrine held out his arms and legs and received a blow from the yucca whips to remove bad luck and bad dreams. Then the hosts came to the front of the room and repeated prayers. Some mudheads then entered the room and made jokes about the hosts. They all smoked a "long reed filled with a mixture of wild tobacco and inner-bark shavings from red-willow stems". [45] She refers to the personators as maskers. Then the elder and younger brothers began a long recitation of the migration story. They began,

"I have come from the sacred lake to see my people.

For years I have heard about my people living here at the

Middle Place

For years I have wanted to come.

I wish them to be happy.

Especially I want the women to be fortunate with their babies.

I bring my people all kinds of seeds…

We are all here bringing you good fortune

I wish you to be happy.

I wish you to be well and to have strong hearts.

I have brought you seeds to plant with your crops next spring.

I want your houses to be full of seeds.

I have prayed that you may be fortunate with your babies.

That no one in this house may drop down…

So I have come that you may all be happy here tonight." [46]

Once the recitation was completed the feast starts and she describes the dishes including barbecued deer, mutton, turkey and beef, along with a special soup called kalhiko with deer meat, chilis, onions, wolfberries, chinchweed and mint. They have piki bread, fry bread, sourdough and sunflower and wheat bread, along with jalapenos and pinto and white beans, pumpkins and potatoes. They serve corn pudding, cattail-flour muffins and Oreo Crème cookies for desert. First they served the dancers and then they served the crowd of people attending.

When everyone had eaten the dances started, with the Shalako and his alternate both dancing, the unmasked Shalako scuffling sideways along the east-west dance floor while the masked Shalako moved gracefully back and forth. Later in the night a group of fourteen Navaho dancers came in and joined in the dance with rows of new dollar bills pinned to their fancy shirts. The dances went on untill sunrise, when the hosts washed the Shalako performers in a ritual bath.

After a brief rest the Shalako were remasked and did a procession through town where they were liberally sprinkled with cornmeal and made their way back to the river. They held the traditional race in the field just south of the river and then, on the way out of town, were chased by the young men who threw them down calling out, "I've killed a deer".

Thomas Mails 1977

He says that the Shakalo ceremony is a reenactment of the emergence and migration legends, as well as an invocation for rain, health, fertility and general well-being. The kachinas are the spirits of the dead who come back to the village. The ceremony is also a hunting ritual which comes as the finale. The whole event lasts forty-nine days and requires ten months of preparation. When he attended there were eight houses that hosted the event, six for the Shalakos, one for the Long Horn and Little Fire God, and a house for the mudheads.

Mails attended the ceremony in 1977. On the day of the main ceremony the Little Fire God came to town in the early afternoon and visited six shrines around the town, planting prayer sticks at each accompanied by prayers for abundant rain. He and his father then met the rest of the procession and visited all six shrines again. This time Long Horn and Hututu danced at each shrine stomping the ground and bowing to one another crying "Hu-tu-tu-tu-tu". When they depart the holes where they deposited the prayersticks are filled. After visiting the shrines, they go to the house which will be hosting the Little Fire God. The main room has an altar on the north wall and a "House of Clouds" ceiling shrine hanging from the middle of the ceiling. There were nine singers in the northeast corner of the room. The kachinas were lined up on a bench on the west wall. There were also nine priests facing the kachinas. Once they were all seated, they removed their masks and began long chants and smoked special cigarettes. This was accompanied from time to time by a priest who twirled a bull-roarer.

He reports that, "About 7:30 P.M. the six Shalakos and their attendants crossed the specially prepared bridge, placed their masks on the riverbank, and entered the village. Once they reached the streets, trucks and crowds led each Shalako to his sponsor's house with auto lights and police car lights piercing the mist and the familiar Hu-tu-tu sound echoing about. An hour and a half later each Shalako had returned for his mask and was again escorted to his sponsor's house." [47]

Each house had a specially prepared room that is forty feet by twenty feet. The impersonators smeared cornmeal on the walls and conducted a blessing. There was an altar at one end of the room with bowls of meal and a basket of prayer sticks. The floor of the house had been excavated about twenty inches deep to allow the Shalakos to dance. There was a sipapu hole where special offerings have been made. There was a bench by the dance floor where members of the kivas sit. The walls are covered with blankets and there are shawls hanging from the top of the walls. He counted nineteen mounted deer heads in the room, each one ornamented with turquoise necklaces. When the initial blessing is complete the Shalako enters the room and removes the mask. The two impersonators are seated beside the mask facing a priest and the three of them recited lengthy chants recounting the emergence and migration myths. After this, the feast is served and the impersonators take the first food and carry it to the river and give it as an offering to the ancestors. After the feast, the dancing began at 1:30 A.M. when the Shalako puts on the mask and the singing and music began. The Shalako moved gracefully, bird-like, looking for the middle place. His beak clacked and his bells sounded as he danced. Every forty-five minutes the impersonators change out behind a curtain of blankets held up by the priests. Other dancers including the mudheads appear from time to time to join in the ceremony.

At 7:20 A.M. the choir sprinkled the Shalako dancers with pollen and the dance ended. The dancers are then fed and given a well-deserved rest. At the Long Horn house as dawn breaks the Long Horn climbed to the roof, faced east and recited a long chant and the participants all got a ritual hair washing and are given time to rest.

Around noon all the dancers moved from their respective houses back to the bridge in processions. By 2:30 the entire assembly of the gods had arrived and danced in the field before the Shalakos spent about an hour racing back and forth across the field from east to west, depositing prayer sticks. The prayer sticks were deposited in holes and sprinkled with cornmeal in a re-enactment of the myth of how the Zuni found the middle place where they built Halona village. After this, the entire party joined together and proceeded out of town.

After the Shalakos left the village there was a week of continuing celebration and dancing at all the houses. Wild-looking ogres appeared at these dances with bear feet and bear mittens and they roamed through the village during the day on the lookout for wanton children.

SHALAKO   2017

My friend Sifu and I arrive in Zuni about 3:00 PM and go straight to the The Inn at Halona where we were lucky enough to have a room during the festival. The level of excitement in the hotel and on the streets is palpable and we are anxious to get out and roam around. The village is full of traffic and there are police cars with lights flashing blocking some of the streets. I know that the procession to town probably won't happen for another hour so we decide to go for a drive around Corn Mountain. There is a dirt road that runs around the base of the mountain and we slowly proceed along the road, stopping every few hundred yards to get out and take pictures. The weather is perfect, the sun shining and the sky cloudless and deep clear blue.

Back in the village we stop in the Visitor's Center for an orientation which they are holding each hour on the hour. We are between sessions but they have a map showing where all the Shalako houses are located with Do's and Don'ts on the back of the sheet. The man behind the desk gives us a little orientation and then tells us it is getting close to the time for the gods to come to town. He shows us on the map where we should go to get the best view. The Little Fire God is already at one of the houses and he and Long Horn and Hututu and the Wood Carriers have visited the plazas and planted prayer sticks and have gone to the house where they will be dancing tonight. We moved the car back to the hotel and walk over to where the guide had indicated. It wasn't hard to figure out since there is a big crowd of Indians standing around waiting for the procession. The sun is getting low on the horizon and I expect they will be coming sometime before sunset, so it must be getting close.

Before long we hear the sound of bells in the distance along with the sound of distant drums. Everyone's concentration has shifted and we are all looking across the river. We are standing on the north side of the river and there is a walking bridge across the river, which is now a dry river bed, just in front of us. But we are obviously supposed to stay here on the street and watch without getting any closer. I notice there are a couple of fires burning across the river at the edge of the field and along the street. Then we catch sight of the tall Shalako masks approaching in the distance and slowly they come into view, one after another, all six of them. Each of them is accompanied by a person dressed in a blanket with a headband. Behind them is another group of men dressed in blankets with headbands who are drumming and chanting and shaking rattles. The bells seem to be coming from the Shalakos. They cross the bridge one by one and then gather in a group about half-way between the bridge and the road where we are standing. After a bit of milling around we see the masks move lower to the ground then become stationary. It is obvious the impersonators are demasking and in a few minutes the six masks are lined up, unmoving, side by side.

A few of the Indians stand near the masks but everyone else drifts away and that marks the end of this part of the event. In a few minutes I get a call from Otto. He has just arrived back in the village from Albuquerque, where he was attending meetings all day. He tells us to go back to the hotel and he will pick us up there.

1ˢᵗ House

Otto shows up with Francine and they are both excited about the evening. He is taking us to one of the houses and says we will stay for a few hours and then move on and work our way around to all the houses. The house is on the edge of town and the area around the house is full of trucks. It is like a big parking lot all around the house, with trucks lined up in rows in an empty field beside the house and cars and trucks all up and down the street in front of the house. It is a large house, obviously unfinished, with a concrete block main room and other rooms added onto the main room. There is a stream of people moving toward the house. Otto takes us in and we move into a side room that has a dirt floor and is filled with metal folding chairs. We move to the back and lean against the wall behind the last row of chairs. The room is about half full but there are two big windows looking into the main room. The main room is full of folding chairs, except there is the dance gallery which goes around two sides of the room that is excavated about a foot deep to accommodate the ten-foot-tall Shalako. On the third side of the room there is a Zuni altar but we can barely see it since all the chairs are occupied and the altar is sitting on the floor. All I can see is the top part of the tallest part of the altar. And beside the altar is a group of elders sitting in a circle; they have drums, rattles and flutes that accompany them as they chant. Along the fourth wall is a bench and it is lined with men all wearing headbands, sitting solemnly, no one talking.

I have never seen anything like the main room. The walls on all the sides are covered with beautiful colorful blankets and rugs with traditional geometric designs. Every bit of the wall is covered with fabric. There are brightly-colored shawls with long fringe draped from the top of each wall. But what jumps out immediately are the stuffed deer heads hanging in rows along each wall. To top it off, on one wall is a huge elk head. All the heads are hung with turquoise necklaces. It reminds me of a Tibetan temple which tradition-ally has lots of fabric on the walls and a shrine in the room, but this is very different. I look around the house. There is a large kitchen where we entered. The main room is rapidly filling with people. I don't see any other white peo-ple so I am happy to be in the back and hopefully not in a conspicuous place.

I am studying the big room intently. The excavated gallery for the Shalako has a trail of cornmeal down the middle with crosshatches every foot or so. I have been looking at the main room for about fifteen minutes, trying to notice how it is set up when all at once I see there is a stuffed bear by the altar in the front. It is standing on its hind legs and must be six-feet-tall. I am shocked, it has just jumped out at me. I marvel how I failed to notice a full-sized bear in the room, but the room is incredibly rich with ornamental detail, more than anyone can take it at first glance. Otto and Francine know some of the people in the room and they converse with them in low tones. I am still intently studying the room and then suddenly I notice a huge bi-son head hanging on the wall, as if it just now materialized in front of me. I was looking all around the room and somehow had been so overwhelmed by all the color and fabric and the other stuffed animals and only now see the buffalo head wearing an ornate turquoise necklace hanging on the wall just through the window in front of me. I am shocked. How could this huge thing be hanging there all this time and go unnoticed? I can feel the room is vibrating with anticipation. I have never seen anything like it. The people are waiting for the god to come into the house and there is a palpable sense of awe and reverence. The energy is already intense and they aren't even here yet.

Then we hear the sound of bells and low chanting and drums in the distance. Otto comes over and whispers, "Here they come." The sounds get louder as they approach, having walked out from town in a troupe. They are congregated just outside the main double doors that lead into the center room. Everyone has gotten totally quiet and all attention is focused outside those doors. After a few more minutes of the chanting, the doors fly open and in comes two men. They are not kachinas, or at least not wearing masks. But they have a special headdress, a white cloth draped over their head and a beautiful Indian shirt. It appears to be made of silk with wide ribbons draped over their shoulders in the back. They each have a yucca whip in one hand and basket full of prayer sticks in the other. They are scattering cornmeal all over the dance gallery and then they go to the center of the wall of each side of the room and smear cornmeal on the wall and then the other person strikes the wall a loud blow with the yucca whip. The sound reverberates in the room, sharp and staccato. When they have done all four walls someone shows up with a ladder and they go to the center of the room and there is a hanging piece suspended in the air. It is painted turquoise and has an elaborate design but I can't make it out. I watch as the priest climbs up the ladder and deposits a couple of prayer sticks in the center of the hanging shrine. During all this we can still hear the chanting and drumming going on outside through the doors, which are now open. Then one of the dancers sits down beside the altar in the front. The next thing we know the Shalako bends low and steps in the door and down into the dance gallery. As he does so the choir doing the chanting steps up to the door and we can see several Indian faces at the door and they are all projecting the chant into the room with gusto. They are blasting out the chants, plus they have drums and rattles in hand. Suddenly the room is full of the sound and the Shalako is swaying and moving back and forth in the dance gallery and the room is electrified. The Shalako moves back and forth in the dance gallery; the sound of his beak clacking echoes in the room. My attention is riveted to the choir at the doorway. They are young men and chanting in loud enthusiastic voices that fill the room. After a few minutes the Shalako makes his way to the front of the room and the chanting and drumming come to a halt and several of the men dressed in blankets with headdresses gather around and hold up blankets to make a curtain and we see the head of Shalako settle down and stop moving. Then the blankets come down and the mask is sitting in the corner of the room and everyone takes a seat.

I notice a group of men have moved into the dance gallery and are sitting on the ground in a line on the gallery floor. The two Shalako dancers are sitting next to the mask and then slowly the drumming and rattles begin and the two dancers start chanting. The room is totally quiet as every ear is attuned to the sound of the chant. They are chanting in unison, in a sing-song way. I surmise it is some form of verse since they raise their voices slightly at the end of the lines and the lines seem to be about equal length. At some points in the recitation, all the Indians in the gallery and those along the wall join in with an exclamation. They all join together in an exclamation that sounds like AH. This happens from time to time in the recitation so it is obvious the people in the room are following the storyline. This goes on and on and gives me time to observe the room and the people. The house is totally packed with people and I can see faces at the windows looking in. The chanting goes on and on. I am mesmerized by the sing-song tonality and can distinguish a bit of the verse structure. The recitation continues for over two hours. It finally comes to a crescendo and then, with a final beat of the drum and shake of the rattles, it comes to a finale.

There is a sense of relief in the room. Otto motions for us to move out and we all make our way out of the room and into the kitchen area and out the side door. Once outside Otto and Francine huddle together with Sifu and me and tell us a bit of the storyline of what was happening. Otto tells us that it was a recitation of the creation story of the Zuni and how they came up out of the earth and they had to come up through various stages of the underground and then emerged in the Grand Canyon. Then they went on a long migration and the story names all of the places they stopped along the migration. Then Otto and Francine consult in Zuni for a minute and Otto says the story included all the different types of family relations in the Zuni kinship. Then he loads us into the truck and they tell us that we have a few hours before the next event starts and they are going back to their place to rest a while. I tell them to drop us at the Inn at Halona and give us a call when they are rested and ready to go out for the next round. When we get to the motel I ask if it will be ok if Sifu and I walk over to the closest of the Shalako houses, which is in easy walking distance from the hotel. They encourage us to go ahead and they will call about one o'clock. They drop us in the parking lot and we look up in the sky to see the brightest moon of the year shining over Zuni.

2nd House

We are too excited to hang around in the hotel room for long so we head over to the Lule Street house which is only a few blocks from the hotel. It is isn't hard to know which house because there are cars parked everywhere and a crowd streaming toward the house. We go in and stand around in the back of the crowd beside two long tables that are filled with newly-baked loaves of fresh bread. There are hundreds of loaves of bread stacked on the tables. We look around at the big room and study it and the people for a few minutes. Then we decide to move to another room where they are sitting up tables. Sifu heads right across the center room and is about to walk into the dance gallery when I call him back. It immediately feels like a taboo for him to enter that room or to walk across the excavated gallery where the Shalako will be dancing. So we go back out and around the house to the back door and go in.

It is not so crowded in this room and they have several long tables and women are coming and going with huge bowls of food. The tables are surrounded by people and the cast of characters is changing all the time. In a few minutes a couple of places open up and the woman who appears to be the hostess, encourages us to sit down and eat. The table is loaded with big bowls of food. There are platters of ham and fried pork chops and enchiladas and several kinds of salads, and a shredded pork mole. Having two white guys at the table seems to slow down the conversation and there is a bit of a cloud over the table, so Sifu starts filling his plate and wading into the food with gusto. I'm a vegan so there really isn't much that I want to eat but I want to respect the feast day tradition and not worry about dietary restrictions. I load my plate but can't bring myself to eat the ham or pork chops. I have a plate full of salad and a little of the enchiladas which doesn't have too much meat. When I put my plate down in front of me I sense I am a center of attention for the people around me so I announce that I am a vegetarian and then there is dead silence around the table so I say, "My friend here eats all my meat." Then everyone looks at his plate where he has ham, pork chops and the mole and is digging in and he heartily agrees saying, "Yes, yes that's right, I eat all his meat and mine too." And everyone around the table breaks out laughing and now the ice is broken and we all settle in.

I ask the tribal affiliation of the people around me. The guy beside me is a young Navaho with a gorgeous turquoise necklace. There are other Navajo at the table as well, plus a woman from Hopi and the rest Zuni. Once that is established I pipe in and say that I am a full-blood myself. This gets everyone's attention and I say, "I'm 100% full-blood cracker." That gets another big laugh. Once we have eaten we get up to make room for the next people. I take a piece of bread with me. Plus they have a whole table full of cinnamon rolls and pies. Sifu finds a chair and sits down next to a guy and they strike up a conversation. He later tells me the guy is a Zuni and was telling him how he remembers the Shalako events being more solemn when he was younger. He says everyone had more respect in those days and people don't believe in the prayers the way they used to. He remembered how there would always be young women from Hopi who would attend and there was always an air of expectation about all those Hopi girls. He said that previously the dancers would all help the people who were building the houses and it was a community effort and now it was more the responsibility of the family to see that the house was constructed.

We go back outside and stand around in the cool air and look up at the full moon. It is what they call a super moon. On this full moon the orbit of the moon brings it closer to the earth than any other month of 2017 so this is the biggest full moon of the year and it is spectacular. We wander around to the front of the house and there are some kids building a fire in a horno oven. The top of the oven has worn away and flames are shooting out the door and out the top. The heat feels good. There is a man there supervising. He is on crutches and we talk with him. Turns out he owns the house and is the host for the whole event, along with a brother and their wives and the rest of the extended family that will end up living in the house when it is finished. For now the house is only a shell. It was built to accommodate this event so the floor is dirt so it can be excavated to make the dance gallery for Shalako. Once this is all over they will build it out, put down the floor, and divide the big room into separate rooms like a regular house. He tells us that the dancing won't start until 1 or 1:30 so we decide to walk back to the motel and take a break for a few minutes and then come back closer to that time.

When 1:00 AM rolled up Sifu and I walked back to the Lule Street house and came around to the back door and walked in. The tables were cleared and the women were folding up the tables and chairs and moving them to the far side of the room. The house was fairly still and not too crowded so we had a chance to get closer to the main room, which was separated from the kitchen/dining room by two large windows through which we could view the main room. In the main room the walls are covered with colorful blankets and rugs, all with traditional pueblo designs. Even the doorways are wrapped in colorful fabric. Around the top of the room there are colorful scarves with long fringe hanging down. There must be a dozen or more conca belts hanging on the wall. Then there are the stuffed animals, mostly deer heads but also a huge elk in the front of the room. The elk head looks gigantic, and all the animals are wearing elaborate turquoise necklaces. There are over a dozen stuffed deer heads in the room.

There is a long dance gallery down the far side of the room excavated about a foot deep and there is a ladder-like design done in corn meal laid out on the dance floor. At the head of the gallery two Shalako masks are sitting on the ground. Each house usually only gets one Shalako but this year there are only five houses hosting so this house gets two of the Shalako. The two Shalako impresonators are sitting near the masks. Next to the masks there is a blanket over a door and men are coming and going through the door.

We edged up next to the windows and had a great view of the altar in the front of the room and the shrine that is hanging from the beams in the center of the room. I told Sifu, "This is one of the best views you can ever see of a Zuni altar." It is constructed from a few slats, consisting of a series of uprights, each one a few inches across with two in the back that are the tallest, about two feet tall. There is a graduated series of sets of uprights, each one a bit shorter in three or four stages with two uprights in each stage. The whole thing is about three feet wide and three feet long. All of the upright pieces are painted turquoise blue and the ones in the back are topped with designs that are like abstract faces which I take to be the sun and the moon. In the front row is a series of Corn Mothers, also called milis, which are ears of corn beautifully wrapped with feathers and they stand upright. There are feathers around each ear of corn with a bonnet of feathers that stick up above the ear. There is a row of them in the front and there is a blanket on the floor and on the blanket is an offering bowl in traditional Zuni design with stepped edges and tadpoles and dragonflies painted on the sides. The bowl is full of corn meal. There is also a bigger bowl that is full of prayer sticks with feathers sticking out on all sides.

The choir is in place beside one of the windows into the kitchen area. They all have headbands and are dressed in fancy Zuni dress, with bright colored shirts and lots of jewelry. There is one person in the center of the group with a bundle of bright red fluffy feathers on the top of his forehead. There is some movement happening and the level of excitement in the house is growing. Then the drums begin, followed by the rattles and a flute. Once they are all playing the chanting starts. When it does several men approach the Shalakos and hold up blankets and the masks starts to move. When the Shalako heads appear above the blankets there is a wave of excitement across the room. The inner room is packed with people but the two side rooms still have a little standing room in the back and around the edges. Then they remove the blankets and the Shalakos are up and moving. The chants are going full blast and now there is a bullroarer added to the music of the drum and rattle and flute. The two Shalakos move down the gallery, one after another.

There are two other dancers as well. These are the two alternates. Each has a white cloth on their heads held down with a chinstrap, and long pigtails hanging down the back. They have on fancy shirts and they both have wide, brightly colored ribbons draped across their backs. They each have prayer sticks on one hand and a yucca wand that is their whip in the other. They are dancing in tandem with the Shalakos. Their dance can take a different tangent, sometimes facing out toward the audience, moving together up and down the dance gallery. One of the Shalakos leans over slightly and runs down the gallery. From our point of view it is like they are on wheels; moving very smoothly with remarkable speed. The Shalakos have a long wooden snout and from time to time they make a loud clicking noise, accenting the sound of the rattles and drums. Sometimes the other dancers interact with the Shalakos and get a clack in return and occasionally the two Shalakos interact, facing each other and snapping their beaks at one another in a clattering contest. At one point they chase each other down the dance gallery. Meanwhile the chanting is continuous, as is the drumming and rattles. Every now and then the chorus of chanting and music comes to a crescendo and there is a change of tempo. This is done without a pause. As the time progresses, I start wondering if any of them are going to take a break. After an hour of solid dancing the guys come out with the blankets and make a curtain and we see the Shalako mask settle down as the dancer gets out of it; but, in just a moment we see it rise up again as his alternate has replaced him. Then the curtain is dropped and the dance goes on. The men doing the chanting alternate on and off as well so each person is not chanting or drumming continuously through the night.

About a half hour into the dancing I feel my phone vibrate. It is Otto and he says for us to stay put. In about twenty minutes I see Otto and Francine making their way across the crowded room. Sifu and I stand by them and Otto whispers to me and says it is unusual to have two Shalakos in the same house and they want to watch for a while. As the Shalako dance back and forth the two alternates are dancing in tandem. They seem to be having a great time, dancing first in line with one another and then turning sideways to face into the room and dancing down the length of the gallery sideways, one of them smiling and looking like it is the happiest day of his life. The owner of the house had indicated he was expecting the mudheads to show up later in the night, so we are watching for them. After an hour or so Otto waved for us to come outside and we waded through the crowd and squeezed out the back door. The cool air felt great and the full moon was so bright we could see everything. Otto and Francine were ready to move on to another house and said the Little Fire God and the Long Horn were at another house. I really wanted to see Long Horn since he is the most regal figure in the pantheon of kachinas.

3rd House

Once we are in the truck I wonder where the mudheads are and Otto says they have a little bus and we can watch for the bus and see where they are. Francine mentions that her father had been chosen to be a mudhead when she was a little girl. She remembers that he was gone a lot that year. She says it is a big responsibility to be a kachina; each kachina is designated by the priests and the head of the kivas and it is a big job that lasts all year. The men responsible for reciting the legendary history of Zuni get together weekly to learn the long chants and on each full moon they recite what they have learned and by October they are expected to have the entire story memorized in Zuni. The story is divided into four parts and they learn each part in order and work on it until they have the story right.

As we pull up to the next house the area around the house is full of trucks. Otto has to drive around to find a place to park. When we get out of the truck there are people streaming toward the house and a crowd standing in the yard with people peering in the windows. Otto takes us around to the back and when he tries to open the door it will only open wide enough to let us squeeze into the room which is packed with people. We make our way across the back of the room. There is a wood stove in the back corner and there is space by the stove. From there we get a view into the main room. Shalako is there and I immediately see Long Horn and then the Little Fire God and Hututu and a Wood Carrier. It is difficult to see. They are dancing in the excavated dance gallery and the room is filled with chairs and people are crowded in. Shalako stands out with his head well above the level of the crowd but it is harder to see Long Horn and the others above the crowd. As we settle in we maneuver around the room and get closer to the windows and then we can see better. I am mesmerized by the sight of Long Horn and the Fire God. The room is similar to the ones we had been in, the walls hung with beautiful blankets and shawls with stuffed deer heads on the walls. I can't see the altar or the men who are chanting and drumming but their sound fills the room. There is one part of the gallery I can see between the people, and I watch as the dancers move, one behind the other, up and down the dance gallery.

Long Horn has a solemn and dignified attitude. He moves in a ponderous way, slowly, every movement exaggerated, raising each foot, holding it poised in the air before coming down hard on each long stride. He has a rattle made of a deer bone scapulae tied together on a string and as he moves they rattle together. When each step comes down it is accompanied by the rattle of the deer bones banging together in a sound distinct from the other rattles. It shakes my bones and I feel it in my marrow. Long Horn has a bow in one hand, along with a bundle of prayer sticks. He is wearing a beautiful long white shirt with turquoise necklaces. Just behind him is his assistant Hututu. His mask is very similar except he does not have the long horn on the side. But the rest of the mask looks identical. It has a rounded black and white cloth ruff around the base of the mask. The mask is crowned with a line of feathers that come up from the center line of the head. The feathers are slanted forward with a downy white feather draping down over the forehead.

There is also a Wood Carrier in the line of dancing kachinas. He has a turquoise blue head mask and a black and white stripped ruff around his neck, but the similarity ends there. His mask has two round eye holes and an identical round hole for the mouth. But on his head is a wooden stick about two feet long with colorful tassels hanging from both ends. There are yellow feathers in the center of his head. He is bare-chested and there are a bunch of necklaces, both long and short, hanging around his neck. He has a white deerskin robe and is carrying prayer sticks in both hands. After him, bringing up the end of the line is the Little Fire God. He has a black mask with a black cloth ruff and just a couple of feathers at the top of the mask. His whole body is painted black. He is wearing a breechcloth and has a fawnskin bag over his shoulder. The mask and his body are covered with red, white, blue and yellow dots. He has a long stick in one hand and a bundle of prayer sticks in the other. The stick is a piece of cedar that he uses to start fires. Little Fire God is usually accompanied by his ceremonial father but he does not have a mask. I don't see him dancing and can't see around the room well enough to identify him.

The dancers move in time with the music. The sound of the rattles accents their movements. Long Horn seems to set the pace and sometimes he moves faster, sometimes slower and more deliberate. The Shalako leans in and out and clicks his beak and seems to glide across the room. Sometimes he passes the line of dancers then he drops back and gets in the back of the procession and moves more slowly, clacking and bobbing along. The people in the room are transfixed, watching in silence. It is deep into the night now and the house is packed with people, all watching intently, almost solemnly. I wonder at the stamina of the dancers and the chanters. I wasn't so sure about my own stamina but the energy in the room is intense and, while I feel tired, I am not about to leave and don't feel any need to sleep. There is nowhere I want to be but right here. It is exciting knowing that it only happens once a year and only here at Zuni. I am befuddled that hordes of tourists don't inundate the event. I look around and I don't see any other white people in the house; there must be some, but I can't see them.

4ᵗʰ House

In a few minutes Otto comes over and whispers in my ear that we should go to the next house, that maybe the mudheads will be there. I get Sifu and we work our way to the back door and slip out. It is a relief to get outside. The moon is slipping down toward the horizon. We find the truck and climb in, Otto has the map and the next house is on the edge of the village on Silt Road. Zuni is typically quiet after dark but tonight, at 3 AM there are cars on all the roads, coming and going in both directions. It is wild out tonight. In a few minutes we are at the fourth house. There are cars parked all around the house and people standing in little groups in the yard.

We make our way inside and the dances are going, the chanting filling the house, the Shalako moving in the dance gallery. Sifu and I stand discretely in the back but we still have a view into the main room. This looks like the biggest house so far and has the longest dance run in the main room. Shalako is dancing and his alternate is trailing behind him, dancing with him. The sound of their rattles accents the night. Then suddenly the atmosphere changes; the door in the main room opens and in comes two mudheads. They run into the dance gallery and circle the Shalako and then start dancing up and down the gallery. They are funny to see, their masks an anomolaic vision of grotesque features, their eyes and ears and mouth weird round balls, like warts on their faces. They have a cloth around their neck and are bare-chested with their chests painted brown like mud, their fat bellies flopping, nothing on but a breechcloth and moccasins along with the fawnskin pouch they have draped around their shoulders. There was a mood of hilarity in the room as the mudheads danced back and forth. One would lean over to tie his moccasin and the other would come up behind him and rub his butt and the room would break out in peals of laughter. Then the mudheads would go mess with the Shalako. They would approach him with their hands up in the air and the Shalako would lean toward them clacking his beak. They would hold their hands up and clap to provoke him to clack at them more and all the while continuing a dance step in the gallery, everything done in time with the drum and the rattle. The mudheads follow the Shalako back and forth, darting in front and behind him with quick movements. Then they would run in front of the Shalako, holding their bodies upright in imitation of the Shalako and try to move smoothly up and down the dance floor. Once the Shalako bent over and one of the mudheads managed to get his hand caught in the beak and was carried along for a few feet making funny faces all the while. Another time one of the mudheads sat down in one of the chairs on the front row and then the other one came along and sat on top of him, much to the amusement of the crowd.

I felt like I was watching some ancient drama, some mystery play for which I was not initiated. It is a mythic tale being enacted in front of my eyes, a grand repetition of a story told over and over on this night of the year, year after year; a ritual repeated annually in the grand drama of Zuni tribal awareness. Meanwhile our hosts were passing around big aluminum bowls filled with bottles of water and soft drinks. They were floating over the crowds in both rooms and you could see hands reaching up taking something to drink. We stood watching the whole scene for about an hour and half until Otto indicated we should push on; there is still one more house where they are dancing.

5th House

The fifth house was across town. It is still pitch black outside. There are cars all over the place as we come back into the village and pass through the heart of town. Then we head north and find our way. This house isn't nearly as large as the last one but it is surrounded by vehicles and people milling around. Inside it is not quite as crowded and the dance run is shorter. There is one Shalako and his alternate but no mudheads. The dancers are going strong when we make our way in the back door. We find a nice spot to watch where we don't feel too conspicuous and look around. This house is not as grand as the others, it doesn't have as much fabric or ornamentation, but still, if we hadn't seen the others first, this would have been impressive. The main room was filled with people. From our side room the dance gallery was in front of us and we could observe the dancers closely. I am wondering when the sun is coming up; I am getting weary and look forward to getting some rest. By this time the dance has been going on for over five hours. When the alternate dances by anyone who seems to be nodding they rush over and brush their face with the feathers on their prayer stick. That gets the person moving. Since the priests have a yucca whip in the other hand it seems nice they are using the feathers instead of the whip. Just when everyone is feeling totally exhausted, the doors fly open and two mudheads enter the room. That gets everyone's attention as a wave of excitement sweeps across the room.

The mudheads get in with the rhythm of the drums and start up and down the gallery. Then one gets out of step with the other and they start making fun of each other. One of them lays down like he is taking a nap, so the other one stands over him and acts like he is peeing on the one laying down. Then they are both up and circling around the Shalako, who is leaning toward one and then the other and clacking his beak. After a bit of this I look at the window and for the first time sense the coming of the dawn. The darkness is lightening up to the east. I give a big sigh. In a few minutes Otto comes over and motions for us to go out. When we get out in the yard the moon has moved low on the western horizon and the first rays of sunlight are appearing to the east. It is cold and there is frost on the windshield. We drive back toward the hotel. Otto drops us off and says the kachinas will all gather for a race about one o'clock and he will call us before then. We have a room on the second floor and when we go up the steps we can see Corn Mountain catching the first rays of the new rising sun. It is a moment of stunning beauty that caps off the whole experience.

We are grateful for a few hours of sleep at the Inn at Halona. But it is not easy to fall asleep even after staying up all night. We nap for a few hours and then can't stand it any longer and head out to look around the village in daylight. We walk across the bridge over the Zuni River into the heart of old town. I want to show Sifu the plazas and we walk over to the old mission church and the graveyard. The church is now completely closed. The Catholics were paying rent on the lot where the mission sits and nobody was coming to any of the services so they stopped paying and now the building is seriously deteriorating, especially on the back wall which looks like it is about to collapse. The front is the graveyard surrounded by an adobe wall. It is totally neglected and overgrown but filled to capacity with graves, many marked only with a cross or a stick. There is a large plaza beside the church and I show Sifu pictures taken in the plaza in the 1800s. At that time there was a multi-tiered adobe pueblo with a five-story complex at the top of the hill. Just up the hill is the central plaza which they call the center of the world. There are two alleys leading into it. We walk up one of them until we come to the plaza and then stay in the alley and don't step into the plaza. I show Sifu pictures that Cushing drew of dancers in the plaza and we can see how it has remained much like it looked in the drawings. The plaza has two and three-story houses surrounding it on all four sides, making for stadium-like seating for the dances. While the old buildings that Cushing shows in his drawings are long gone the new houses around the plaza reproduce the architectural features of the old buildings, including the flat roofs. While the buildings have changed from adobe to stone the basic configuration of the plaza has remained exactly the same. The new buildings still rise above the plaza in stair- steps making rooftop seating for the villagers to watch the dances. Then we walk around the village and up to the top of the hill. At the top it is easy to see the foundation stones of the old buildings. It is possible to clearly demarcate the size and shape of the rooms based on the foundation stones still visible at ground level. Then we go over the hill and down to the main street where we cross and go into one of the only markets in town.

As we come out of the market the police have closed off the street at the stop sign and there are a bunch of Zunis standing in the middle of the street. We move up that way and then hear the sound of bells and drums in the distance. We stay back a short distance and watch as a procession of kachinas comes up the street. At the head of the procession is a Zuni priest wearing a blanket and a headband and a fancy shirt. He is holding a bowl in his hands that is full of cornmeal and he has a Corn Mother standing upright in the bowl. Behind him are two of the Shalako alternates with their white head scarves and ribbon shirts. They are carrying yucca whips and a bundle of prayer sticks. Behind them is the Shalako and the orchestra/choir drumming and chanting as the procession moves along. The Zuni form two rows and the procession moves between them. The Zunis showers the procession with corn meal as they pass and puts corn meal on the road in front of them. We follow the procession and watch as they go up the hill and down to the bridge where they turn and go up the road beside the river. There are more police cars at this turn and they have flashing lights and officers out in the roadway.

We stop and a young man comes up to us and asks if we would like to buy a fetish. He reaches into his coat pocket and pulls out two beautiful corn maiden fetishes. They are the same basic design; one is five inches tall and the other one about three inches tall. They are made of the same type of stone with a stack of corn maiden heads going up the stone like the kernels on an ear of corn. It is really exquisite. I buy the large one and Sifu buys the smaller one as a gift for his young daughter, Tara. The guy moves on and we stand there marveling at the fetishes. It is not uncommon to have someone come up to you and offer to sell a fetish or a piece of jewelry; what is uncommon is to have it be a beautiful work of art. But the Zuni are master carvers and later we show the corn maidens to Otto and Francine and they immediately recognize the work and identify the artist and sure enough he has signed it on the bottom.

The procession has moved down the road and stopped at the bridge which they crossed when they entered the village. We wander down to the main bridge and cross to the other side and run into another procession much like the one we just saw. It is the same lineup, a person with the Corn Mother and the offering bowl leading the procession, then the alternate, then Shalako, and then the drummers and chanters. Again the Zuni people line up and sprinkle corn meal in their path and on them as they pass. Now I'm catching on: the Shalakos are converging, one by one, back to where they started by the bridge. We watch as the procession crosses the bridge and takes the same route.

I get a call from Otto and they are ready to join us. Otto leads us up the road where the Shalakos are congregating. Along the way Otto and Francine run into some of their relatives and we stand and talk. People are streaming by us. We can see several Shalako have converged and the masks are sitting on the ground by the river. As we are standing there we hear bells and drums and see the procession of the gods coming down the street. They pass by and cross the bridge to the field where the final race will happen.

We see the Shalakos are moving as well, their tall heads sticking up in the distance. We watch as they cross the bridge. Apparently no one is allowed near them as everyone stays on the road or down by the river bank and no one crosses with them. The kachinas all gather in the middle of a small field across the river. We are about a hundred yards away. Now all the kachinas are assembled and I see the Shalakos and Long Horn and Hututu and the priests and alternates. However, there must be drummers and chanters and representatives of the kivas since it is a large gathering, more than just the kachinas and their entourages. We can hear the drumming and chanting which goes on non-stop. After about a half-hour I see movement in the crowd. I see Long Horn and notice the mudheads are there as well. Some of the kachinas break out from the gathering and run across the field and circle back and then another kachina follows in their path. When we see a Shalako running across the field, we can't see his feet so it looks like he is gliding across the field. One Shalako after another takes off and glides in the same pattern. Other players start running as well and we can hear the clacking of the Shalako's beaks. Finally the running seems to be over and the whole group is gathered back together. There is more drumming and chanting as the group begins to move in a long procession away from the river. Otto leads us back across the main bridge over to the parking lot behind the grocery store. From here we can see Zuni people lined up on the road just a block behind the store. I ask Otto if we can go over there and watch the procession as it goes by but he says that area is restricted. I tell him and Francine to go ahead, that Sifu and I will watch from here. They take off and join the people lining the road. All we can see are the tall Shalako heads moving down the roadway. In a little bit Otto and Francine come back and tell us we are invited over to their place. We load in the truck and go over to their house where Francine makes some Zuni tea. Otto shows us his room where he makes jewelry and some of the pieces he is working on. We visit for a while as it is getting dark. We invite them to come out to dinner with us and all head over to Chu Chu's. After dinner they drop us off at the hotel and we pack and get ready to head back to Albuquerque early the next morning.

It has been an experience of ancient religion. We got to watch the gods come to town and got to be in the same house as the gods. We entered Zuni mythic time and space. It had a dream-like quality to it, and was invigorating and tiring at the same time.

THE BIRTH OF THE GODS

It has been an archaeological mystery to discover when and where the kachina cult originated. The Native American residents of the Southwest have gone through two major periods of population displacement. The most dramatic was in the 1200s when the people moved from the Chaco Canyon and Mesa Verde area to the Rio Grande valley. The causes of this disruption are still not fully understood except there was a period of extended and extreme drought. But there is more to the story which includes a political aspect where there was a major shift from government by a divine emperor to a more egalitarian plaza-oriented village governed by a council of priests. The Chaco model had great houses for the residents of the ruling elite and scattered villages that provided food and came together for grand ceremonies. The changes during the 1200s included moving to a new location, a new form of governance, and a new architectural style.

The kachina cult was a part of the cultural dynamic of change that was taking place. The kachina cult became a means of religious and cultural expression that brought the population together. The ceremonial calendar of the kachina dances involved the whole village and cut across old kinship lines. The scholars now agree that the kachina cult came from the south. There have been several lines of evidence coming from studies of painted pottery showing kachina-like images, images on excavated kiva walls that can be clearly dated, and petroglyphs and pictographs that depict kachinas and masked dancers.

There are stone carvings from Mexico depicting images of Tlaloc, the Aztec rain god. Those images as well as images of the plumed serpent have iconic religious significance similar to the kachinas. There are resemblances between the images on the pottery, the murals and the petroglyphs that suggest that the kachinas evolved out of Mexican prototypes. The Mimbres culture that stretched from northern Mexico into southern New Mexico was the bridge between Mexican religion and the kachina cult in the pueblos. One of the foremost rock art scholars, Peggy Schaafsma, concluded there is a historical and cultural continuity between Tlaloc and Quetzalcoatl and the iconic images of some of the kachinas. Other lines of cultural continuity include: a period of four days of fasting and continence before the enactment of important ceremonies; the association of foot races with ceremonial events; the annual kindling of a new fire; certain types of divination; burned

offering of food; the depiction of ritual shields; and similarities in the structure of the calendar. All of these point to cultural influence on the pueblos
from Mesoamerica.

When the people abandoned the Four Corners region and moved to the
Rio Grande valley they left the great houses and cliff dwellings and moved
into multi-storied terraced pueblos arranged around a plaza and governed
by a village polity. There was also a change in population dynamics as some
villages had up to 2,000 rooms. This aggregation and village planning indicates a very different politico-religious orientation. The social and economic
reciprocity demanded by the kachina dances and the fact that the kachina or-
ganizations draw from the entire village served as strong social mechanisms
to reinforce a new village dynamics. Evidence suggests that the kachina cult
was well-established in the pueblos by 1300. When the people moved from
the Four Corners they quickly adopted the kachinas to serve as supernatural
intermediaries to bring good fortune. The kachinas were adopted from the
Mimbres who were influenced by the great Mesoamerican cultures to the
south. The Mimbres' kachina iconography predates the pueblo kachina cult
by three hundred years.

The kachina dances pervaded the pueblo culture starting in the early 1200s
and by 1300 are well established all along the Rio Grande, as well as at Zuni
and Hopi. The Spanish invasion and the subsequent religious repression in
the Rio Grande valley drove the kachina dances underground everywhere,
except among the Zuni and Hopi. The kachina dances survived more intact
at Zuni and Hopi due to their separation from the larger population centers
in the Rio Grande valley by a desert that required up to ten-days travel. There
is evidence that there were kachina dances in all the pueblos, except perhaps
Taos, when the Spanish invaded. Today they are still pervasive in the pueblo
world, although in many places they are disguised or hidden as a result of the
centuries of Spanish, Mexican and American persecution and suppression.
In the archaeological record the kachinas did not enter the picture until after
the people had aggregated into villages, learned to cultivate corn, practiced
burial, and had rain-making specialists. There were two great periods of aggregation: the first after the collapse of Chaco Canyon and Mesa Verde; and
the second time between 1600 to 1650, when the Spanish invasion created
large-scale disruptions in pueblo culture. After the first great dislocation the
people adopted the kachina cult. After 1600 the kachina cult was violently
suppressed by the Spanish and driven underground in many of the pueblos.

THE ASSEMBLY OF THE GODS

To the Zuni the kachinas are multidimensional representations of the
forces of nature, especially the rain, but also of many other aspects of nature: the earth, and the sun and moon and all the heavenly bodies; the corn
and all the plants; the prey animals; the trees; and on and on. They are called
"the ones who hold our roads". In the Zuni spiritual hierarchy humans have
no dominion over the earth. To the Zuni, nature has dominion over humans

and the forces of nature are personified as the kachinas. The kachinas are above the humans and must be propitiated to keep life in balance. Humans are dependent on the kachinas for the rain, for their crops, for their entertainment and for religious fulfillment. Maintaining all the forces of nature in the proper balance requires prayer, purification, periods of abstinence, and sacrifice. The kachinas are the ancestors, the dead who have gone before, but they don't represent the dead as individuals. When a Zuni person dies they cannot be identified as a specific kachina, rather they have gone to the village under the lake and their life force is part of the life force of the kachinas. The kachinas spend their lives in their village dancing and singing. The kachinas like offerings of cornmeal and expect the people to put food in the river as offerings for them. The kachina dances encourage the kachinas to bring the rain and keep all the forces of nature in order so the crops grow and animals stay healthy and reproduce so they can be hunted and the people continue to propagate and have children. All the kachinas have a container of seeds somewhere on their body or in their clothing. They bring corn and other seeds to the people when they dance. The people believe that kachina seeds grow better and faster than regular seeds.

The kachinas are also the masks that the dancers wear when they impersonate one of the kachinas. The masks are identified with the kachinas and to wear the mask is to be the kachina. As a result of this Zuni transubstantiation the dancers are the kachinas and not just some person wearing a mask. Finally, the kachinas are the little wooden images that are carved and displayed in the village. These are often available for sale but for the Zuni the image of the kachina holds the whole meaning of the kachina and is a kachina. To assume the role of a masked kachina provides a direct connection with the supernatural and affects your status in the afterlife. When the kachinas are in the village it clearly evokes a sense of devotion, even fear, and definitely respect.

The beliefs that surround the kachinas involve the use of masks, elaborate painted altars, stone fetishes, feathered ears of corn, prayer sticks, paintings made of pollen and cornmeal, and a rich iconography. Some of the masks are ancient and are the property of the tribe; others are individual and will be buried with their owner when the dancer dies. A person wearing a mask must not speak and no one must touch that person while they are in the mask. The activities that encourage the kachinas to bring the rain include rolling rounded stones called thunderstones across the floor in imitation of the sound of thunder, blowing smoke from wild tobacco and willow bark reed cigarettes to encourage cloud formation, and planting seeds under the floor of new houses.

Ruth Bunzel's research published in 1930 identified 115 different kachinas. Later research by Barton Wright found over 200. Bunzel confirmed that many of the masks are ancient and belong to the tribe not to any individual. Thomas Mails reports over fifty-two ancient masks in the possession of the tribe in 1977. The kachinas are such a part of the Zuni idenitity that every male is a member of a kachina society at birth. Each society has their own kiva and each kiva has assigned roles for members as part of the tradition.

Taking on the assignment of impersonating a kachina is a major responsibility. For some of the dancers, especially the Shalako and the mudheads, there are daily meetings to memorize the chants and learn the dances. There are regular tests of their ability to recite the chants, prayers and songs along with monthly visits to various shrines where prayer sticks are planted. The process of making and planting the prayer sticks is a complicated and time-consuming affair. There are long prayers associated with every aspect of the manufacture and planting of the prayer sticks. When the sticks are planted the priest says, in part,

"This day

We shall give you plume wands.

Keeping your days,

Throughout the cycle of your months,

Throughout the summer,

Anxiously we shall await your time...

To this end: My father,

My mothers,

My children,

Always with one thought

May we live together.

With your waters,

Your seeds,

Your riches,

Your power,

Your strong spirit,

All your good fortune,

With all this may you bless us" [48]

The Zuni legends tell the story of the birth of death and the afterlife scenarios that arose in reaction to it. When the Zuni emerged from the underworld they knew nothing of death. The first death occurred in a bargain with a witch who offered to trade corn in exchange for the life of a child. The rain priest gave up one of his children, who died as a result. For four days the people made prayer sticks and mourned. Then two Bow Priests returned to the place of emergence and were surprised to find the child. This was the first intimation of afterlife; that the dead would go to the place of emergence and continue living there. The place of emergence was a watery place and when the people first emerged they were covered with moss and looked like salamanders. Only after the migration began did the gods wash away the moss and change their appearance to what we see today. It was during the migration, before the people found the middle place, when the kachinas first appeared. Before the people reached Haloma they were crossing a lake and some children wriggled loose and went to live in the bottom of the lake. There, at the bottom of the lake, they found a village where the people danced all the time. After this the place of the afterlife shifted from the place of emergence to the kachina village at the bottom of the lake.

The kachinas have not attained eternal life; they can and will die. They go through four deaths before their ties to this existence are extinguished. Then they return to the world of nature and are totally absorbed into the processes of nature, without specific human or spiritual embodiment. They return to the conditions of life that existed long before the kachinas or humans inhabited the earth. This was before the birth of death, before self-awareness. In this state they may become an animal: a bear or a badger or a wolf or an eagle. The only humans who do not go through this process are the Rainmaker Priests. These priests are picked by the people; no one asks to be a Rainmaker. It is a burden that requires great sacrifices. They must never kill anything, not even a plant or an insect. They must devote their entire life to prayer and preparation for ceremonies that includes fasting and abstinence from sex. They must pray not just for the Zuni and not just for humans but for all life, all forms of life, for all beings. In the earliest creation myths the Rainmakers lived by the ocean and eventually joined the people who made their way up out of the underworld. When a Rainmaker dies they go back to the ocean.

To the Zuni kachinas, animals and humans all live in different kinds of time. The animals have a kind of reincarnation where a deer will always be a deer and all deer have all the qualities of being a deer. Plants share in this as well. The kachinas live in the land of the dead so time doesn't mean the same to them as it does to humans. Kachinas look like humans and wear masks when they dance. Being fully spirit they do not give birth but they wear clothes and need food to survive. They depend on the people to sacrifice food for them. The kachinas' numbers are increased not by birth but by death. When a Zuni dies they go to live with the kachinas. The kachinas come back to the village, first in the form of rainclouds. The kachinas can sing but they can't talk. When they speak it is more like the sound of the deer or the sounds other animals make. The kachina village is not the only realm of the dead. Members of the medicine societies go instead to a special mountaintop. The medicine people can visit the kachina village but they do not live there. The kachina village is to the west of Zuni and the mountaintop is to the east.

The kachinas give beauty to the people. The term for beauty in Zuni has

shades of meaning not present in our dictionary. Beauty refers to a variegat-
ed quality with bright, contrasting colors. They consider multicolored irides-
cent shimmering colors the most beautiful. Beauty manifests as bold patterns
with striking designs. The same applies in their chanting and music. Dennis
Tedlock says that their musical tastes, "require as much as a two-octave range,
make use of semitone embellishments analogous to Western chromaticism,
and juxtapose themes that are highly contrastive." [49]

Chants, prayers and songs are all integrated into the ceremonial complex.
The chants are in verse form and tell the stories of the myths and legends.
The songs accompany the dance and prayers start and end each ceremony.
Prayer is considered sacred and if anyone is praying everyone is expected to
show the proper respect. Prayer is a source of spiritual power and the success of the prayer is based on proper recitation. The dancers all go through
months of training, much of it devoted to learning the chants and prayers.
Each kiva has one person who is in charge of keeping all the prayers. A
person's status in the community can be enhanced by the number of prayers
and chants that can be properly recited. A person who knows no prayers is
a poor person. There are prayers that are associated with numerous daily
activities: there are prayers to greet the sun; prayers to accompany all aspects
of making a mask; prayers to be recited while you make prayer sticks; prayers
associated with planting the sticks; there are prayers at each stage of dressing
for a masked dance; for the dedication of a house; for blessing food; for
thanking your hosts and on and on. Dancers are tested on their knowledge
of the prayers and chants before they are allowed to take part in the ceremonies. Prayers are always done for the people and never as an individual
request. Prayers are for rain or long life and deal with external circumstances
rather than internal states of personal well-being. Zuni prayers are not like
prayers in the Christian tradition. They are not spontaneous outpourings of
devotion accompanied by personal requests for divine intervention. Rather
they are formulistic devices that must be memorized and repeated verbatim
in the proper order.

The language of the chants and prayers is highly esoteric. Translations of
these chants contain language that is difficult at best since they include words
with highly symbolic poetic meaning. If you don't understand these symbolic
meanings, the words seem nonsensical. For example, when they refer to the
flesh of their mother they are referring to a piece of cotton, and when they
refer to water-filled rooms and water-filled woodpiles these are symbolic of
smoke from reed cigarettes and bonfires where the smoke is associated with
clouds; and hence with rain and water. The white cloth cap that is worn by
the Shalako impersonators is called a cover of thin clouds, and an elder is
referred to as having snow on his head. Marking the walls of the host houses
with cornmeal is called rooting about.

There are songs that accompany ritual and everyday activities. There are
songs that are sung while the women are grinding corn, songs for planting,
songs that accompany healing rituals, and songs that can be used as love

charms. The songs at the kachina dances are sung differently from the other songs and have a special musical notation. Songs are associated with all the different dances. Dancing is considered a form of worship and is not a secular activity. The Zuni consider dancing the most pleasing activity for the gods. The joy of dancing is a delight for the gods and any sadness is a sin against the gods. At the kachina dances the dance itself is an essential part of the ceremony.

Offerings are a vital part of the prayers and ceremonies. The primary offerings are, first and foremost, cornmeal which is mixed with ground shells and turquoise; then, food that is either put in the river or burned in the fire, tobacco mixed with willow bark which is smoked in reed cigarettes; and prayer sticks. The prayer sticks are made of red willow sticks and are measured by the length of the hand or sometimes from the tip of the finger to the elbow. The sticks are painted and feathers, typically either turkey or eagle, are tied to the upper part of the stick with cotton string. Most are painted black but blue and gold are used for the sun and the moon. Each person makes prayer sticks which are incorporated into the kachina dances and used as offerings accompanying prayers. The prayer sticks are planted by the priests and the person making the prayer stick must refrain from sex for four days after making the stick. Ceremonies begin and end with the planting of prayer sticks.

Each ceremony includes veneration of the ancestors in the form of kachinas or fetishes, followed by offerings. They involve purification and abstinence, along with fasting and seclusion, which are followed by public recitation of prayers and chants, and all-night dances accompanied by song and music. The events are highly colorful and dramatic. They have a quality of graciousness and benign splendor. The ancestors are called "the keepers of the roads", they are protectors who watch out for the people and bring what they need to prosper. The ancestors are not individual people or specific family members. They are identified with the clouds and the rain. In death they go to the place of water at the bottom of the lake to live in the kachina village. Then they return to the Zuni village clothed in the rain. When the people see rain clouds on the horizon they call out, "The ancestors are coming." Rain itself is a living being with supernatural qualities and all the divine emanations are associated with water. Clouds are the house of the rain, mist is the breath of the rain, and tadpoles and other water creatures are their children.

To anyone who is not a Zuni the Shalako is an otherworldly adventure. It is an ancient ceremonial celebration that has survived into the modern world. The various accounts of the Shalako start well over a hundred years ago and continue to the present. In all these accounts there are some basic features that appear to be standard parts of the Shalako ceremony. All the accounts tell of the procession coming to town and going to designated houses where they recite the history of Zuni followed by a feast and all night dances. At the end of the long night of Shalako dancing the priest goes to the roof of the house and recites a prayer to greet the sun. The last lines of this prayer are:

"Verily, so long as we enjoy the light of day,

We shall greet one another as kindred

Verily, we shall pray that our roads may be fulfilled.

To where your sun father's road comes out

May your roads reach.

May your roads be fulfilled." [50]

The Zuni are a small tribe but they have a rich social, religious and ceremonial structure. The main characteristics that the Zuni strive to achieve in
their personal lives are beauty, dignity and kindness. The matriarchal household is the basic social unit. The sons move into the household of their
wives when they marry. The tribal structure includes thirteen matrilineal ex-
ogamous clans, these are warrior societies which in the old days were for
those who have taken a scalp. There are also twelve medicine societies for
those who have survived serious illness, as well as many other secret and cult
groups such as the kachina cult, the cult of the sun, the rainmaker cult, and
the cult of the beasts. Each of these is devoted to a specific supernatural
and has a separate priesthood, with its own ritual systems, its own fetishes,
its own particular places of worship and a cycle of ceremonies. There are
six dance groups which represent the six kivas. Kinship and clan are fixed
at birth but a person can be a member of multiple other groups as well. At
puberty every male is initiated into a masked dance society. Each of the kivas holds three dances per year plus there is an intense ceremonial calendar
based on the solstices and equinox. Consequently it is impossible to hold a
forty hour per week job and be deeply involved in the Zuni religious and
ceremonial calendar. The Shalako and the other ceremonies are the containers that have held the traditions intact. The people who participate in these
ceremonies have to speak and understand the Zuni language, and those who
serve as kachinas are required to memorize the myths, legends and prayers
that have been passed down for countless generations. In this way these
ceremonies serve to maintain the survival of the Zuni culture and traditions
now and into the future.

SAN FELIPE: THE GREEN CORN DANCE - 2015

INTRODUCTION

Flying west I get a window seat and enjoy looking down on the newly-green forests, passing over the great rivers, the Cumberland, the Tennessee and the Mississippi. I see the dams where America tries to hold back the forces of nature, like trying to dam up the tectonic plates. It creates a sense of calm that belies the forces that move beneath and which will one day come due. We are heading to the pueblos where they have traditions that honor the earth in ways we have only the slightest premonition. These traditions have survived in areas which are so desolate, so hard and indomitable that the great waves of American capitalist exploitation have ignored them as useless. And there lies hidden small kernels of cultures that bespeak an entirely different style of life that miraculously still survives.

Upon arrival in Albuquerque we head for our favorite restaurant where they serve vegetarian cuisine done in the Ayurvedic style of Indian cooking. The next morning Susan and I pick up our friends; Paul and Becca, and head to Acoma. We tour Sky City and have a great walk down the ancient steps and then drive to Santa Fe. Next day we give Paul and Becca a tour of Santa Fe. We walk to the Palace of the Governor and shop for jewelry with the Native American vendors who sit in the shade of the porch. The next morning we drive to the San Felipe pueblo, about 30 miles south of Santa Fe.

THE GREEN CORN DANCE

The green corn dance has a long history in both the Southwest and the Southeast, where corn was the primary crop. Many tribes had a planting ceremony, a harvest ceremony and, most importantly, a green corn dance held a few weeks before the corn is ripe. It has components of purification, renewal and fertility.

For the Southeastern mound-building tribes, this ceremony marked the end of the old year and the beginning of the new. It was a time for people to confess their misdeeds and repent of their wrongdoings. There would be ball games, races, dances and rites of transition for young members of the tribe. They used an emetic, known as "the black drink", to induce bodily purification. This was accompanied by special prayers and chants so that when the dance began they were physically and mentally purified. This way they achieved a state of innocence so that when they consumed the first corn of the new year this fresh corn did not come in contact with any polluted food. After fasting for at least a day, they would have a feast. In the Southeast it was customary to do ceremonial scratching as part of the green corn dance. The Cherokee, Creek, Seminole, Yuchi and other tribes in the Southeast would inflict deep scratches across their back as a form of personal sacrifice. Thorns or snake teeth embedded in a wooden handle were used to make the scratches.

The twenty pueblos in New Mexico and Arizona have four main language groups, but all of them share a lot of common ceremonies. Each pueblo is divided into clans and into secret societies which are in charge of war, hunting, control of weather and the various ceremonies. Ethnographic and anthropological reports from the early twentieth century indicate that the green corn dance ceremonies included fasting for up to four days, but only from certain foods, as well as maintaining sexual abstinence during this time. Even now special altars are built, prayer sticks placed and certain people are designated to visit special shrines. Ceremonies are conducted in the kivas and the whole event culminates with a public dance and a feast. The dances are midsummer events that are done in gratitude for the earth's provision of corn and other crops, along with gratitude for the rain that contributes to the maturation of a bountiful harvest. The dances at San Felipe and at Santo Domingo are thought to be the closest in form and content to the ancient religious ceremonies that took place before the Spanish invasion.

Nearly all the pueblos participate in the green corn dance which is often held on the Saints day associated with the namesake of their pueblo. The sacred clowns, the keshares, are a part of these ceremonies in some, but not all, of the pueblos. The keshares are a vestige of ancestor worship or ancestor veneration. They represent the ancient spirits of the ancestors who still exercise a protective influence for the village. As the spirits of the ancestors they have special powers to cure disease and control the rain. They also control fertility and as such have total license to make obscene jokes and gestures. Everyone is expected to accept this behavior without bitterness or embarrassment. They are costumed and painted head to toe with black ringed eyes, they wear dry cornhusks as a headdress. Rabbit skins girdle their ankles, symbolizing death, and sometimes they carry pine fronds or tie them to their arms to symbolize renewal. Their hair is matted with gray clay and plastered down with tufts of dried corn husks sticking out. Their only clothing is a black loincloth with a small buckskin pouch on their right hip. The people believe when the keshares are present they are, in fact, the spirits of the dead and have their powers in full. During the dance the other dancers act as if they cannot even see the keshares since they represent the invisible spirits of the departed.

I read several accounts of green corn dances and learned that males and females come out in equal numbers. The men wear fox skins tied to their belts in the back with the tails hanging to the ground. They have turtle-shell rattles tied to their knees and moccasins with skunk fur to keep away the witches. The women dancers wear a one-piece black garment with the left shoulder bare. Their dress is tied at the waist with a red embroidered belt. They wear their fanciest jewelry, with multiple necklaces and bracelets. They dance barefoot to contact with and absorb the fertility of the earth. Music consists of drumming, chanting and a notched stick that is rubbed across a gourd. The dance is a form of prayer for the renewal of life for the corn, the animals and the humans. The dancers come up from the kivas in two groups, one for the summer and one for the winter. During the course of the dance they alternate, winter following summer, reflecting the turning of the seasons in each yearly cycle. The summer dancers are the first to come out of the kivas with the men and women coming out alternately. The summer dancers enter the plaza from the west and do four different dances, each with its own chant and distinctive movements. When they retire after the four dances, the winter group emerges and takes over the plaza. The dress is identical for both groups. Each group is led by a pole carrier who is the rain priest. Although he typically turns the pole over to an assistant who carries it for the main part of the dance.

The pueblos have a common belief that witches causes disease to humans and animals and blight for the crops. Thus, they must be courteous to all people to be sure they don't offend any witches, since nearly anyone could secretly be a witch. Any evils that befall a person or the pueblo as a whole are thought to be caused by the evil influences of witches. There are special societies in each pueblo who are charged with determining which members of the tribe are witches and exorcising them.

As the time nears for the green corn dance a special priest prepares for a retreat. He goes to a designated spot where he plants two sticks; one forked, one straight. They are set in a pre-designated pattern. He must keep his mind free of all mundane thoughts and pray incessantly for as many days as it takes until the shadow of the straight stick falls into the crotch of the forked stick. This marks the change in the ceremonial calendar and from then on ceremonies are dedicated to growth, fruition and rainfall. Certain preliminary ceremonies then begin and lead up to the green corn dance. It is also called the tablito dance. Tablito is a Spanish word for "little board" and refers to a small wooden plank that is used as part of the headdress for the women dancers. It has a stair step design at the top, like the surrounding mesas, and is decorated with tuffs of feathers that represent the clouds and is painted blue like the sky.

On the day of the dance the villagers all come to the church for early mass and then tour the village, ending up by the kivas where a special shrine built of leafy boughs has been erected. A statute of the local saint is carried in procession from the church and enshrined at the arbor where he can observe the dances. Once the saint is in place, there is no further reference to anything post-colonial in the ceremonies.

Meanwhile, the keshares have been in the kivas all night, fasting and doing ceremony, and when the time is right they come out of the kivas. The first thing the keshares do is a bit of theater, enacting a scene where remote sentinels come running into the pueblo to announce that enemies have been spotted approaching the village. Runners are dispatched in all four directions and when they return each runner is surrounded by an excited throng as he delivers his message with dramatic gestures. There is a flurry of mock activities in preparation for battle. This causes great excitement and lines of protection are formed. Once the protection is in place, the keshares summon the dancers who come up out of the kivas. The dancers come out of the kivas in two lines, one for the men and one for the women. They are all costumed and have rattles and bells which sound in rhythm with their movements.

The dance itself is a prayer or supplication to the supernatural forces of nature to protect the crops and bring them to maturity. While the dancers, both male and female, perform, the keshares are going around doing various antics which are ignored by the other dancers who go about their duties and pay the keshares no mind.

The leader of the dance has a special pole topped with bright macaw feathers representing the sun and the life-renewing energy it brings. At the base of the pole are parrot and woodpecker feathers. Just below the feathers is a foxskin with the tail hanging down. The flag itself runs nearly the full length of the pole and is painted with green corn stalks and decorated with eagle feathers. The pole is the most sacred object in the dance and the dancers all pass under it at various points in their procession as an act of purification. The pole represents all life, all of nature, and has special potency to bring the rain upon which all life depends.

The men wear eagle feathers in their hair, shell beads around their necks, turtle rattles on their legs and spruce boughs on their arms. They sometimes stomp their feet to call up the forces of the earth. The women carry pine boughs in their hands and wave them in time with the drum. The dance lasts all day and at the end of the day all the dancers join together for the finale.

HISTORY OF THE PUEBLO

The pueblo was named San Felipe Apostol in 1598 by the Spanish but to the Indians who live there the name of the pueblo is Katishtya. It is on the west side of the Rio Grande, six miles north of the junction with the Jemez River. It is on the lower slope where the Santa Ana Mesa rides down to the river valley. There are ruins in the area that may have been earlier prehistoric locations of the pueblo. When the Spanish did their first census in 1680 the population was only 600. In 1990 the census reported 1,859 people living on the pueblo. The current population is 2,080. The language is a dialect of Keresan which traces its roots back to Chaco Canyon. By 1200, Keresan-speaking people moved south from the Mesa Verde/Chaco Canyon area in response to years of drought.

In 1539, when Francisco Vasquez de Coronado's invasion force made is way up the Rio Grande, they passed by the pueblo. It wasn't until 1598, when Juan de Onate came up from Mexico with troops, priests and settlers, that they had to begin seriously dealing with the consequences of the Spanish invasion. Onate proceeded to enslave the people of San Felipe and forced them to accept the Catholic missionaries who made every effort to eradicate

Native religion. By 1600, they were forced to build a Catholic mission in the village and the Spanish renamed all the Pueblos with saints' names. In 1620, a Spanish decree forced a new form of government under Spanish control gave the office of governor full control over the pueblo.

In 1680, San Felipe joined in the famous Pueblo Revolt and forced all the Spanish out of the Rio Grande valley and back into Mexico. The Spaniards had practiced insidious torture to force the practice of the Catholic religion and had instituted a system of forced labor. Anyone who did not follow their orders was sold into slavery. They also forced farming and grazing practices that quickly led to famine and massive erosion. By 1691 the Spanish were back with a huge invasion force and the San Felipe people escaped to the top of a nearby mesa where they watched as the Spanish destroyed their pueblo. In 1692 they were coerced into allowing the Spanish back into the area and were again forced to be baptized in the Catholic Church. By 1696 they had rebuilt their village on the site where it still exists today. After this, relations with the Spanish improved and the practices of torture and forced labor stopped.

The next consequences of the Spanish invasion were severe epidemics which killed a large percentage of the people. As the epidemics raged through the pueblos they were experiencing constant fighting with the neighboring Apache and Comanche. In 1821, the Spanish were forced out of Mexico and the pueblo came under Mexican rule. This offered the warring tribes even more opportunity to raid the pueblos. In 1837, another rebellion took place and the governor was assassinated and the Indians regained their autonomy. But by 1848 the United States replaced the Mexicans and took over all the pueblos. They recognized the Spanish land grants and the pueblos were allowed to stay on their own ancestral lands. However, the United States sought to continually restrict and take land they considered their own. In 1880, the railroads crossed New Mexico and once again forced greater and greater acculturation on San Felipe. In 1920 all the pueblos joined together, this time to form the All Indian Pueblo Council, which tried to fight the government's attempts to take away what land they had left. During the 1900s the pueblos had to fight off numerous attempts by Protestant churches who wanted to establish missions on their pueblos. In the 1940s the government attempted to dam the Rio Grande in such a way that the land occupied by San Felipe would be underwater. During this time the hated Bureau of Indian Affairs instituted a policy that forced Indian children to leave the pueblo and go to boarding schools where they were not allowed to speak their own language. This was followed by a wave of anthropologists who invaded the pueblo and tried in every way possible to get the Indians to reveal all the secret aspects of their religious ceremonies and everything about their way of life.

In the traditional religion of San Felipe the sun and the earth are venerated and they believe they live in the center of the world, which is defined by four sacred mountains. The ancestors are considered kachinas. San Felipe has two main kivas, with Squash and Turquoise societies associated with each

As a consequence of the Spanish invasion, the religion of the pueblos was violently suppressed. Indians could be tortured and mutilated for practicing their indigenous religion. As a result some strange syncretisms developed. After being forced at gunpoint to adopt the Spanish religion, the Indians managed to subvert much of the Catholic beliefs, especially the worship of the Catholic saints. The Indians disguised the ancient figures from their religious heritage in the garb of the saints and celebrated their own deities in the guise of the saints. For example, an extremely remote church in the mountains of northern Mexico was well-known because of the extreme devotion it inspired in the Indians for miles around. The Indians would come from great distances on certain days to show their devotion and would decorate the altar with extravagant displays of flowers. The rural priest was baffled that so many Indians came from so far to show their faith since otherwise he had to force the local Indians to attend. Then one year an earthquake shook the church and destroyed the walls and beneath the altar they found an ancient Aztec statue.

This practice continues to this day. In downtown Santa Fe there is a Catholic church with a famous statue of Our Lady of Guadalupe. The image is iconic in the town and in the state. She is the Patron Saint of New Mexico and all of Mexico. This came about as the result of a vision that took place around 1530 when an Indian named Cuauhtlactoatzin was on his way to the village of Tlaltelolco in northern Mexico. As he was crossing a mountain he had a vision of a dark Indian maiden clad in a blue robe arrayed with stars that looked like grains of toasted maize. She instructed him to build a church on the spot. The Indian had been baptized and given the name Juan Diego and he reported his vision to the priest and it went up the line, all the way to the Bishop. The Bishop refused to act upon the vision until he had seen a sign so the Indian went back to the exact spot and prayed for a sign. Sure enough, Our Lady of Guadalupe reappeared and at the spot where she appeared a spring came up from the ground and, as he watched, a rose bush grew out of the desert and roses appeared on the bush. She instructed him to gather the rose petals and take them to the Bishop as the sign. He put the roses in his serape and folded it up and took it to the Bishop. When he opened the mantle the roses were gone and, in their place, was an image of Our Lady of Guadalupe on the fabric, just as she had appeared in the vision. The Bishop had the painting examined by his superiors who declared it a miracle and the church was built on the spot indicated by Juan Diego. The serape was hung behind the altar and Our Lady of Guadalupe was declared the patron saint and protectress of all of New Spain.

However, in later years it was discovered that the spot where the vision happened and where the church was built happens to be the exact place the Indians had used to make sacrifices. The church had been constructed on the ruins of a temple the Spanish had destroyed. It had been a temple to Tonantzin which in Aztec meant, "Our mother" and the Indians began calling Our Lady of Guadalupe the Mother of Gods or, in their language,

Tonantzin. In ancient times Tonantzin was the Mother of all the Aztec Gods and the Goddess of the earth and the corn that grows out of it. Gradually all the Indians came to call her Guadalupe or "the brunette virgin".

THE GREEN CORN DANCE AT SAN FELIPE

The Green corn dance at San Felipe is a magnificent event. It is incomparable, unlike anything in modern life. No NFL Superbowl game, no world-class soccer match, no movie, no opera, no ballet, no megachurch service or revival, no rock concert can begin to compare. I had no idea what I was walking into on this hot dry day in early May.

It was a short drive from Santa Fe on I-25 to the pueblo. We crossed the Rio Grande River and were in a line of cars leading into the village. Cars were parked all along the road and the road was full of slow-moving traffic. We drove until we came to the community center, where they administer what pueblo business takes place with the government, and found a place to park. We fell in with a crowd of young Indians walking along. I could feel the excitement before we heard the first drum beat and then, as we followed a growing stream of people, nearly all of them Indians, the deep booming sound of the drum seemed to be coming up out of the earth. In a few more minutes it clarified and, with it, we could hear a resonant chant of voices in a singsong verse of unknown sounds, completely unrecognizable sounds that adamantly refused to constitute itself into language. They were sounds of the ancient world, sounds from the earth, sounds in a tongue that could not be configured into words, even in their own pueblo language. They were singing songs of the ancient earth like the sound of the corn growing, the sound of the rain falling, of the mist rising, of distant thunder, of the river running, of man and woman in intimate deep embrace, the sound of the horse, the sound of the bison, of the mountain lion, the sound of the sun rising, the sound of moonlight falling on the desert. There were hundreds of dancers in a fabulous spectacle of sound and color. It was a sight beyond words, beyond comprehension, beyond the frame of our modern abstract understanding. What a feeling. I wanted to cry tears of joy at being there, tears of sorrow at what we as white people had lost so long ago, tears of immense sadness at how these people had been treated for hundreds of years, tears for the lives and land they had lost, tears like the rain to join in the cycle of nature, tears of union with something so primordial, so primeval, so pristine, so immediately present that words could not express it. I could not even begin to say what I was feeling, since the saying put the feeling into another realm of experience that was alienated from its source so words fell away, unable to give expression to the sights, the sounds, the feelings that arose. I stood there in wordless wonder, tingling with joy and amazement.

We made our way through a line of vendors to stand behind a row of young Indians where we had a good view. It was a plaza in front of an adobe church. The plaza was defined by the tents of the vendors, a large space completely filled with movement and sound, men and women who were no longer themselves but rather were the movement and the sound and the color and the spirit of the forces of the springtime earth, of the growing corn, of the falling rain. The men were painted with earth tones, browns and grays, their long black hair shining in the sun, with white skirts. They had green juniper boughs tied to their arms, a fox skin hanging down behind them, its tail just touching the ground, their white moccasins fringed with black and white skunk skin, a rattle in one hand, a turtle shell attached to their knees, a long necklace of seashells around their necks. The women had on dark dresses, knee-length, drawn in with a belt at the waist, one shoulder bare, no moccasins on their bare feet, and a tablita on their heads, blue with stair steeped design cut out on the top and white clouds painted on it. In each hand hold juniper boughs, which they waved up and down in time with the music. The men's bodies moved bent over, the women upright. In the center of the plaza a group of men in colorful ribbon shirts are bunched together, chanting around a drummer as the dancers move like a huge chorus around them. Then another figure appeared holding a tall pole with a long flag attached to it, the flag decorated with painted stylized corn stalks bright green against the yellow cloth of the flag. At the top of the pole there is a garnish of feathers. The pole was moving through the crowd, swooping low from time to time. Then there was a crescendo of sorts, the rattles all sounding in unison as the drum hastened to a final beat and all the movement stopped.

A strange silence fell over the people. The dancers slowly gathered in small groups and moved away from the plaza. We walked over to the church and into the chapel. There is a big sign at the front gate to the church saying Stay Out, Visitors Not Allowed, but people are coming and going so we check it out. It is a typical pueblo church with a low adobe fence around a courtyard entrance. The church has two bell towers and is two stories. The front of the church has painted horses on either side of the main door and painted images of two poles like they are using at the dance decorating the second level of the front of the building. The poles are leaning in and are stylized with green corn stalks on them so it is a striking and unusual design. It is cool and nice inside the church and there are murals around the altar with corn plants and Indian motifs. There is one small, sinister-looking mural of a man on horseback with Indians on the ground in front of him.

We tour the vendors and no sooner get started than we run into Otto. He is there selling his jewelry and Zuni fetishes. It is great to see him and now we have a place we can come and rest in the shade if we want. We catch up on all the news from Zuni and move along so he can do his business. We stop at a lemonade stand and sit for a minute and watch all the people. Standing in line the Indians around us are all speaking in pueblo so it is nice to hear them speaking their own languages. The crowd is swirling around and before too long we hear the sound of the drumbeat in the distance and move in that direction.

We walk past the church and a few other buildings, then follow the crowd as they funnel into an alley. I am surprised when we come out at another plaza. It is already filled with dancers. There is an arbor on one side of the plaza covered with green juniper boughs. This is the famous sunken plaza of San Felipe. The plaza is actually a couple of feet lower than the ground level of the houses all around. This is the traditional plaza for the pueblo. Many of the houses are two- story affairs and there are people standing on both levels of the flat roofs and there are chairs on the roofs so people can sit and watch. There are also chairs and benches set up all around the plaza at each corner so people can sit and watch the dances. The roofs and porches of all the houses are packed with people. The chairs are filled and the dancers are in the plaza. In the center of the plaza is a group of about twenty men in bright silk shirts who are chanting and in the center of this group is a drummer. The sound of the drum reverberates off the buildings. I can feel the sounds deep inside my chest; it feels like the heartbeat of the earth in tune, in time with my own heart.

I try to estimate how many dancers are in the plaza. It appears there are at least six hundred dancers in the plaza. I can't believe there are that many dancers. They are equally divided, men and women. The pole carrier is there and he is moving around the circle. The drum, the chanting, the sounds of the rattles, and the jingle of the bells are all in sync with the movements. The dancers are in two circles, men on the outside, women on the inside, all slowly moving round the plaza. Then a couple of young Indians come by with sashes on that say Security and they ask us to take off our hats. We hadn't realized this was a rule so I quickly pull off my broad-brimmed hat. There are benches open on one side of the plaza so Susan and I sit down for a bit. It is great to sit and watch; it is a hot dry day and I can feel the heat of the sun. There are lots of kids out there dancing as well and the two groups separate a bit and the kids fall in between the lines of men and women, so now there are three lines in concentric circles all moving gracefully. The women are waving the green boughs they carry in their hands, the men shaking their rattles in time with the drums. I notice some of the older women sitting on the porch of a house moving their hands in the same motion with the women dancers. There is movement everywhere you look in the plaza.

Susan and I decide to get a change of perspective and move to another corner of the plaza. There are entrances into the plaza at each corner. The plaza has houses fronting it on all four sides and several of the housing groups are tiered, with a second set of rooms on the upper floor set back somewhat so it is like a porch facing the plaza. They are obviously set up to do this event. So we take off and walk one street back and head over to the other corner of the plaza This takes us right by a large kiva. The street in front of the kiva is filled with dancers. I remember there are two troupes that dance, one for the summer and one for the winter; so,here is the other group. The kiva is really impressive; it looks new and it has circular walls that are ten feet tall and a grand staircase going up from the street. The stairs are heavy timbers. We can see the roof of the kiva and there is a big ladder sticking up. This ladder has steps instead of rungs so it would be easier to get up and down. There are dancers all over the roof of the kiva and we see a couple of dancers coming out of the kiva. It is quite a sight and we don't want to get in the way. There are police and the street is blocked off with yellow tape but there is a space like a sidewalk opposite the kiva and we quickly maneuver our way down to the other corner of the plaza and make our way to where we can get a good view.

I have learned that where the majority of the audience is Native American it is better to stay back. Don't push in to get a frontrow seat. If there are people standing, stand in the back. So we were in the back row but had a great view. Then, out of the arbor came these two big Indians with a large galvanized washtub filled with ears of corn. They worked their way around the crowd, passing out ears of corn, offering them to one person after another. We were totally surprised when they made their way back to where we were standing and offered us each an ear. It was delicious fresh corn on the cob and we immediately ate them. What a wonderful offering to have at the green corn dance. I had expected it was only for the Indians and maybe only for those who had been fasting, but here we were, enjoying our corn.

Then the dancers adjourned once again. There was a movement from the man holding the pole and I noticed a young man with long black hair made a distinctive sound with his rattle and the sound was echoed by each man down the line so it quickly traveled around the circle and, when the sound moved around the entire circle, they all sounded their rattles together while the drum beat hastened to a crescendo and it appeared to be over. All the movement stopped and the lines of dancers broke up and started drifting off to the corners of the plaza. I had read there is another kiva but we hadn't explored far enough to find it yet. But they seemed to be moving in the direction of the other two corners of the plaza and I suspected their kiva is in that vicinity.

We headed back to see more vendors and get another drink. We found the lemonade stand and went over by the river to sit and relax. The pueblo is built on the west bank of the Rio Grande and there is a small flood wall to protect the village. We saw a tree growing next to the wall and found a place to sit in the shade. The river is about fifty feet wide and is rolling by at a fast pace. It appears shallow all the way across and from time to time kids came and stood in it for a few minutes or threw rocks. We sat still and quiet, listened to the ripple of the rocky shoals, the chatter and suck of the water reeling past us, the whisper of a gentle breeze in the reeds. We finished our drinks and by the time we got back to the center of the pueblo the other troupe of dancers were back in the plaza. This time we knew to take our hats off and moved around to yet another corner.

It was a very cinematic experience but, of course, no pictures were being taken. If the pueblo didn't have a rule against photography there would be people all over the place shooting videos and stills. It is a beautiful and moving experience; the movement and the sound and the visual impact of watching it all combine into an ethereal, otherworldly experience, like stepping outside time, outside the typical American frame, outside all the norms of day-to-day life, at least for us. I feel like I have been taken to another world, a world where people are not alienated from their environment or their community, a world where people make art as part of life not as special events.

I can't take my eyes off the spectacle and stare transfixed at the movement, the colors, the interaction of the dancers with one another and with the music. The dance brings us closer to the origin of things, to the origin of dance, of music, of song, of the land, of the rain, even of life itself, to the plants which transform into the life of our flesh. Just as the adobe of the pueblos rises up out of the earth and eventually settles back into it, so the life of the people, individually and collectively rise out of and fall back into the self same earth. The corn dance is primal and creative in ways that our dance and music have long lost. It is the heartbeat of the earth calling for the rain to fall, to flow in its rivers and to rise to form the clouds in the great cycles repeated and reflected in the cycles of the dance. The cycle of dance is a fractal of the cycle of the seasons, which is a fractal of the cycle of the movement of the earth around the sun, which is a fractal of even larger cosmic cycles that extend beyond our universe, beyond our imagination. The dance is an infinite act of fertility from the seasonal planting of the corn seed, to the planting of the human seed, to the seed of the earth, the ancient seed of the sun.

Finally, it is time for us to go, so we walk through the vendors one last time and say goodbye to Otto. We walk through the pueblo to where the car is parked. In the car we follow the road as it loops around and brings us back by the river. We crawl along watching the swirl of the people. Everyone is very quiet, tired from being out in the sun all day, but mostly astonished and unable to speak, still glowing, basking in the experience, not wanting to put it into words. That will come soon enough. This will certainly be the highlight of the trip. One of the purposes of the dance is to bring the rain and when we left the dance at the San Felipe pueblo we pulled onto I-25 and headed north towards Santa Fe and there were dark rain clouds on the horizon and a few raindrops fell on the windshield.

THE EARTH MOTHER AND THE CORN MAIDEN

In the pueblos they acknowledge the Earth Mother and Sky Father. In the Keres-speaking pueblos her name is Iatiku "Bringing to Life", since all plants, animals, birds, fish and people all come directly from the Earth Mother. In the pueblo tradition they recognize the winter as the time when the Earth Mother is staying still, and from early in December until the tenth of January everyone must move back into the pueblo from their summer homes in the fields. During this time no one is allowed to dig in the earth or repair the adobe in their dwelling or even chop wood within the walls of the pueblo. Everyone must walk softly; the Earth Mother is sleeping under a beautiful white blanket of snow. It is the time of rest and renewal. This period is called, "The Time of Staying Still". Then, on January tenth, everyone takes a sunrise bath and activities resume. From here on it is the time of gestation and preparation for the new life that is coming.

Of all the crops, corn is the most important. While Asia has its rice and Europe and the Middle East have their wheat, corn is the American grain that has sustained the life of the pueblos for countless generations. The corn we know today has been cultivated for over 7,000 years. It originated as a wild grain in central Mexico called teosinte. It is the oldest of domesticated grains in the Americas and could no longer survive in the wild without human cultivation. Corn has been found in the Southwest dating back 4,500 BP. Corn may well have been the single most important factor in the evolution from hunter-gatherer bands to tribes. As such, it is what made the birth of the people possible; it is the thing from which the people sprang.

The only older cultigens are the gourds, which may have been brought here in the initial migration for their utility. It is ironic that the first cultigens were not a food crop. But it was corn that allowed them to settle into communities and expand their population. The earliest corn was much smaller and had a small cob, but either through expedient hybridization or by fortuitous mutation or both, it grew into the many varieties that are now grown by the Indians and by people all over the world. In Peru, the Inca developed hundreds of varieties of corn. The blue corn is the favorite at some of the pueblos. Archaeological evidence indicates that the earliest cultivation may have been done while the people were still nomadic. They would make a camp and stay there long enough to plant and grow a corn crop before moving on to follow the animal herds and wild food crops. But once they developed the skill to grow corn it started them on a path that brought monumental changes to every aspect of life. When they added beans to their garden, they were no longer dependent on the hunt for protein. A diet of corn and beans could give them all the protein needed for survival. Then it became possible to settle down and build villages.

The people moved into areas along rivers with flat fields and learned to irrigate with the water from the streams and rivers. The implements for grinding corn and making cornmeal can be found in archaeological ruins all over the Southwest where they used handheld grinding stones and stone troughs. The cornmeal was an all-purpose food. They made it into a mush for breakfast called atole, and of course made tortillas and the wonderful paper thin piki bread made by the Hopi, along with many other uses. Cornmeal is an integral part of the ceremonial equipment for any ritual and the pueblos start the day making an offering of cornmeal to the sun to greet the day at sunrise.

Growing corn at the pueblos has little resemblance to the techniques used in modern farms. The pueblo farmers make hills and plant with a sharp planting stick. They put multiple grains in each hill and plant it up to a foot deep so that it takes advantage of moisture deep in the earth. The farmers allow the weeds to grow to protect the soil and grow clusters of corn here and there without formal rows. Some pueblos celebrate planting with a planting dance in which young maidens dance with ears of corn in their hands. An old man, painted with black and white wearing a corn husk headdress, carrying a planting stick and a bag of corn, leads the dance. Just before the corn is ready to harvest the Indians do the green corn dance, which in many pueblos is one of the most important festivals of the year. The Indian garden is an ancient scene that is dream-like for non-Indians but represents the very life of the village, of the people, of the past and future for the pueblos.

TAOS PUEBLO:
THE SAN GERONIMO FESTIVAL - 2008

Skyborne, westward bound, back to New Mexico for another visit to Santa Fe and then on to Taos for our third visit to the San Geronimo festival. Susan and I attended the great festival the two previous years and this time we are bringing our ten-year-old son,Coby. I have been reading anything I can find about the Taos pueblo, starting with Merton Miller's *Preliminary Study of the Pueblo of Taos*, published in 1898, which turns out to be a Ph.D. thesis for the Anthropology Department of the University of Chicago. I was amazed at the standards for this thesis which reads more like a journal than a scientific study. Miller stayed in Taos for about three months and learned precious little from the few Indians who would even speak to him at all. Nonetheless, it is a quick but interesting snapshot of the pueblo in the 1890s.

Then I moved on to Elsie Clews Parson's wonderful book *Taos Pueblo*, published in 1936. She was a professional anthropologist with years of academic and field research when she went to Taos. She was connected to Mabel Dodge Luhan and had, probably through Mabel and her Taos Indian husband Tony, as much access to the natives as it was possible to attain. She certainly had to rely on Indians who were living "outside the walls", and were therefore more willing to talk than the Indians who lived "inside the walls" at the old pueblo. She had already done an enormous amount of field work in other pueblos and was able to extrapolate from what she learned to understand what was happening inside Taos pueblo. Her book, along with the second book she wrote called, *Taos Tales*, which records a hundred and eight pages of myths, legends and stories, provides the most detailed analysis of the ritual and ceremonial life of the pueblo.

These books, in tandem with Frank Waters' magnificent book *The Man Who Killed the Deer*, give the most reliable account of what the life of the pueblo must have been like. More recently Nancy Woods, a longtime resident of Taos, published a lengthy book in 1986 called *Taos Pueblo*. These few books show the evolution of Taos culture from 1896 to 1986 during which time the pueblo was transformed from a living pueblo into a heritage site where families have rooms but live in houses outside the walls. Now only a handful of families still live inside the walls, without electricity or running water.

The pueblo has been a tourist attraction for all of its history. In its earliest days it was already a place other Indians came for trade, serving as a crossroads between the Plains Indians and the pueblos that line the Rio Grande. But for most of the 20th Century, and up to the present day, the crush of tourism has been intense. They close the pueblo on the days they are preparing for big ceremonies and during initiations but otherwise it is open, for a small fee, to anyone who wants to walk in and most days you can take pictures. Even in the early 20th Century the plaza would fill with people on

feast days and people would visit the pueblo anytime day or night in a per-
petual flow of often unwelcome visitors, everyone drawn by the great adobe
multistory apartment houses. It is a World Heritage Site and is a remarkable
place where you can experience a great monument of the ancient times that
still survives relatively intact.

Even under this continuing assault the pueblo still guards its secrets with
intense furor and threatens anyone who would reveal them with severe punishment, including public beatings and even death. The publication of anthropological books about the pueblo was a catastrophic event to the elders
and it caused great consternation in the pueblo. I read them with fear and
trembling, anxious to learn and understand but guarded in what I want to
know or talk about. There is precious little literature about Taos pueblo and,
other than a few other small books like Bodine's book, *Taos Pueblo*, written
mainly for tourists and a few chapters in other books, like Thomas Mails'
study of pueblo culture. This illustrates how the efforts of the elders have
managed to keep a tight lid on any information coming out of the pueblo,
despite the onslaught of anthropologists who have worked every conceivable
angle to get information about their secret ceremonies. They have managed
to maintain their secrets better than perhaps any other tribe. Still, much has
slipped out, mostly by bribery and pay-offs to off-reservation Indians.

New Mexico was controlled by Spain up to 1822, during which time it
was closed to foreign incursion. Before 1822, any American, Englishman or
Frenchman who crossed into the mountainous deserts was quickly arrested,
imprisoned, and shown out of the territory. In 1822, the Spanish were kicked
out of Mexico and the Mexican government opened the door and the first
American traders and mountain men began to show up in the New Mexico
territories. At that time Taos was nothing more than a few Mexican farming
compounds with walled haciendas scattered through the valley around the
Indian pueblo. Trade to Taos and Santa Fe began when the Santa Fe Trail
opened and brought a new influx of culture. At that point they learned a
lesson repeated all over the West: once you open the door the Americans
will flood the area with trade until they dominate the lifestyle and soon take
over to the extreme detriment of the indigenous cultures. It didn't take long
before American Manifest Destiny saw the opportunity to seize the Mexican
territories north of the Rio Grande, which were acquired in 1848 as a result
of the Mexican American War.. It was another half century before these
territories became states.

I never tire of the drive across New Mexico. This landscape has drawn
artists of all genres and has been described as one of the most aesthetically
satisfying on earth. When we arrived in Santa Fe, I drop Coby and Susie at
the old town square and go over to Canyon Road to visit the little complex
of Tibetan stores, where I roam around lost in the amazing jewelry, statues,
bells, rugs, books and clothes, picking up a few gifts, a couple of books and
a mala from old Tibet.

Next morning we head out to Bandelier National Monument and walk the trails and explore the ruins. Bandelier has a valley lined with cliffs formed from volcanic ash millions of years old. The ancients built their homes nestled up against the white cliffs and they would cut additional rooms back into the soft white stone of the cliff face. Coby had a great time climbing the ladders up into the shallow caves. A group of dancers were there, a troupe from Zuni, and they did dances in the courtyard of the Visitors Center. There were a dozen of them, all in traditional regalia, male and female, along with a couple of drummers. The ranger came out and told us the names of the dances and a crowd of about fifty people watched. They did a Turkey dance, the lead dancer with a headdress of turkey feathers arrayed on his head and a black fringe that hung down over his eyes so all he could see was the spirit world. The dancers, mostly teens, danced and chanted under the clear blue sky in the beautiful courtyard in the canyon. There were several Indian vendors set up around the courtyard and Coby hung out with an old Indian woman who showed him how to make a traditional style paint brush out of a yucca leaf. She gave him a flint shard that he used to scrape the skin off the yucca leaf until only the inner fibers remained, forming a perfect little paint brush. He got some paper and painted a picture with it.

Then it is back into the car and up the road to Taos along the Rio Grande. The road runs along the river where it cuts a passage through the mountains. It is an extraordinarily beautiful drive with the semiarid desert in contrast to the green river valley and the sheer rocky mountains. When we went over the last pass we see the Rio Grande gorge with Taos in the distance. Just at that moment the sun was low on the horizon and about to drop out of sight and the sky suddenly turned a blood red in the west. High above, the sky was still blue and a few billowy white clouds were bottom-lit by the evening sun and tinged with colors, some pink, some red, others scarlet to purple. There is a pullover at the spot where you overlook Taos and see the great gorge with the mountain in the distance, so we pulled in to watch the light show. The western sky was filled with color and now the sun was just over the horizon and the colors moved from scarlet to deep, deep orange to brightest red. And then in a few more minutes it faded into darker and darker tones and we jumped back in the car and drove into town.

From Bandelier to Taos we went from semi-arid desert filled with sage to steep mountain terrain with tall fir trees, to areas with exposed rock faces carved in incredible shapes by wind and water, then into strange white ash cliffs pockmarked with holes. It was Sunday and we went straight to the Mabel Dodge Luhan Bed and Breakfast where we checked in and took off to find some dinner.

In the late 1890's a couple of artists from New York City, Ernest Blumenschein and Bert Phillips, came to New Mexico to look for interesting landscapes to paint. While they were touring around their wagon lost a wheel just a few miles outside Taos. They came into town to get their wagon wheel repaired and immediately fell in love with the place. Blumenschein stayed in Taos while Phillips returned to NYC to gather their stuff and move back.

That was the beginning of the Taos art colony.

Blumenschein's house is now a museum and he is a recognized name in local and national art. They sent word back and other artists started to migrate to the area. By 1915, there were enough artists to form the Taos Society of Artists. It has continued to grow from then to now. They were eventually followed by Mabel Dodge, who came about 1919, and in her wake came Georgia O'Keefe, D.H. Lawrence and another huge wave of artists from both coasts. In the 1960's Taos became a refuge for the counterculture and the town is still a haven for artists.

While the story of Taos as an art colony is fascinating, it is the pueblo that really attracts my attention. The people of the pueblo have miraculously withstood incredible pressures of assimilation which have exerted intense demands on them for over 450 years. While Coronado was staying along the Rio Grande River he sent scouts out to explore. One of them, Hernan Alvarado, was the first European to visit the Taos pueblo, arriving in 1540. The name Taos was derived as an adaptation of the Tewa word "Towid", which means red willow. The name was first recorded as a place name in 1598. It seems the Indians have been living on this spot since at least 1350. The Spanish settled here in 1615 but didn't form the town until 1796, when sixty-three families received a land grant from the Spanish Crown. It was a part of Spain at the time and, of course, later part of Mexico until 1846, when it became a territory of the United States. The town wasn't incorporated until 1939.

The pueblo has withstood these onslaughts from the Spanish, the Mexicans and then the Americans, all who have a history of incredible cruelty and violence. In the face of this, the Taos pueblo had two factors that aided their efforts to maintain their culture. First, the pueblo itself: the two amazing complexes of adobe buildings inside the walls of the pueblo; and second, their language. Although many tribes have been forcibly removed and relocated, the Taos people have retained their pueblo and some of their lands. Except for one period of nineteen years, when they lived in exile in the mountains, they have lived on the land where their creation myths tell how they came forth from the elements: from the sky, the lake and the land, where they learned to hunt and to farm.

From my review of the literature, I learned about the development of the trends toward modernization in the pueblo. Up until World War II, the people lived within the walls and the pueblo itself was the container of the tribe and the culture. Then, after World War II, it was no longer economically feasible to remain a farming/hunting culture and the onslaught of tourists coming to the pueblo day after day disrupted the traditional lifestyle inside the walls. This tourist invasion occurred concurrently with the forcible removal of the children, who were sent off to BIA Indian schools. This disrupted the culture in a huge way by forcing the kids to learn English and constantly punishing them for speaking their own language. Then, in the 1960s the people began to move into HUD housing outside the walls. The population inside the walls has been reduced to just a few families. Now the elders in the kivas can no longer talk to the youth who lost the ability to speak their own language. Then, English began to be used even in the kivas. By the time Nancy Woods wrote her book in the 1980's it was a sad commentary in comparison to Parson's account of life in the pueblo in the 1920s. By the 1980s most of the people no longer lived by farming and hunting orlived within the walls,and the younger generation could no longer speak their own language.

Now I can only observe from afar that the yearly cycle of dances and ceremonies are still being carried out and the religious life and the language have managed to survive, along with the adobe walls which appear like a time capsule, a revenant of prehistory. This provides a glimpse of a living tradition flowing from ancient times with a small trickle in modern time. It is a miracle that here in America we still have this treasure. It is time travel to find these places, like the villages in the high mountains of Peru, the Taos and Hopi pueblos, the Tibetan and Bonpo monasteries, and the remaining aboriginal cultures that have, by hook or crook, survived. Perhaps in some small way the tide has turned and at least some people are coming to learn their ways;not in an academic way and not to watch them like creatures in a zoo, but to show good faith in their efforts and to take back into modernity something of their culture in the distant hope that these lessons create a counterforce to the capitalist industrial imperialist juggernaut that is destroying our planet. To bring a voice to stop the terrible destruction that is forced upon the planet by the horrific greed and hostility that it takes to preserve the lifestyle of palatial homes with two cars in the garage, while we waste more food in a day than many third-world families see in a week.

The Taos Indians have managed to guard their ancient ways and keep them alive inside the walls. Here at the pueblo the life of the air is also the life of the clouds, which is the life of the lightning, which is the life of the thunder, which is the life of the rain, which is the life of the rivers, which is the life of the oceans, which moves by the power of the sun and the moon, which creates the life of all life. The pueblo beliefs have a primitive beauty that expresses the pathos of nature in a religion far older than the Judeo-Christian god.

The Taos pueblo is a time capsule that carries in its adobe walls religious beliefs that reach deep into prehistory where the Sun and the Moon are prayed to; the Sun to help the hunters, the Moon to help the farmers, and where the Earth, called "Our Mother for Corn", is given thanks at each meal. Here at Taos they still remember when the Stars, called the Night People, ruled the sky; Spider Grandmother had medicines for any illness; the Cloud People brought the rain; the Big Red Bear bestowed courage; the Stone Men gave strength; and the Cloud Boys were named Lightning and Thunder. This pantheon included Rattlesnake, Big Water Man, Gopher, Coyote, the Winds, Echo Boy, Dirt Boy and Red Boy. The supernatural forces, called "thlachinas", bring forth all the good things of the earth.

They have their own creation story. In it long long ago the Sun and the Moon mated and people came forth. These people slid down the handle of the Milky Way into Blue Lake. At first they lived below the surface of the water, and the first people to come out of the water were called the Feather People. Then, the Day People emerged and the Water People swam out of the lake until a Feather Girl saw them in the creek and they stood up and became people. They were followed by the Knife People, the Big Earring People and the Old Axe People. All the people lived around Blue Lake in harmony with the animals. When the weather grew cold the people followed Taos Creek down the mountain until it came to a beautiful meadow filled with grass where the people built houses out of earth and water on both sides of the creek. It is these houses we still see at Taos Pueblo.

When Coronado made his way into northern New Mexico in 1540 he sent Hernando de Alvarado with twenty soldiers and a few small-bore swivel guns to Taos. They visited the pueblo and described it much as we find it to-day, with two parts divided by the stream. The archaeologists estimate it was built around 1350 and is made entirely of adobe. The five-story complex on the north side of the river is the largest continuously inhabited adobe struc-ture in existence. Up until 1900, the only entrance to the rooms was via a ladder that extended through a door in the ceiling. The village includes seven subterranean kivas, six of which are still in use. By the mid-nineteenth centu-ry the population had declined to 360 people but by the 1920s the population had come back to over 600, and has grown into nearly 2,500. In the 1930s Elsie Clews Parson counted 175 housing units in two large clusters on either side of the Taos River. In 1992 Taos pueblo was designated a World Heritage Site, along with the Egyptian pyramids and the Great Wall of China.

Coronado's expedition was followed by a steady stream, a slow-motion invasion, of Europeans showing up at the pueblo. At first the Indians let the Spanish stay at the pueblo but after a while the Indians told them they had to get their own place and it had to be at least a league away from the pueblo. So the Spanish followed Taos creek downstream until they were a league away and built their own adobe houses, which became households in the hacienda style with big families living in a compound with a courtyard in the center. They settled by the creek and soon other haciendas appeared in the valley. The place was called Don Fernandez de Taos, which was eventually shortened to Taos.

Our first morning in Taos we go to the old square where I feel the strange horrors of the past, remembering that the square once served as a slave market where Taos Indians were sold as Spanish slaves. Later, it was the site of the famous Indian revolt against the Spanish; then later still against the Mexicans and finally of a revolt against the Americans. In each case, the invaders were repulsed only to return with a vengeance and hang the rebels in the square. These days, this site of so much conflictis now all commerce, surrounded by shops and restaurants. The place, though, still holds a long, ugly history of violence.

We walked the square, stopping at all the stores. In one an old Indian tells us to watch out for the people who run a couple of the stores where their wares are cheap knock-ffs made to look like real silver and turquoise. There are a couple of bookstores which catch my interest, but mostly there are tourist shops with cheap knick-knacks and tee shirts. There are a few Indians working in a nice jewelry store where we look at the concha belts. Some of the stores carry pottery. There is a nice rock shop with big crystals and fancy fossils next to the old La Fonda hotel. There are a couple of restaurants and that is about it. The only remnant of Taos' past is the architecture. The stores are all one-story adobe with connecting porches that run the length of each side of the square, all of it looking somewhat like it looked when the wagon trains were coming down the Santa Fe Trail through the Taos square. The square was the location for a brisk trade in hides brought to town by the mountain men who spent the winters trapping beaver. The old hotel, the La Fonda, has been on the square for many years and was started by an eccentric Westerner who managed to buy some of D. H. Lawrence's erotic artwork, which is still on display for a small fee. When you pay, one of the staff takes you into a locked room and then pulls back a curtain to show you about a dozen erotic paintings. They are tame by today's standards, but Lawrence painted himself as a satyr cavorting with naked women.   The annual Taos Open art show is held at the Civic Center just off the square. The most prestigious section of the show is reserved for "Taos Masters".

Just off the square is a hotel and restaurant called Doc Martin's, which is an old adobe house that was owned by a doctor who lived in Taos at the turn of the 20th century. It is a great building with an interior courtyard. Mable Dodge Luhan had written about it and when she first came to Taos she stayed at Doc Martin's house, which served as a boarding house for people coming to town before there were any hotels.

Ranchos de Taos is south of the main part of town. Here, right beside the road, is an amazing piece of architecture, an old adobe church built by the Indians in 1815. From the back there are adobe buttresses jutting out from the tall adobe walls. It is one of the most photographed and painted buildings in the West. Ansel Adams has a famous picture of it, Georgia O'Keefe painted it, and there are images of it in all the art books about Taos. We park in the lot and circumambulate the building, taking pictures from all angles. The front is somewhat more conventional and has a statue of Saint Francis in the courtyard.

The San Geronimo festival starts the next morning. We have dinner and when we come out the sun is below the horizon and there is an ominous dark cloud hanging over the pueblo. Lightning flashes illuminate the interior of the dark thunderhead, the night sky becrazed, rent by the lightning, then immediately mended back by the darkness. Lightning flared and faded and flared again inside the wind-whipped darkness of the clouds but we could hear no thunder. It must be raining under the cloud and I wonder what the Indians do if it rains on festival day. Then it is back to the Mabel Dodge Luhan House. We stand in the courtyard and look at the sky; the stars overhead being born and dying in the far enormity fill me with a strange sweet woe.

The distant mountains darker still against the star-lit sky. The constellations, assuring that the heavens are locked into place, wheeling in their great arcs; the north star a guiding beacon for lost travelers, a constant mote of light that tethers the small bear, held firm by the fidelity of the earth to the night sky in the ever-turning firmament. We turn in early in anticipation of being at the pueblo at sunrise to watch the footraces. When we crawl into bed I have a copy of Elsie Clews Parson's *Taos Tales* and I read one of the tales to Susan and Coby to get in the mood for the events of the next day. We propped ourselves up on a bunch of pillows and I read:

"Coyote thought he would go hunting at the edge of the wiregrass. Little Yellow Fox was already there hunting in the same place and by the time he saw coyote coming it was too late to get away.

So he called out, 'Grandfather coyote!'

'My grandson, where are you going?'

'I am going to the big feast.'

'Where is this feast?'

'Oh grandfather, the settlers are hosting a big feast.'

'Let's go together.'

'Oh yes grandfather, let's go.'

They came to a place where a large tree was growing beside the trail.

'Grandfather, a big hailstorm is coming quick. There is no shelter here. We will be killed by the hailstones. Quick get inside this buffalo skin bag and I will hang you to a limb from this tree and you will be safe.'

'Hurry grandson! The sky will be getting dark soon.'

So he tied coyote in the bag and hung it from the nearest tree limb, then he picked up some rocks and started throwing them at the bag.

'The hail is coming grandfather, the hail is coming.'

'Oh grandson the hail feels like rocks.'

And Little Yellow Fox went running off and left coyote hanging in the bag." [51]

After the story we were all tired and turned in. I slept lightly in excited anticipation of the day ahead.

Something about the air, or the altitude, or the excitement of being in Taos wakes me early after a series of vivid dreams. At about five in the morning Susan whispers, "Are you awake?" By 5:30 we are dressed in several layers. We pull out before dawn. The car thermometer reads thirty-two degrees and it feels brisk and cold compared to the heat of the day, which can get up to eighty degrees. We arrive at the pueblo just before the sun comes over the horizon. San Geronimo is what the Indians call Saint Jerome of the

Catholic tradition. Every year the festival falls on September 30th. The event includes four main features. First is the "race" in the early morning. Second is the trading fair, with vendors from all the pueblos. Third is the pole climb by the "dark eyes". Finally, there is the great feast. All of these go back into prehistory and now overlap the Saint Day for Saint Jerome.

The race is a semi-annual event. Many pueblos have a racetrack in their pueblo. The Taos racetrack runs east/west in front of the five-story northside pueblo building. It runs over a quarter-mile from the arbor at the west end of the track. The arbor is covered with cottonwood branches with the leaves still on and, at this time of year, the leaves are golden. The racetrack runs the entire length of the main building on the north side and then through a break in the wall and out into a field beside the creek. The "race" pits the northside kivas against the southside kivas, with three kivas on each side of the river. The "race" is not a contest in the way we think of a race but is a ceremony that influences the year's hunting and farming and keeps the sun and moon in place. The racers go into the kivas the night before the race, where they chant deep into the night. Early that morning the racers use turkey feathers and offer cornmeal to the local deity called Pachale, which means Blue Water. They take some pollen and blow it into the air as an offering to the sun. Then each racer is brushed with eagle feathers to give them strength.

As we pull into the Taos pueblo there are police lights flashing and road-blocks. An Indian policeman stops us and directs us to the parking lot. I am surprised to see that we don't have to park in the meadow where they bus people into the pueblo. We are among the first to arrive and get a prime parking spot in the little lot just outside the walls. That makes it much more convenient to leave stuff in the car and come and go during the day if we need anything. As we enter the pueblo, the first light of the day is brightening the eastern horizon. We watch in the dawning light as the vendors are setting up shop. The sky is clearing and there is not a cloud in sight. I marvel at the weather, remembering the lightning storm we watched hanging over Mt. Wheeler at sunset. The pole is standing tall with the dead sheep and the bundles of bread and melons at the top. The sheep's head hanging down, penitent looking, sacrificed to the feast day.

People are gathering at the church, so we go in to see the mass and stay warm until the sun gets above the horizon. The church slowly fills with a mix of Indians and whites, mostly older. The early morning mass in the Catholic Church starts the festival. The church is a dark adobe building with massive walls, stained glass windows along the sides and sculpted vigas in the ceiling. In front of the church doors is a courtyard defined by an adobe fence with a beautiful gated entrance. We go into the church and take a seat. It is early still and we watch as Indians, men and women, all dressed in bright festival shirts and shawls, make their way into the church. Behind the altar the wall is painted with murals that depict corn plants entwined with beans. These frame the alcove which holds a doll-like statue of Mary, who is elaborately dressed. The sun is depicted on one side of the alcove and the moon on the other. The atmosphere is both calm and quiet and charged with an air of excitement and expectation. Two priests come in, dressed in fancy robes and followed by younger men swinging censers that are releasing incense that fills the air with a sweet juniper aroma. I see Nancy Woods. I recognize her from a picture on one of the books she has written about the pueblo. The priest goes through all the rituals of the mass and gives a little sermon about the life of Saint Jerome, who is ostensibly the patron saint of this event. Saint Jerome was a penitent and the penitent tradition is still alive in the hills of New Mexico. It is strange how the festival, which dates further back into prehistory than the feast day of St. Jerome, has been overlaid on the Catholic tradition. The Saint's Day for Saint Jerome falls on the same day as the festival and the Indians, no doubt forced by the early church fathers, had to include the Saint's Day into their festival to carry on their own tradition. I get a little worried that the race might be starting and wonder if they coordinate it so it doesn't begin until after mass. Just as soon as the mass is finished we hurry out into the plaza.

The sun is just appearing and the plaza is filling up with people. We walk over to the racetrack. People are beginning to gather along the edge of the track, where you get the best view. We go down to the spot where the racetrack goes through the wall that surrounds the pueblo. From here we can see the three kivas on the north side. They are restricted and no one can go into the little plaza where they are located but the roofs are in plain view and we can see the long ladders protruding from the ceilings of the kivas. The racers are in the kivas and every now and then we hear a loud cry or whoop. It is cool in the morning air. Some of the Indians are beginning to appear on the roof of the north-side pueblo where they get the best view of the race.

The sun is just illuminating the top of the mountain behind the pueblo when we hear the Indians whooping and yelling and they start boiling up out of the kivas. It makes me wonder if the sun on the top of the stone peak is the signal to start the ritual of the race. They are coming up the ladders of all three kivas. The runner's bodies are painted with red and white clay from head to toe. They are wearing nothing but a breechcloth and moccasins. Small downy feathers are stuck in their hair. As they emerge they let out wild whoops and piercing yells and line up in two lines just outside the kivas. The racers range from very young to very old. They come out onto the racetrack, staying in two lines. A drummer appears and an elder takes his place at the front and back of each line. The drum starts up and the racers sing a chant and dance to the beat and then break up and walk down to the start of the race track, where they bunch up in front of the arbor. Then we hear the racers from the south side coming toward us, letting out wild piercing whoops. They walk past us to the east end of the track.

Soon the sun's rays are coming straight down the race track, shining into the arbor and making the cottonwood leaves glow like polished gold. Since the racetrack runs due east/west the sun just past the equinox shines its first morning rays directly into the arbor.

With the Indians gathered at both ends of the race track, I am expecting them to start the race when I see a procession coming from the church. It is the priests in their long white robes, followed by choirboys, also enrobed, swinging censers of incense; white clouds of fragrant smoke clouds the air. There is a group of Indians behind them, carrying the big doll-like statue of the Virgin Mary, dressed in silk, riding in a platform and followed by someone carrying the statue of Saint Jerome. They make their way from the church past the tall pole over to the arbor, where they climb up to the chairs waiting for them. They brought the Virgin Mary and Saint Jerome out to watch the race, marking some level of recognition and approval of the traditional religious rituals enacted on the feast day.

Suddenly the race has begun and young Indians come running by in both directions. The racetrack is lined with elders, each one painted like the racers and wearing only a breechcloth. They hold willow branches in their hands. We see the governor of the pueblo standing by the race track holding three straight staffs, each festooned with multiple ribbons of various bright colors. The ribbons are about a yard long and are streaming down as he cradles the staffs in his arm. These staffs are the insignia of office; one was presented by Abraham Lincoln. The first runners whisk by us, running barefoot, raising little puffs of dust when each foot hits the ground, the elders urging them on, lightly whipping them with the willow branches as they race by, calling out encouragement to them in their native tongue. Women and children from the pueblo line the roofs of the northern building, like stadium seats, with each tier of the building filled up with women and kids dressed in colorful shawls and blankets, ready to cheer on the racers. When the racers come by the women make a high-pitched trilling sound, almost like a Middle Eastern trilling wail, and urge the racers on. It is a beautiful sight with three levels of the pueblo filled with spectators high above the racetrack, all reenacting a spellbinding scene from the past.

After a bit Coby grows impatient asking, "How much longer?" The runners are zipping by in each direction, in no discernible order. It is not what we think of as a race where the runners are lined up and race against each other to see who crosses the finish line first. Rather it is runners racing by in one direction or the other, and when they get to the end another runner takes off, like in a relay race. While I understand that one side or the other is ultimately declared the winner, from our point of view, there is no way to tell who is winning and who is losing. All we see is runners going by every few minutes. The little girls are in spectacular bright-colored dresses and, as the racers come by the adobe building, all the women continue to let out piercing trills. The old men lining the racetrack call out encouragement and whip the racers with their willow branches. All this in the bright morning sun with a spectacular clear blue sky. It is a spectacle so removed from our everyday mundane life that it casts me into the past, jerking me from our modern 21st century life into a prehistory that is so glaringly distinct that it creates a dislocation at once intimate with the past and so removed from our present that I stand in dream-like awe.

After about an hour the race is over and all the racers congregate in front of the arbor. The drums reappear and there is more chanting and dancing. Then the racers move in a tight pack along the racetrack in front of the pueblo and the people on the roof and the spectators on the ground rain down goodies on the racers. Each racer produces a plastic bag and begins catching the candy and bags of popcorn and other assorted stuff. A mood of hilarity fills the air. We have a big bag of stuff we bought the day before and when they reach us we start tossing our stuff up into the air. I have small bags of redhots and Doritos. Coby has mints and Susie has small chocolates and in a few minutes we have tossed them all up. When the racers have passed by all the kids in the vicinity, with Coby joining in, jump out into the racetrack and pick up any candy that has been left behind. Then the parade moves to the south side, where the procession continues and the people appear on the roofs and start tossing down more stuff until each racer has a bag stuffed with goodies. When they reach the area of the kivas on the south side they all disperse and the race is over. After the racers left the track there are eagle feathers scattered all over it. Susie went to pick one up but was cautioned by an Indian lady not to touch them.

By this time the vendors are all set up and when the race ends everyone gravitates toward the tents. Now is the time to eat and shop. The plaza between the north side and south side is bisected by the Taos creek and both sides are filled with vendors. On the south side are food vendors and a few booths filled with plastic toys manufactured in China with kids buying toy guns. On the north side of the creek are vendors with over a hundred covered booths filled with beautiful silver and turquoise and fine pottery and clothing and other items. All the vendors are full blood and each booth has a sign with the vendor's name and tribe.

We get a sopapilla covered with honey and a fruit drink and go to the shady spot beside the creek where we set up our folding chairs and establish our resting place and enjoy the sweet bread and drinks. Then we are anxious to tour the booths and to shop for presents. We work our way along, booth after booth. Otto is in one of the booths selling fetishes. We stand and talk for a few minutes, pick out a couple of fetishes and then move on with the flow of the crowd as the aisles between the vendor's booths are filled with people streaming through in both directions. The Taos Indians stand out as they are wrapped in blankets against the chill of the morning, most wearing moccasins.

I am interested in going into the shops in the pueblo. There are several rooms in each part of the pueblos where we can go inside the building and talk with the Taos Indians and see the stuff they have. In the stores in the pueblo we get to see how the rooms are configured. In one of the stores there is a young man tending the store. There is a glass case on one side of the room and it is filled with artifacts. I examine them carefully and when everyone else left I ask him about them. He says there was a lake nearby that they drained and when they got all the water out of the basin they found the ruins of an old village and the artifacts were from that village. The best of the artifacts is a hafted axe with the handle still perfectly intact. The wooden handle is about a foot long, with the broad stone axe firmly placed in the handle and wrapped with sinew. As I stood in the store looking at the artifacts, people were streaming in and out, most of them only staying a few minutes. Some of them asked questions, which the young man answers patiently.

One woman asked, "What's in those bundles at the top of the pole?"

He answered, "Sacred stuff."

"Are the clowns really going to climb the pole?"

"Well they are going to try but they aren't really clowns."

"It must be really hard for them, I heard they grease the pole."

"Yeah, it isn't easy."

And then she was out the door without buying anything.

I looked at him and shook my head. I had been advised by people around town that it wasn't a good idea to ask a lot of questions at the pueblo. They said the Indians resent it, that those who know won't say, and that if anyone does answer your questions the answers will all be bullshit. I could see why.

From time to time we return to our chairs, which are beside one of the bridges, and relax for a few minutes. Coby plays with the Indian kids who are coming and going by the creek. Now that the race is run and we have made our first pass through the vendors it is getting near lunch time and we are ready to head out to John Suazo's studio to join in the feast and visit with Juanita, John's mother. Their house is a short walk from the pueblo but we have food to bring so we take the car. When we pull into the yard there are people sitting at a table under a big shade tree between the house and John's studio. John has a small studio in the shape of a hogan. It is roughly circular, about fifteen feet across. John gets up and greets us and invites us in.

We carry in our food offering and find the house full of people and a big table in the living room covered with food. Juanita is sitting in a big chair in the living room watching over everyone as they come and go. We sit with her and give her a gift of an old book called *Pueblo Boy*. She had told us at one of our previous visits about the book. She said when she was a little girl a photographer had come to the village and asked if he could get her family to pose for pictures in traditional dress. They agreed and he took a bunch of pictures and then disappeared. She opens the book lovingly and shows us a picture of herself when she was three-years-old, back in the nineteen-thirties. We get to see her mother and father and all her relatives who are depicted in the book. They are all in the pueblo so it is interesting to see how it looked in those days. The photographer said he would send payment to the family when the book was published but nothing ever appeared. Susan also presented her a turquoise-colored shawl encrusted with beads from India and she immediately draped it over her shoulders, smiling.

She said it was wonderful to live in the pueblo and all sorts of things would happen. She said one time when she was a little girl her father and grandfather would take their horses and go up the mountain, hunting for deer and elk and bear. She remembered one time they killed a bear and brought it into their living room. She said they had to do a lot of ceremony over the bear and that it was laying there stretched out on the floor and she was afraid of it and wasn't at all sure it was dead. But she was fascinated by it and wanted to touch its hair and she went up to it and was touching it and all at once it farted and scared her. She thought it must be alive and was going to jump up and attack them. She went running out of the room and hid and says she has never liked bear meat since that time.

John comes in and joins us and asks who won the race. I have to say that I couldn't tell whether the north or the south won. He said the old people told him that the breath of the racers was food for the sky. At Zuni they build fires to feed the clouds so here the breath of the runners feeds the sky and the energy of their feet touching the earth gives energy to the earth. A number of the racers were barefoot and the rest wore only moccasins so that might explain why they run barefoot. I asked John if he had been a runner and he said oh yeah he had run in the race many times and that he had even climbed the pole in 1976. He said in those days it was a lot harder, that they didn't have ropes. Now there is a big rope tied to the top that they use to help get up the pole and to lower the bags and the sheep.

John invites us to the studio. He has a new sculpture, as he always does, since he creates about three per week. It is a great feeling to step into his studio and there, across the room, is a beautiful sculpture made of gleaming white stone. It is a bear sitting on an Indian and he explains the story. He says the man depicted is a friend of a relative who had gone bear hunting and shot a bear, which then charged him and knocked the gun out of his hand and knocked him down. When he came to and opened his eyes the bear was sitting on him and when he tried to sit up the bear fell over dead. Next he pointed out his grandfather's snowshoes hanging on a leather thong attached to a ceiling beam. I wouldn't have recognized them as snowshoes. They were circular and made of willow limbs that have been pulled around to form a circle about a foot wide, just wide enough for your foot. Then it was woven with some fiber that formed the base of the snowshoe so they looked a bit like a dream catcher.

Then it was time to eat and we went inside with the dozen or so people, including John's son, his wife and their two small kids. Juanita had made stew and hominy and there was a table full of food. We had stopped at a bakery and brought pies and cookies. It was an eclectic crowd of old friends of the family, mostly anglos and mostly artists of one kind or another. After everyone had eaten, we sat under a big tree in the yard and talked. When the conversation died down I wanted to question John about the Anasazi.

I looked at him and asked, "What was the relationship of the Anasazi to the people here at Taos?"

He responded, "They were our ancestors."

I was a bit surprised since the Taos Indians have their own creation story which I have heard from John and it doesn't include anything about the people of Chaco or any of that. There is an older man across the table from me and he wants to get into the conversation and he says that calling them Anasazi is a misnomer since that is the name given to them by the early explorers who questioned the local Navaho about who left all the ruins and they replied, "The Anasazi", which means Ancient Enemies. I concur with that and ask if John or anyone has any idea what they called themselves but neither John nor the other guys have a clue. Then I ask about the religion of the Anasazi and how it relates to the religion of the contemporary people and whether we know anything about the old religion. John mentions all the kivas at Chaco and says they were used as initiation chambers for the young men and women who had to go through long initiation ceremonies. He says the women had it easier than the men and had shorter initiations that only took four days.

John was born in 1951 but looks ageless, like a piece of weathered stone. He is a very gentle man of tremendous accomplishment. He has a gallery in the northwest corner of the pueblo in a couple of rooms that belong to his family. He also has the studio outside his mother's home and a large house he built for himself. He is a big guy, over six feet tall with long hair in a ponytail, dark complexion with a mustache, very soft spoken. We met him the year before at his gallery in the pueblo where he has six or eight pieces of his work. He talked about each one. Most of them illustrate mythic themes dealing with the various clans and the story of creation. He told us how after you are born your parents take you to one of the kivas and then you are a member of that kiva for the rest of your life. He is a member of the fish kiva and says that the fish people came up the stream from Santa Fe and when they got to here there was an ancient kiva and the people came from the kiva over to the stream and pulled the fish people out of the water and as they came out of the water they became human.

He asked if I had read *The Man Who Killed the Deer* and I told him I had as had Susan. He said his grandfather was the man who killed the deer in the story. He said Waters never talked to his grandfather but obviously heard the story and wrote the book largely based on the story of his grandfather's life. He said he had grown up in the room where we were standing. The walls in his gallery are white and he says that it is not paint or whitewash but a special kind of clay that they plaster on the adobe for the interior walls.

He told a story about his father and said he had only gone to school for a total of five minutes. He arrived at the school and five minutes later they had a recess and all the students got to go outside and when he got outside he took off running and went home where he said he was needed to help with the farm work. Even though that was the end of his formal education he learned to speak three languages; Taos, Spanish and English.

He said his great-grandfather had been a famous traveler and had made three trips north to the Missouri River, starting when he was only sixteen. He had gone with some Mexican buffalo hunters on the first trip to act as their guide. About one hundred miles from the pueblo he had been out in front of the Mexicans leading the way and was captured by some Comanche Indians who were ancient enemies of the Taos Indians. They held him for two weeks then one day dressed him in fine clothes with beautiful beaded moccasins. This meant one of two things; either they were about to kill him as a sacrifice or they wanted him to marry a Comanche woman. He said he needed to go out to answer the call of nature and when he got out of sight he took off running. The Comanche chased him on horseback but he was a fast runner and, as luck would have it, there was a big gorge nearby and he ran to it and the horses couldn't follow. It was cold weather and, as he made his way back to Taos, he had to cross a river and his leggings got wet and froze and he was lucky to run into two Indians from Taos who were out hunting. They had some whiskey and rubbed it on his legs and kept him from freezing to death.

John said he doesn't do any drawings, he just puts water on the rocks to show him the colors and lines in the stone and then he sees what shapes are most natural to the stone. I really enjoy being in the studio; the walls are covered with interesting photos and there are sculptures everywhere you look. He reached over into a little alcove and pulled out a catalog from a Thirty Year Retrospective of his work at the Harwood Museum and asked if I would like to have it. He signed it and gave it to me with a poster of the piece that took first place at the last Taos Art show. Just outside John's studio he had the larger pieces. One of them is eight-feet-tall and another one four-feet-tall with a sculpted Great House sitting on top of a mesa.

Coby comes in and wants to know when the clowns will appear and I look at my watch and see it is about one o'clock. We tell John and Juanita that we are going back to see the koshares and move the car closer to the pueblo. We return to our chairs and I tell Coby that we will know they are about to appear when the excitement level in the plaza becomes more intense. Sure enough, about one-thirty we feel it; the excitement becomes palpable. We all look up on top of the north side pueblo to the roof of the very topmost apartment. There they are at the very top of the five-story pueblo. Ten of them. It is a jarring sight, dream-like, out of a distant past. They are the Black Eyes, painted with black and white stripes from head to toe and wearing only a breechcloth. Their faces are painted black, thus the name "Black Eyes", they are wearing straw headdresses in fantastic shapes that stick out both sides of their heads. The Black Eyes standing on top of the pueblo silhouetted against the blue sky are a chthonic revelation, stirring some deep inner forces of the psyche. It is a startling sight: their sacred mountain behind them, the deep blue sky overhead, the koshares whooping and yelling.

They bound down the pueblo, jumping from one roof down to the next, out into the plaza where they begin to wreak their havoc. All the kids go crazy and start running around looking to hide or get away. Coby doesn't know what to do. At first, he hides behind a nearby adobe oven but then runs out and then runs back and then runs out again. He doesn't know whether to be excited or scared. The vendors start covering up their goods and putting out offerings like apples, oranges, cigarettes, melons and knick-knacks. The koshares start going through the vendors' booths, picking up the offerings and messing with the people, acting fierce or funny. Otto told me that if you don't cover up your merchandise and leave a nice offering for them they will take everything you have in your booth. Once they make their way through all the booths then the real fun begins.

Coby is fascinated by them and we start trailing them around. He can hardly stand it and wants to run up to them but when he does he loses his nerve and runs back and hides behind me. Then he finally runs right up behind one of them and the koshare turns at that moment and jumps at Coby with a fierce face and it catches the attention of a couple of other koshares in the vicinity and all at once they have him surrounded and one of them grabs a bottle of water from a booth and pours it over his head. They all give him a collective yell and he runs back to me soaking wet. He is scared out of his wits and thrilled to death both at the same time. We go over to our chairs and Susan pulls out a towel and dries him off and then he is ready for another round and wants to go back into the crowd and find them again.

It is easy to tell where they are; you can see the crowd reaction wherever they happen to be. They don't have any patterns and sometimes group up and sometimes spread out. At any point they can grab a kid and head for the creek. Once I see them running by with a little baby and I follow and watch as the mom goes with them and they hold the baby, which is screaming its head off, and sprinkle it with a little handful of water and hand it back to the mom. They corral some of the teenagers and escort them to the creek and point at the water, when the kids gets in the water they make sure they get wet front and back before they let them out of the creek. There is an old Indian elder who is moving around with them. He has long braids and is wearing a blanket and moccasins.

The three of us are hanging out by one of the log bridges and here comes three koshares with a couple of kids about Coby's size. They dunk them good and when they are coming out of the creek Coby runs over in front of them. They surround him and grab him. I am standing right beside them and before they take off to the creek, which is only a few feet away, one of them looks over at me to make sure it is ok, a courtesy they wouldn't extend to a Taos Indian, and I nod and say, "Dunk that kid." And off they go into the creek and they ease him into the cold water and he comes out totally soaked from head to foot. The elder is with the koshares when Coby comes out of the water and he pulls Coby aside and says, "You have nothing to be afraid of." We take him over to our chairs where Susan pulls out the towel and dries him off and Coby goes over to the porta potties and pulls off his wet clothes and changes to something dry. We hang his wet clothes on a tree limb by the creek to dry.

Then we are curious and go back into the crowd to watch the action. One of the clowns was given a watermelon as an offering and he gets a big knife from somewhere and cuts the big melon in two and scoops out the red fruit and hands it around to anyone in the area. When he has it all scooped out he spots some teenage Indian and runs up to him and puts the rind on his head like a helmet. The kid shakes it off and runs to the creek to wash his hair. Someone has put a pack of cigarettes out for an offering and a couple of them tear it open and they each put about ten cigarettes in their mouth; a lighter appears and they are both smoking like chimneys. They run around with the mouthful of cigarettes and one of them goes by me, stops in front of me and pokes a cigarette in my mouth. I lift my head and in an exaggerated gesture blow smoke into the sky. He runs on and I snuff out his cigarette, feeling a bit honored that they had picked me out of the crowd for some action.

At one point they all gather in front of the arbor, someone shows up with a drum and the deep bass beat of the drum rings out and the koshares dance around in a circle in front of the arbor and then break off and start pulling the aspen boughs down and throwing them on the ground. They keep at it until the arbor is bare. People gather around and pick up the branches and leaves which are, apparently, a special offering, blessed by the korshares. Wherever they go a crowd quickly gathers, watching to see what will happen. People come running over to pick up branches and golden leaves as souvenirs. Then the clowns move to the pole.

The pole is thirty feet tall and about the size of a telephone pole, with a pair of crossbars at the top. These two sticks go through the pole just a foot or so from the top and stick out on each side, one just below the other. I have heard that they go up on the mountain and find a tree and cut it and clean the limbs and the branches off and when it is ready they have to carry it down off the mountain without it touching the ground. When it arrives they close the pueblo and have ceremonies associated with the arrival of the pole and plant it in the middle of the plaza on the north side of the creek. They put up police tape around it and a couple of Indians stand guard to be sure no one tries to touch it.

Now all the people form a huge circle around the pole and the koshares act out in various ways, pulling people out of the audience into the circle to goof with them, pour water on them or steal their hats. Then after a while they pull out little miniature bows and arrows and shoot or pretend to shoot little arrows up at the top of the pole. There at the top is the dead sheep and the two bags, one full of bread and the other full of melons, all suspended from the crossbeams that go through the pole.

Eventually they start to climb the pole. Various koshares make it a little way up then slide down to the ground. After a number of unsuccessful attempts they form a human ladder, with one on top of the other while a third climbs up to get a good start at making it to the top. There are ropes tied to the crossbeams and eventually one of them uses the rope and climbs up to the top. When he gets to the top crossbar the crowd breaks out in applause.

Once up there he perches on the top of the pole and sits there for a while and spreads his arms and looks up at the sun. After a few minutes he lowers himself to the cross beam and lowers the sheep and the two bags of food down by the rope. Then he uses the rope and slides down and when he hits the ground that is the signal for the feasts to begin. All the women of the pueblo have been cooking, some for most of the night, and each household has big pots of food ready and everyone who is a Taos Indian and anyone lucky enough to get an invitation goes into the various apartments in the pueblo to enjoy the feast as all the tourists make their way back to the parking lots.

As the crowd swirls around me heading for the exit, I walked over to the pole. Suddenly I remembered one of our trips to Mexico where we saw some Mexican Indians, Mayas, recreating a pole ceremony where they had five young Indians climb to the top of a pole and four of them tie their feet to a rope attached to a device that turns around the top of the pole. One man stays at the top playing out the ropes, extending them further and further, as the young Indians swirl around suspended upside down, spiraling in ev-er-widening circles until they slowed down and righted themselves for their return to the earth. I wanted to connect the dots to find some cultural con-tinuity between the pueblos of New Mexico, which were the northernmost manifestation of the great culture of indigenous Mexico, and the Maya cul-ture. I wondered if the Taos pole dance was a ritual enactment in a tradition still echoing this cultural impulse.

We go back by Otto's booth and say goodbye. He is heading back to Zuni that evening and we make plans to meet again at Zuni to see the kachi-na dances. Then we head back to town. It feels good to get back to Mabel Dodge's where we can rest after the long day. Mabel's house is an historic building and played a huge role in the history of Taos as an art colony. Mabel was a remarkable woman who had visited Gertrude Stein's salon in Paris and then settled in New York City and established a place in the Village modeled on Stein's. It was a huge success and she was able to attract the artists and literati of her day, along with the radical political element. She came from a family with money and married an Italian architect. She heard about Taos and came for a visit in 1919 and knew immediately that she had found a place to call home. Taos was already an art colony and she bought land adjacent to the pueblo and started building an adobe house. She hired a crew of Indians who were supervised by her husband. The Indian in charge of the crew from the pueblo was named Tony Luhan, a beautiful man, who she quickly fell in love with. She consequently kicked out the architect and moved Tony in and put him in charge of getting the house built.

Once the house was complete she began to solicit the people who fre-quented her New York salon to come to Taos. From then until her death she had a constant stream of artists, writers, musicians and intellectuals who came to stay for varying lengths of time. Among the most famous were Georgia O'Keefe, D.H. Lawrence, Carl Jung, Ansel Adams and many others.

It was a who's who of the early 20th century and many of them fell under the spell of the northern New Mexico landscape and moved to the Taos area.

The stream of visitors was as enchanted with Mabel's husband, Tony, as they were with her. He wore his hair in two long braids down the front. He, of course, had lived in the pueblo and was from a family whose heritage reached back into prehistory. He once took D.H. Lawrence on an adventure and they drove to the Hopi reservation so Lawrence could see the famous snake dance where the Hopis dance with rattlesnakes in their mouths. They took off in Mabel's car with Tony driving. They soon left the road and drove the car straight across the desert, camping out along the way.

The house is a big rambling adventure in itself. The courtyard in front of the house is paved with flat stones. The house is three stories tall, with Mabel's solarium on the top floor. It has a long portico across the front leading to the main door, which is ornate and has the date 1922 carved and painted on the door. Next to the door is a ceramic tile decorated with a picture of Don Quixote.

Opening the front door is like stepping into an altered reality; the place hums with the collective energy of its residents. It is classic Southwestern adobe architecture with traditional vigas across the ceiling. The ceiling is Indian style, made with branches stripped of their bark and cut to a uniform length and laid in a herringbone pattern. There are carved posts from floor to ceiling, worn dark with age, in the center of the main room. Each room has a corner adobe kiva fireplace that seems to grow out of the wall. The atmosphere in the house is organic and alive.

We are staying in Mabel's bedroom on the second floor. We go up the narrow stairway and down the hall to Mabel's room. They recently added a bath to the room. The bedposts are like the carved poles that support the downstairs ceilings. There are windows looking out to the east. There is also an exterior door with curved adobe steps leading out to a courtyard. They had to build the bed in the room as it was under construction because it wouldn't fit through any of the doors once the construction was complete.

At the top of the stairs is a bathroom where D.H. Lawrence painted the windows. I go in and study them and take pictures. The little bathroom holds an old tub, sink and commode, with no room left over. But there are six big windows and each window has eight panes and each pane is painted with bright colors with abstract designs. The narrow stairs leading down to the office are a work of art, with an Indian design painted in a repeating pattern on each step so that as you look down at the steps it is like looking at the design on an Indian blanket in three dimensions. There is more art in the hallway: murals by Indian artists on the walls of the hallway and on the steps leading down from Mabel's bedroom.

Under the portico on the outside there is a row of single rooms and each of them has some claim to fame. One of them was used by Ansel Adams on his visits and each one is named for the famous artist or writer who stayed there. The room at the end was used to edit the film *Easy Rider* back in the Sixties. After Mabel died, Dennis Hopper bought the house and lived in it for several years and set up an editing room where they did the initial editing for the famous movie. He got a reputation for loud parties and shooting off his guns. He didn't own it for long and afterward he sold it to a non-profit group who run it as a Bed-and-Breakfast for artists. They hold a series of events of all kinds. The most famous are probably the Writer Workshops hosted by Natalie Goldberg. We were lucky to get rooms between the events.

There are giant cottonwood trees across the front of the main plaza, which forms a barrier that separates the house from the rest of the world. The back of the house borders on land owned by Taos pueblo. The next morning it was reported that a bear came down out the mountain and was looking around in the trash cans.

We had a couple of places we wanted to see before leaving town. We drove over to Ledoux Street, a very narrow one-way street, more like an alley, lined with galleries and museums. R.C. Gorman had his studio there and it is now a gallery of his works and we always drop in and see his art. Down the street is the Blumenschein Museum. He was the founding father of the Taos art colony and the Museum was his house. He arrived in 1897 when he was traveling through the area with another artist painting landscapes. Once he saw the town he knew it was a special place where he wanted to stay. His daughter continued to live in the house until the 1970s and then it became the museum. It still has a lot of the original furniture and all his books are in his library. All the rooms are filled with art from the very first generation of artists who established the Taos art colony. His art in particular is outstanding: landscapes of the mountains and portraits of the Indians in the pueblos, all done with great style and beauty.

We came to one room full of drawings he had made of the San Geronimo festival in 1898. I studied the drawings intently. I couldn't believe it; the details were exactly the same as what we had seen the day before. He depicted the race and the racers and their body paint, and they looked exactly the same. He had drawings of the pole and the koshares climbing it and even the pole looked exactly the same; the same size and the same crossbeams at the top. I felt I was part of a recurring ritual, an eternal recurrence, played in identical repetitions.

Then it was back to the mundane world and off to the airport in Albuquerque.

TAOS GREEN CORN DANCE - 2015

I had a schedule of dances at the pueblo and this year we were on hand for the Green Corn Dance. We headed to Taos in time to check into La Fonda hotel on the town square. We were up early the next morning to get out to the pueblo to see the footrace. Taos pueblo holds two footraces each year. The one we were familiar with at the San Geronimo festival at the end of

September and now this one, held during the Green Corn Dance. We were early enough to get a good parking space up close to the old pueblo buildings. There wasn't nearly the crowd that we encountered at the September festival, but it is still a glorious sight to walk into the pueblo just as the sun is lighting the granite top of Taos Mountain. We head down to the racetrack where we can see the kivas on the north side. The Indian women, some with their daughters, are gathering on the roof, wearing their most colorful scarves. They have long dresses and beautiful scarves with long fringe. They gather on the first two levels of the roof. A few men show up with them, and there is a small crowd lining the racetrack. Anglos, like ourselves, and Indians from the pueblo; the Taos men wrapped in their blankets, the women wearing their long scarves. The main difference from the St. Geronimo festival is they haven't built an arbor and there doesn't seem to be a mass at the church associated with this event. Plus there are no vendors. Another difference is that this race is for the kids and they have children as young as four-years-old participating. The racers are all in the kivas, where they have spent the night singing and chanting to gather their strength.

Then we hear loud whooping and watch as they emerge from the kivas. Once out, they circulate around, letting out war whoops and piercing yells. They are dressed in breechcloths and moccasins, their bodies painted earth tones, tufts of eagle feathers stuck to their hair and on their bodies. They have a little ankle bracelets on as well. They gather in two lines at the middle of the racetrack. There must be about twenty-five or thirty racers lined up. The young boys have the same breechcloth but they are covered with white paint, their hair slicked back and painted white as well. Then I notice there are a few young boys who are painted black from head to toe. Their faces are painted black with a white circle around one eye. The elders are in line with the racers, painted like the dancers but with willow boughs in their hands. The governor is there, holding the staffs of office. A drummer shows up and stands between the lines and begins a beat; the men all start to dance and chant. Once they finish they move down the racetrack and gather at the west end of the track.

They no sooner congregate at the end of the track when we hear whooping and yelling coming from the south village. In a few minutes the runners from the south side appear coming across the log bridge over Taos creek. They move to the east end of the track and the elders take up their positions along the runway. Now the racetrack is lined with spectators and the roof of the pueblo is filled with Indians. Then without any apparent signal the racers are racing by. Some of the runners are barefoot, others have moccasins. The racers are all ages, from very small kids to teens to elders. The young men run like the wind with a look of determination on their faces. It is really touching to watch the little kids run by. They go in pairs, their bodies painted white, a few eagle feathers fluttering in the wind and settling to the racetrack as they pass. The elders wave their willow boughs as the runners pass by and call out encouragement saying "Oom-a-pah! Oom-a-pah!" Occasionally one of the elders will step out onto the track to swish his willow branch and emphasize his encouragement. It is eerie to hear the women on the rooftops trilling as the runners go by. They grab their scarves and wave them and let out a loud trill to encourage the runners. The morning sun is up in the sky and it is warming up; the sun is bright and the light is magical, illuminating this scene as it has for generations of the ancestors of these runners. The racers aren't racing against time but rather to exert themselves to their fullest so that their energy is a sacrificial offering to the sun. They are giving their energy to the sun to encourage its life, giving it force to pour down on the earth to make the corn grow and to give fertility to all life, plant and animal.

The racers pass by, back and forth, until everyone at both ends has run and, after about forty-five minutes, it is over. I have no idea who has won or what it means to win or even if it is a meaningful concept to them in any competitive sense. All the runners and the elderly gather at the west end of the track and the drum appears and they create a circle and chant to the drum beat. Then suddenly plastic bags appear and they parade down the racetrack with all the women on the rooftops and the spectators throwing candy and apples and oranges. The little kids scramble to catch the goodies and quickly gather up anything that falls on the ground. We follow along, watching the spectacle of the tightly-bunched group of Indians, all in their breechcloths and body paint and moving under a shower of treats. Everyone is smiling and laughing. We follow them over the bridge to the south village, where more people appear on the roofs and the shower of treats continues on the path as the runners move toward the kivas.

We are scheduled to visit with John and Juanita Suazo at ten and once the runners disperse we head back to the car. It is a short drive out to the studio where we find John at work. He has a sentinel outside the workshop that is a tall abstract-looking Indian with a headdress on a narrow column of stone. We enjoy spending time with him and with his mother. Juanita informs us that the green corn dancers will be in front of the church at the pueblo about two and that this morning they are making the rounds, dancing at other places around the village outside the walls and will do the dances inside the walls starting then. So we have time to visit for a while and then drive into Taos for lunch.

I read in a Frank Waters' book that the green corn dance was not a very big deal at Taos so we knew not to expect anything like what we had seen at San Felipe. When we got back to the pueblo there was a small crowd gathering in front of the church. We went in and sat in the cool quiet atmosphere of the church, looking at the artwork around the altar. There are murals that are clearly pueblo-inspired and not the Spanish iconography of the suffering Jesus and the anguished stained-glass saints. Rather, there are stylized corn plants with the bright sun shining in the sky. Not to say that Jesus on the cross and the Virgin Mother don't appear prominently in the statuary and get central place on the altar, with the native motifs as murals on the surrounding walls.

We wander back out and stand by Taos Creek, watching the water rush down from Blue Lake on its journey to the Rio Grande. The water is shallow, riveting over rocks and casting a million points of lights, with each crest reflecting a star-like glint of white light, twinkling in the constant flow. Haulms of tall grass quiver in the current. I can sense faint movements of nesting fish unseen beneath the surface. I see pebbles furred with algae lying on the floor of the creek. The creek is lined with willows standing in clumps, cut back in places so the people can fetch water. I squat by the creek and put my hand in and dip up a palm-full to drink. The cool water tastes fresh; it has a metallic hint, bringing something from the mountains, something from the sky. The rippled silted floor of the stream is furrowed by the changing currents. A waterspider glides across the surface on jointed horsehair legs, the water spins and flares in its wake. Filaments of mossy underwater plant-life sway below the surface. I see my visage, trembling, mirrored on the surface of the stream with white clouds overhead, clouds above and below me, at the same time.

Acoma, Hopi and Taos all lay claim to being the oldest inhabited villages in America. Standing here surrounded by the pueblo is an experience that has greater antiquity than anything produced by the European invaders. Here, a small piece of the ancient world has managed to survive. It is probably eight or nine hundred years old but no one knows for sure. The tribe has kept the archaeologists out and no firm dates have been documented, it has simply been here as long as we have written records and as long as the Taos people have any tribal recollection. As far as they are concerned the pueblo has been here through their entire history which is tied to those buildings, to that creek, to Blue Lake and to the mountain that cradles Blue Lake, and feeds it and sends it on its way rushing by us. The buildings are revenants where the dead are alive, the past vibrant in the complicity of the aged, remembering held in the adobe walls permeated by the past, an earthy incense of sage-smoke wafting across time. I look at the stacked architectural features and sense the antiquity of the place gazing from these walls, wan and serenely ageless. A picture forms, the world forever spinning and these buildings gazing out, a mask of tribal identity, the face of a people confronting the sheer velocity of time, a racial artifact risen from the mud, held recurrent, unchanged, redundantly preserved by the will of a people, remembered to us this day by ancestors long departed, preserved against the incertitude of time. I take this as a herald of racial distinctiveness that is both a fragment of humanity and a facet of our shared nature.

In a few minutes there is a sense of anticipation that runs through the little crowd standing in the plaza by the church, a palpable feeling, and then we see them, a line of dancers coming from behind the main building. Everyone moves toward the church. It is a small crowd, not a throng, but an audience for the dancers, mostly Anglos, a few residents of the pueblo, the men in their blankets, the women wearing their colorful shawls. The dancers line up in two lines with the women facing each other and the men at the end of the lines. But I can see immediately Frank Waters was right, there are only about thirty dancers and the women far outnumber the men and most of the men are teens. But they are all nicely appointed with apparel that closely parallels what we saw at San Felipe. The women don't have tablitas, but they have the dress with one shoulder bare and have the evergreen boughs in their hands. The men mostly have long hair and they are wearing breechcloths and have the fox skin and a rattle. One of the men gives his rattle a shake and the dance begins. They have a drum and a few men standing in a circle around the drummer chanting. The dance lasts about a half hour and then they proceed across the little bridge next to the church and go down to the smaller plaza that is in front of the kivas in the south side of the village. We follow along and watch as they recreate the ritual dance, carrying on the traditional ways. The rattle and the drum echo off the walls of the pueblo as they have for generations. When they finish this round the dancers troop off behind the kivas, deeper into the pueblo where visitors are not welcome. We watch them disappear and turn to go back to the car.

The next morning we go out to the gorge, where we stand on the bridge and look down into the depths. The gorge is enclosed with sheer cliffs of black volcanic rock layered in tiers that step down, one after another, descending toward the Rio Grande several hundred feet below us. Ragged boulder fields are at the base of each layer. It is a strange combination of water and desert. All around us there is nothing but the high desert sage fields, and there, far below us, is the river, the water so deep in the gorge there is no way for it to water the adjacent fields. Visually it is stunning, the depths of the gorge opens beneath us like a huge abyss. The sage fields in the high deserts surround us and in the distance Taos Mountain stands snow-capped with deep green forests on its slopes. The landscape is aesthetically rich, challenging and rewarding to the senses.

The next morning we have to leave for the airport but before we leave we go by the old adobe church in Ranchos de Taos, just south of town. The parking lot is empty and it is a perfect time to take pictures. Then we head south to follow the river down to Albuquerque to catch a plane. The plane flight seems to drop us into a different world.

HOPI: PEOPLE OF PEACE - 2016

The Hopi refer to themselves as the Hopitu-Shinama which is translated, "little people of peace" or "all peaceful people" or more simply "peaceful people". The Hopi reservation has twelve villages with ten of them clustered on three mesas. The mesas are exposed stone ridges protruding from north to south out into the desert plains. On First Mesa there are Tewa Village, Sitsomovi Village and Walpi Village, lined up almost contiguously and perched on top of the narrow ridge of the mesa. Second Mesa has three more villages, Shungonovi, Sipaulovi and Mishongnovi, along with the Visitor's Center and Museum. Third Mesa has Kykotsmovi, Oraibi, Hotevilla and Bacavi.

The Hopi are most likely descendants of the people who left Mesa Verde about 1300 CE. It seems appropriate when we leave Mesa Verde to go see the Hopi, going from their past to their present. It used to be there was only one hotel on the Hopi reservation but now they have built a new one in Tuba City called Moenkopi Legacy Inn. It has adobe-style architecture in a stepped design. There is a courtyard on one side which has a huge fountain flowing into a stream that runs about 100 feet, this in the middle of a desert where the temperature is often above 100 degrees. But we are glad to have a room. I ask at the desk about getting a guide for the next day and the clerk gives me the number for a man named Donald Dawahongnewa. I call him and leave a message and hope for the best in getting in touch with him. Tuba City is on the edge of the Hopi lands. The town is divided, with Hopi on one side and Navajo on the other.

The Hopi are among the most peaceful of all people. They are among the rare tribal societies that did not send out raiding parties. However, in historic time they were under constant attack from the Navajo, the Apache and the Comanche. Any of these tribes could swoop in and try to kill someone as a war trophy and steal their livestock. A well-trained cadre of warriors was a necessary part of life and as late as 1935 all young Hopi were trained to be warriors. The story goes that whenever the Hopi sent out a war party it was to get their horses back or recapture their women and children. The Hopi had one person in the war party whose job was to sing. They had songs to prepare them for battle and songs that needed to be sung during and after the battle. The success or failure of the battle could be blamed on the quality of the songs.

Today the Hopi reservation consist of about a half-million acres. This represents a small fraction of what they consider their ancestral lands. They are totally surrounded by the Navajo. The reservation only gets eighteen inches of rain per year. They do dry land farming and manage to raise corn, beans, cotton and melons in scattered fields. They are governed by a tribal council but each village has its own chief.

Once we were checked in to the hotel in Tuba City we headed out to tour the Hopi villages on the mesa and drove sixty miles across some of the bleakest deserts in America. Yet the desert is punctuated with spectacular landscapes. Leaving Tuba City the road winds down off the mesa and runs straight as an arrow over a rolling desert plain where nothing seems to grow over a foot tall. However, the desert was tinged with green. We passed a Hopi cornfield and could see the dry farming technique with short clumps of corn spaced about ten feet apart. Then the road exits the flat plain and goes up to a mesa top and presents a vista across the desert plains that fades into a distant haze where the land meets the sky.

The desert has protected Hopi culture and allowed them to retain their traditional ways into the present and beyond. When the Spanish came they concentrated their forces on the pueblos along the Rio Grande as it was an arduous trek across the desert to get to Hopi. The Hopi adamantly refused to allow Catholic priests into their towns and today, unlike almost every other pueblo, there are no big Catholic missions on the Hopi reservation. Then the Mexicans ran the Spanish out and they were in charge of Hopi country from 1822 to 1848. During this time the Hopi had to fight off their tribal enemies without any help from the Mexicans. The Americans stormed into New Mexico and Arizona in 1848 and took over without much of a fight. At each stage it has been a constant battle for the Hopi to retain their traditions in the face of government efforts to force assimilation.

We drove into the Hopi Cultural Center as our first stop. The Cultural Center has a nice craft store, a restaurant, a small motel and a museum. There is a spiral petroglyph on a boulder at the entrance to a museum dedicated to the Hopi. They have displays of old pots and lots of old pictures and cases of Hopi artifacts. There are several other shops around a courtyard behind the main craft center so it is a great place to shop. In the craft shop I asked about getting a guide and the woman working there recommended the same guy they recommended at the hotel. I told her I had a call into him and hoped that he would be available tomorrow. She said she would call him and she got the message machine but then she called his wife, who was home. She knew immediately where he was and what he was doing and assured us he would be happy to take us around tomorrow. So now we were set up for the next day and still had a couple of hours of light to look around.

The artwork in the craft center was of the finest quality, like being in a gallery filled with beautiful art. They had kachinas, jewelry, paintings, prints and pottery. All of the prints were by one artist who was doing detailed paintings of the kachina dances. Traditionally, the people didn't like for anyone to have images of the kachinas and it was strictly forbidden to take pictures or make sketches during any of the dances. The place was full of beautiful pieces and I slowly worked my way around the store. Then a young man entered the store carrying a kachina. When we walked in I noticed a very prominent sign on the door saying they were not buying anything today. But there he stood, kachina in hand. She politely told him that she couldn't buy anything today. I then asked if she minded if I looked at his kachina and she told me to please go ahead. He and I went outside; I asked if I could hold it and he gingerly handed it to me. I was immediately captivated by it. He had one of the finest kachinas I had ever seen. I was planning on buying a kachina but my plan had been to look at everything and then buy tomorrow before we left town. That plan flew out the window when I saw this broadfaced kachina. Carving kachinas for the Hopi is like carving fetishes for the Zuni, it is a sustaining art form that is a primary source of income. This kachina had delicate features and a lifelike design. It is painted beautifully with particular care for the ornamentation which includes rings on his fingers and bracelets on his wrists. The young man and I went out to his truck to bargain and talk to his father, who is sitting in the driver's seat. His father was advising him in Hopi. We quickly work out a price. I had long ago learned the virtues of buying directly from the artists on the reservations.

At the side of the parking lot, under the shade of a few scraggly trees, is a line of vendors set up with tables. One guy is working off the tailgate of his pick-up truck. We walk down the line. One of the tables had an old woman tending the wares and she had several kachinas. I looked at them and one of them was a small kachina with a human body and the head of a mouse. She saw me looking at it and said it was the kachina they call "Warrior Mouse". She told how long ago there was a chicken hawk stealing all the chickens so the people tried to kill it but no one could shoot it. So they called on Warrior Mouse to shoot it with his arrow and he came to the village and shot the chicken hawk and the people gave him a big feast. She even told me the spot where he shot the arrow just down the road from the cultural center. After shopping up and down the line of vendors, I went back across the parking lot and into the restaurant. We had a Hopi dinner of corn and beans and headed back to Tuba City for the night.

The next morning we came back to the Cultural Center to meet Donald. I went into the museum and told the woman behind the counter that we were meeting Donald, and she immediately knew who I was talking about and told me she hadn't see him yet this morning. She gave me a dirty look and asked,

"Why you meeting him?"

"He is going to be our guide for the day."

"You know we have guides here. Donald isn't allowed in the museum."

"That's interesting but I'm afraid we are stuck with him for the day."

That was a strange start to the day, but I understand that in tribal cultures everybody knows everybody and there are a lot of friends and enemies.

We went into the restaurant and had a breakfast of blue corn pancakes and just when we sat down Donald walked into the restaurant. We invited him to join us and after breakfast it was off to see the reservation with Donald as our guide.

He told us that the first clan to come to Hopi was the Bear Clan. The creator told them to watch for a supernova in the sky and in the year 1056 they saw it and settled on this spot and made a village and a plaza. He talked about their history and mentioned that in 1882 the government had taken away a lot of their land and given it to the Navajo. He said the Spanish had used the Navajo as guards when they were attacking the Hopi and that when he was a young man the Navajo would make raids and steal children and crops.

He says there are twelve villages but only one of the villages still has all the ceremonies and it is named Songoopavi. I know there are ten villages on the three mesas so the other villages must be off these mesas somewhere. He says that in all the towns there are two things required of a man; first that he build a house and do it without grants from the government and second that he plant corn.

He started the tour by taking us out into the courtyard between the motel, the museum and the restaurant. The plaza has a dirt yard divided by four sidewalks that converge in the center at a big monument like a stone pyramid. They buried a time capsule in it in 1972 and they will open it in 2072. He pointed out that each section of the courtyard is planted with crops and we could see small corn plants sprouting in one section with squash and beans not far behind in the other sections. He said they had a good harvest last year.

Then we loaded into his truck and drove out to a petroglyph site just east of Oraibi. He parked and we took a short walk to the site. Along the way he pointed out one plant after another and indicated how it could be prepared for food or medicine. When we got to the petroglyph site he said it told the creation story. He told about the meaning in each symbol then said this place is called prophecy rock and showed the symbols that represented past catastrophes and said there was one more coming and at this one the earth would flip over four times and all life on the planet would be destroyed. Then he told how the petroglyph was created in 1969 by four men and the last of them died last year.

While we are looking at the petroglyph he explains the symbols, "The people are doing ceremonies that the creator gave us which are for the benefit of all people, all the animals, all the plants and even the insects and all life on the earth. These are meant to maintain harmony and peace among all life. The roots of life for the whole world are protected by the Hopi. We believe in praying for all life. We have three kivas that are lined up like the stars in Orion's Belt. Women have their own ceremonies in the kivas but they are different and separate from the men."

As we were walking back to the truck he told the story of the split at Old Oraibi in 1906 between those friendly to the Americans, who wanted to adapt new ways, and the traditional people who wanted to maintain the old ways. He says, "The people had a split and it divided the village between the 'Friendlies' and the 'Hostiles'. The friendlies beat the hostiles in a battle that was a sort of tug-of-war and the hostiles moved out and built a new village just up the road. They call it Hotevilla." Then we got in his truck and drove over to Oraibi and he showed us the spot where the hostiles and the friendlies had the battle. He said they wanted to move far away but ended up just a few miles away. When the hostiles left, the rest of the people burned all the shrines and altars and while they still do dances they don't participate in the annual round of ceremonies like the rest of the villages. He said that while other villages were growing, Oraibi was losing population.

Oraibi is a sad sight with only a few buildings scattered here and there along the mesa. As he turns onto the dirt road that leads through Oraibi he says, "Oraibi was the first Hopi village, established in 1020. Other villages were built in the 1700s and the 1800s. The Spanish first showed up in 1540 when one of Coronado's soldiers, a guy named Pedro de Towar, made his way to the village of Awatobi. He immediately demanded total allegiance to the Spanish King. When the people refused, he attacked and had 17 men in full armor on horseback. The people quickly retreated into the desert. He reported to Coronado that there were seven villages with a population of around 3,500. The Spanish didn't come back for over forty years. But when they did they brought a priest who was supposed to stay. When the Spanish came they told the leading Hopi priest he had to convert to Catholic religion. He refused and they stripped him naked and cut him all over, then poured turpentine over him and burned him alive. Others who refused had one hand cut off. They came with troops and forced the people to build five churches and banned ceremonies in the kivas. The people killed the first priests who came but eventually they were forced to attend church with the priests. Then in 1680, when the Pueblos all revolted against the Spanish, the Hopi killed four priests and totally destroyed the mission churches.

One of the churches was in Oraibi and he points out where it had been. All that is left is a low mound, no bell towers or anything you could recognize as a church. If he hadn't pointed it out we wouldn't know it was anything but an empty parcel of land. Before we get out he finishes the story, "When the Spanish came back in 1692, the Hopi refused to rebuild the churches and the Spanish allowed us to live on our own. The village of Awatobi wanted to allow a priest to return and the rest of the Hopi attacked them and killed seven hundred people."

He points out a few old abandoned houses in Oraibi that are from the 1700s and 1800s, made of stone with the roofs gone.

He showed us the ruins of the old Protestant church built on the point at the end of the mesa and said they built it once and it was hit by lightning and burned to the ground. Then they rebuilt it, but it wasn't long before it got hit by lightning again and this time they decided not to rebuild it. Now only a few charred ruins are left. He said the Hopi believe you get sick if you go around the site.

We walked to the plaza and I immediately felt a sense of antiquity. There had once been a great multistoried adobe building on this site. Donald pointed out where the foundations could still be seen as lines of stones at ground level. The plaza still stood in exactly the same location where it was in the original village and they still do dances. Looking at it, I felt a time shift and could sense the life of the place still vibrant, even after all that time and the destruction of the old buildings and the inner-tribal squabbles, I could sense a wave of energy like a heat mirage that hung in the air just above the ground, reflecting all the years, decades, centuries, even a full millennia of people dancing and holding ceremonies that were dedicated to the welfare of all beings.

As we walked back to the truck there was an old guy sitting in the shade of a craggy tree carving a piece of cottonwood. He had a table with a couple of kachinas on it. He waved and Donald took us over and introduced us. The old Indian had long hair and was wearing an old raggedy pair of pants cut off just below the knee. He was barefoot and when I looked at him and he looked back I was a little shocked to see he only had one eye. We stood around his table and looked at his kachinas; they were a crudely carved but he had several other carved items and I picked up one of them and realized it was a bullroarer. It is a wooden slat about six inches long and an inch or so wide, with a hole drilled in the one end with a piece of cheap string wrapped around it. I showed it to Donald and then asked the old guy how much. He took it from my hands and unwrapped the string and slowly got up from the chair where he was sitting. He was lean as a rail and he stood with one foot in front of the other and started swinging the bullroarer round and round and it immediately started giving out a loud roaring sound. I smiled and reached for my wallet. He wrapped the string back around it and handed it to me. I studied it; one side was painted yellow with four ears of corn on it, one red, one yellow, one black and one white with tadpoles painted alongside the corn. The other side is blue and has three clouds with rain falling above a sun sign that is divided into four parts with a different colored dot in each quarter, and below that a swirling symbol with two interlocking lines. All around the sides it is painted with alternating stripes of black and white. I thank him and pay him. I was delighted. The bullroarer is one of the oldest musical instruments on earth and I know that people in the caves of France 40,000 years ago were using bullroarers. I had seen them played at ceremonies at Zuni and it was a nice feeling to have one and to have the experience of watching the old man play it.

It is strange that most of the villages now have electricity and running water to the houses but it isn't allowed in Old Oraibi. This is ironic since it is now occupied by "Friendlies" and they drove out all the traditional people. But they are forced to live without electricity or running water since it is the oldest village. Sounds like the Hopi revenge against the friendlies?

Then it was back on the road to another of the villages where Donald bought lunch at a little deli in the back of the only grocery store in the village. We were the only white people in the store and it was a good feeling seeing all the Hopi, young and old, coming and going in the store, talking to one another in Hopi. Then he took us to his village and then to Walpi to get our tickets for a tour later that afternoon. We were due back to Walpi at 3:00 for the last tour of the day.

In Donald's village each house has a mark near the main door, a square brown patch with four white horizontal striped lines. The brown part is about two feet square with the four stripes across it and we see it by nearly all the doors. He says the kachinas come and paint the four stripes. He says this village was founded in 1680 and is one of the mother villages. When they ceremonies they have especially designated runners carry things to the shrines. At winter solstice they have special ceremonies and you have to wash your hair with yucca and each hair represents a different nation. If anyone builds a house off the mesa, what he calls, "Down below", they lose their rights to come and participate in the ceremonies. He says that when he was a young man he had to do ceremonies in the kiva for six months and when a woman has a new baby the woman has to do ceremonies for twenty days before the father can see the baby. On the twentieth day the baby gets a name and the grandmother brings it out for the father to see. But before the father gets to see the baby the grandmother has to introduce the baby to the morning sun and she goes out at sunrise and tells the sun the baby's name. He says that when it is time for ceremonies there is a village crier who stands on the roof top and calls out. He tells us there are about 15,000 Hopi living on the reservation. With twelve main villages scattered around the reservation, half of them clustered on the three mesas, that means there are about a thousand people in each village.

While we are driving back to the Cultural Center, Donald points to a mesa in the distance and tells us a dragon lives in a cave in that mesa. He says he has seen it four times and that it is like a fireball moving in the sky. The antipathy between the Hopi and the Navajo was apparent with Donald. The Hopi have a philosophy of peace and compassion for all things, perhaps as much as the Tibetans, and surely more than any other people of North or South America. Yet for their recorded history they have been under constant attack and their way of life has been threatened at every turn. And even with a philosophy of peace and love they train as warriors. They are the least aggressive of all the Indian tribes. They believe in fighting primarily in defense of their way of life. Still, they must be constantly vigilant, even today. In the historical record they have been under assault by the Spanish, the Mexicans, the Americans, the Apache, and the Comanche and, even to the present day, the Navajo.

To hear Donald talk, the Navajo were stealing Hopi children when he was a kid and even today raid their corn fields. He says, "The Navajo have a four-day festival where they have total sexual license. During these days anyone can have sex with anyone." Then to make the point he adds, "And they do it even with people who are not Navajo, who just show up during the festival." He says that is why they have such a big population.

Donald says that the books I have read about the Hopi were all written based on information from "Friendlies" and that lots of it is lies and that I shouldn't take everything in those books as the truth about the Hopi. He says that a traditional Hopi would never give information to an anthropologist or white person who wants to write about the Hopi. He named Cushing and Fewkes and Waters and said they based their books on information all gathered from people living at Oraibi that were not to be trusted. I assume I have to apply this same advice to all the information Donald is telling me.

While he was driving around, Donald pointed out a cluster of houses on a mesa top and said they were all from Ute and other pueblos who had moved to Hopi to escape Spanish persecution after the revolt in 1680. He said they are still here and are considered Hopi but some still have some of their old ways. We left Donald at the Cultural Center about 2:30 and drove over to Walpi. When we got to the ticket office we were the only people on the tour. We had a Hopi woman who was to accompany us as our guide. Tree ring records show that Walpi was built around 1700 and has been occupied continuously ever since. Walpi is one of only two ancient multistoried adobe buildings that have made it into modern times; the other is at Taos. Walpi was built soon after the Spanish returned after the pueblo revolt. At that time the people were shuffled around and many of the villages moved and were rebuilt in other places. Walpi has been under more or less continuous rehab ever since. It is likely that the plaza and some of the kivas are at least in the original positions. There are concrete block houses and concrete covering many of the old stone walls to reinforce them and hold them in place. There are about thirty-five houses in the complex but there are no full-time residents. Our guide owns one of the houses but says, like everyone else, she only comes there for ceremonies. She shows us her house and says if we come back for a dance we can come eat at her house.

Walpi is built on the end of a very narrow ridge and there is another village on the same ridge. However, the other village has its own name and identity, and they have running water and electricity with a modern road leading up to it. We park in that village and walk through the village and then along a very narrow part of the ridge that goes a hundred yards and then widens out to accommodate the ancient village of Walpi, with its two-story houses that rise up out of the narrow ridge. As we walk our guide points down to the land below and shows us a spring where the people had to get their water. There are old steps leading down to the spring. From the vantage point of this narrow ridge we are looking across a vast desert landscape in both directions. There is a patchwork of gardens and orchards, with scenes of plentitude in the midst of the arid plains.

As we enter the pueblo, we notice some of the houses still have the low doors that were the first generation of ground-level entries when they diverted from the rooftop entrances. These doors are distinctly un-modern, sized for the Hopi, who are short in stature. She led us into the main plaza. There are many old pictures of dancers in this plaza and many famous people have been here. She shows us where Theodore Roosevelt stood and watched a dance and says that a few years ago the Dalai Lama was here. We sit on a ledge in the plaza and she tells about the Dalai Lama blessing this spot and giving two days of teachings at the visitor's center. He had monks with him making a sand mandala. She was there with the Dalai Lama in the plaza and attended his teachings and said how special it was. We told her about being with the Dalai Lama in Bloomington and Atlanta. We asked if we could sit in the plaza and she sat between us in the shade on the ledge looking out over the distant horizon with our back to the houses of Walpi. We got to sit for about ten minutes and while we were sitting silently a rabbit hopped into the plaza. I gazed at this dreamcreature, an omen of the wildness preserved on this rocky outcrop. At first it sat still, obviously unafraid, then it moved around the buildings and scurried out into the little plaza. Its nose alert, unaware of the three humans so near, yet invisible to its senses, until it disappeared through a crack under a doorsill into the cool darkness inside.

There are three kivas on the outer edge of the plaza. The plaza is not very large as there isn't much room on the ridge but there in the plaza is a natural megalith, a stone rising up out of the plaza about fifteen to twenty feet tall and called Snake Rock. She lets us walk around it and touch it. On one side is a small natural niche in the stone and in the niche is a small stone idol. It appears to be a natural stone about ten to twelve inches long and is shaped like a baby wrapped in snuggling clothes. As we walked away the guide remarked that she had never seen an animal of any kind in Walpi and that the rabbit was a special sign. Then, we went past the plaza to a group of two-story houses and there was a young man sitting on the steps of one of the houses. She introduced us and pointed out he was selling kachinas. I bought a brother and sister kachinas with butterflies at their feet.

She then walked us through a covered alleyway, like a tunnel that connected with the other side of the village overlooking the other side of the mesa. We stood in the alleyway and she showed us the vigas in the ceiling covered with brush and adobe and explained there was a house just above us. It was an interesting experience, like being in a tunnel from one side of the village to the other. They were doing some repairs to a couple of the houses on this side so she took us back through the tunnel and then out of the village. As we were walking back, she pointed out a beautiful Hopi shrine on the lip of the mesa. It is a low stone box, two to three feet tall, with the stone carefully laid up in four walls with a hollow space in the center. The hollow space is crowded with prayer sticks, which are long twigs with small eagle feathers tied to the end of the sticks.

I feel with the Hopi something like I felt in Tibet. I feel in the presence of a people with a profound earth spirituality that reaches deep into prehistory. They have suffered incalculable oppression for many generations but have kept their culture and traditions alive in the face of incredible forces of assimilation, largely at the end of a gun, and in the face of terrible adversity. The degree to which they have maintained their cultural traditions was illustrated by a story I read where archaeologists digging a site called Ridge Ruin in Arizona unearthed a remarkable grave in the ruins of a rather insignificant pueblo. The grave turned out to be one of the richest ever found in the Southwest. They deemed the large male buried there the Magician and dated his death to around 1125. The grave goods included twenty-five decorated pots along with eight elaborate baskets, one with fifteen hundred turquoise pieces and orange rodent teeth used as ornaments. There were four hundred arrowheads, amulets made of seashells, and a skullcap of beads; but, the most unusual things were long wooden pendants with the ends carved like human hands or deer feet. The archaeologist took these artifacts to the Hopi reservation where the elders informed him they were used as ceremonial objects which would give great power to the war chief. They said the shaman would swallow the shafts like a sword swallower with only the carved end protruding from his mouth. The elders then proceeded to tell him what else he should expect to find along with the wooden shafts and these were exactly the things he had found among the grave goods. There was a gap of over seven hundred years between the burial of the Magician and the time the archaeologist dug into the grave but the Hopi managed to retain the information about the use of these ceremonial objects over that time span. To some of the Hopi the archaeologist is just another grave robber, only this time he is sanctioned by the state, but surely not by the Indians who are the descendants of the people in the graves they are robbing and, in the eyes of the Indians, desecrating.

JEMEZ: FALL CORN DANCE - 2017

The Hemish (Jemez) people are one of the nineteen pueblos of New Mexico. Their language is known as Towa. The language was also spoken by the Pecos pueblo but the Pecos people were driven to near extinction and the few survivors joined with the Hemish, who welcomed them. Today the population is about 2,000 on a reservation that covers 90,000 acres. They originally had six villages but have now consolidated into one village called Walatoma. The area in the Jemez River valley known as the Canon de San Diego is lined with dramatically beautiful sheer red stone canyon walls.

The Hemish, like other pueblo people, believe they emerged from the underworld, with the guidance of their creator, Hua-vu-na-tota. They were born out of a lake called Hoa-sjela, now called Stone Lake, which is on the Jicarilla Apache reservation in northern New Mexico. They learned to grow corn and followed a parrot that led them to Crow Canyon in southern Colorado, where they lived for many generations until they were forced to move due to drought. They moved to the Jemez River in New Mexico and built villages in the river valley and on the mesa tops. They developed two warrior societies, the Arrow and the Eagle society, which had the responsibility to protect the people. They did this so effectively that they were later called on by the Spanish and then the Mexicans to fight off Apache and Comanche raiders.

The Hemish migrated to their current location from the Four Corners area between 1275 and 1350. First contact with Hemish came in 1541 when Coronado's expedition visited the canyon. Other visitors showed up in 1581 and again in 1583 but it wasn't until the Onate colony in 1598 that they began to feel the effects of the Spanish invasion. The Hemish people were living in six villages when Onates' entrada arrived in 1598. The first census estimated there were 30,000 people. The largest village had 3,000 rooms in buildings four stories tall. Onate established the first Spanish capital at San Gabriel near the San Juan pueblo. He then assembled representatives from thirty-eight pueblos and assigned Franciscan priests to each region. The Hemish representative, a man named Pe-stiassa, was the first Hemish person whose name appears in the historical record. Onate's forces enslaved the Hemish and forced them to build churches.

The Hemish had their own form of government with a war chief and two assistants. These offices were for life and they were charged with enforcing the rules of the theocratic system of the pueblo. When one of them died the religious council picked their successor. The War Chief had a War Captain who had five aides, all of them selected annually from the two kivas. They were in charge of overseeing the dances, the hunts and the foot races. The Spanish imposed their own system of governance on the pueblos starting in 1590. The Spanish went to each village and erected a large cross and appointed a governor. Each governor was given a silver-tipped cane as the symbol of office.

In 1610 Onate moved the capital to Santa Fe and built the Palace of the Governor, which was completed in 1614. Starting in 1620, the Indians were instructed to elect their governor and lieutenant annually and the King of Spain gave them another cane as a symbol of their authority. Onate appointed the Franciscan friar, Fray Alonzo de Lugo, to Hemish and he founded the first church in the area at the village of Guisewa and a second church at Walatoma. The church at Walatoma was never completed and was destroyed by fire in raids by the Navaho which forced the people to abandon the village and move to the mesa top. By 1627 the Hemish villages were depopulated by war and disease and they were forced by the Franciscans to move into two villages. However, between 1609 and 1628 the Spanish managed to build nearly fifty churches in the various villages in the Rio Grande valley. In 1632 the priest at Hemish was transferred to Zuni, where he was promptly killed, and the church at Guisewa was abandoned. The Hemish fiercely rejected Spanish demands that they give up their traditional religion and in 1644 they allied with the Navaho to kill the local priest. The Spanish hanged twenty-nine Hemish leaders in retaliation, which only led to further resentment.

The mission at Walatoma was reestablished in 1628 and served as the primary mission at Hemish. From 1600 to 1680 the Hemish were in constant revolt. From 1650 to 1700 they joined forces with the Navaho to fight the Spanish. There was a major revolt at Taos in 1650 and the leaders were all captured and hung in the town plaza. In 1680, the Hemish joined a coordinated attack called the pueblo revolt and removed all the Spanish from their region. Twenty-one of the thirty-three Franciscan priests in New Mexico were killed, along with over 400 Spanish settlers. The survivors made a hasty retreat back to Mexico. The priest at Hemish in 1680, Fray Juan de Jesus Morador, was killed at the start of the revolt. The church at Guisewa was then totally destroyed.

The year after the revolt of 1680 a governor of Hemish named Francisco went to Mexico and accompanied an unsuccessful attempt by Antonio de Otermin to return to the area and reestablish Spanish rule. They managed to burn the pueblos at Isleta and Sandia before they were forced back to Mexico. The removal of the Spanish was not the end of hostilities. As quickly as the Spanish were gone, the Apache and the Comanche began raiding the pueblos. In 1688 the Spanish made another attempt to regain control of the area but failed. In 1689 a new Spanish governor, Domingo Jironzade Cruzate, was appointed and by 1692 Santa Fe was back in Spanish hands. The Santa Anna and Zia pueblos were the first to be reconquered. In 1692 the Hemish moved back to the mesa tops in anticipation of the return of the Spanish and to better ward off the Zia and Santa Ana pueblos which were pro-Spanish. The Zia, Santa Ana and San Felipe pueblos acted in coordination with the Spanish upon their return. In revenge for their collaboration with the Spanish the Hemish killed four men from Zia. In return, the Spanish stationed at

Zia went to Hemish and destroyed the main village.

In July 1694 the Spanish stormed the mesa top villages and killed eight-four Hemish men and captured 361 women and children. It took a force of 120 Spanish with backup troops of Keresan warriors to conquer the mesa top villages. The Spanish took all the stored corn and torched the villages. They took the captives to Santa Fe. Hemish representatives negotiated the return of the women and children by offering Hemish warriors to help the Spanish fight the remaining rebellious pueblos. With the return of the women and children they were forced into one village. The Spanish had no sooner rebuilt the missions when, in 1696, there were new revolts at both Hemish and Taos. The Hemish war chief Conejo lead a short-lived revolt when he clubbed to death the priest at the pueblo. He then went to Pecos to enlist their support, instead they turned him over to the Spanish authorities, who killed him and his chief assistants. As a result the people moved back to the mesa top and many of the Hemish people fled to Hopi. Others went to live with the Navaho. In 1704, at the urging of the Spanish, about 500 of the people returned. In 1706 the new mission at Walatoma was complete. Then, in 1716 another 113 returned from Hopi. The Hemish and the Santa Domingo pueblos were the most opposed to the Spanish and, later, the American rule and remain so to this day.

In 1750 the Hemish stopped making pottery and broke all their pots to keep them out of the hands of the Spanish. What is known as Jemez Black on White pottery ceased at that time. In 1821 the Mexicans won their independence and opened the area of New Mexico to American traders. In 1827 the Hemish expelled the only remaining priest in their area and the missions fell into disrepair. In 1848 the Americans sent in troops and claimed all the land in what is now Texas, New Mexico, Arizona, Nevada and California. In 1848, James S. Calhoun was appointed the first Indian agent of the new American government for the pueblo peoples. When American troops visited the Hemish in 1849 the church was in ruins. In 1850, the pueblo peoples signed their first treaty with the U.S. government. In 1864 Abraham Lincoln affirmed the system of governors at each pueblo and gave each pueblo governor a new silver-tipped cane. To this day the governors carry these canes as the symbols of their offices. The governors are responsible for civil government and negotiating the more than 350 treaties between the U.S. government and the pueblo nations. By 1879. the railroad had come to New Mexico. In 1888 some of the Hemish rebuilt the church. In 1904 they established the first school and in 1931 a new Franciscan priest was assigned to the area and built a house at Walatoma. In 1922 the All Indian Pueblo Council (AIPC) was founded. Two years later, Indian people were declared citizens of the United States, except in the states of New Mexico and Arizona, which did not allow citizenship for their Indian populations until 1948. Up until 1968 all these officers of government served without payment.

The Hemish had up to twenty ceremonial groups in the 1930s. Each society had a "Corn Mother" which was an ear of corn decorated with feathers.

There were two clown societies and a flute society. Kachinas appeared at solstices. The kachinas and the dead are believed to live underground in the north where the people emerged. The people made prayer sticks and carried them to Mount Redondo at summer solstice. Ceremonies during this solstice included races and dances. There were flute dances and deer dances. Initiation began at age eight when the young boys were whipped by a kachina. The clown societies were the Tabosh and the Tsuntatabosh. The Tabosh were in the turquoise kiva group and were in charge of the San Diego festival. The Tsuntatabosh were in the Ice and Squash kiva. They would talk backwards and didn't eat outdoors and were called the "Black All Overs". If they touched a dancer or racer they would leave a black mark and it was considered good luck in the hunt to get a black mark. They had a series of races associated with the dances. The women had races as well. They had a Kick-Stick race in the spring and another to open the irrigation ditches.

They had a Town Chief and a War Chief. The War Chief called meetings of the council and was in charge of the races. The Town Chief was chosen by the council. He watched the sun rise and designated the solstices. The Mountain Lion society had the responsibility of bringing rabbit and deer meat to the Town Chief. They had ceremonies associated with killing a bear or a deer. The hunter distributed the meat and then the head of the animal was put in a shrine.

The Snake Society held four snake hunts each year and used them in ceremonies held in a cave. They had two kivas, two kachina dance groups, two clown societies, two men's societies, two women's societies, two eagle societies and two patron saints: Saint James who is celebrated on November 12th and Saint Porchingula, who came from Pecos and has a feast day on September 2nd. The winter dances at Christmas included an animal dance where corn was roasted. At this festival the family would gather round the fireplace and draw pictures of animals on the walls. They celebrated the birth of Jesus as a symbol of the rebirth of all the animals and plants and the images on the walls were there to encourage the animals to reproduce. They have steadfastly refused to allow their language to be written. They are traditionally a militaristic society and have provided troops for other pueblos to help settle disputes.

11/12/17 Corn Dance at Jemez

It is only a few miles from the interstate to the pueblo. As soon as we turned off the interstate it was obvious we were in for something big. Almost immediately the traffic backed up and slowed to a crawl. I knew it was several miles to the pueblo and hadn't expected to see this kind of traffic. We crept along and slowly made our way into the pueblo. Cars were parked on both sides of the road lined up bumper to bumper. The sign for the public parking had a line that was stopped dead so I cut down one of the dirt roads that leads into the main part of the pueblo. The Hemish have a reputation for not allowing anyone into the pueblo except for today so we felt privileged to be there. The streets are all dirt and the pueblo is a warren of narrow alleyways with barely enough room to pass a car going in the other direction. Today there are cars parked in every place where there is enough room to put a vehicle. We wound through the streets until we found a place we could park the car and piled out.

The streets were full of Indians, families with little kids, elders, men and women, all streaming toward the plaza so it wasn't difficult figuring out where to go. In just a few minutes we could hear the sound of the drums, muffled and distant, growing louder with each step. Next the vendors began to appear, tent after tent lining both sides of the narrow streets. Looking around I saw a throng of people and they were all Indians, I couldn't see another white person other than Susan and me and our friends from St Augustine, Enzo and Gayle. Eventually, we saw a few other white faces and a few African-Americans, but non-Indians were few and far between. Meanwhile, the sounds of the drum grew louder and we could hear the jingle of the dance bells and the sound of the singers. There were vendors lining all the streets leading into the plaza, many more than at the Taos San Geronimo feast or the Santa Domingo corn dance. It is a feast of commerce, most selling arts and crafts, some with food and drink.

We cut between the vendors and made our way to the plaza. Once we came in sight of the plaza I was surprised at how large the plaza is and it was completely full of dancers. The plaza was longer than a football field and at least as wide and lined with houses, mostly two stories tall with flat roofs. We had come in by a kiva with a big ladder leading to the roof. It had a built-in bench across the front and there was some empty space on the bench. I asked an elderly lady if it would be all right for us to sit there and she encouraged us to sit down. It was a great location.

At first glance the dancers seemed very similar to those at Santa Domingo's corn dance. The men had similar apparel and were carrying a rattle in one hand, and had skunk skin around their moccasins and a fox skin hanging down in the back. The women also looked quite similar with the dresses down to their knees, a woven belt, and the tablitas on their heads. The tablitas were all painted turquoise blue with different design features painted on them from one woman to another. However, at Santa Domingo the women had one shoulder and arm that was exposed while here their dresses covered both arms. The women had juniper branches in their hands and waved them in time with the music. The men had their bodies painted with an earth color that appeared to be red clay, and a rattle in one hand, and a twig of juniper in the other.

However, I quickly began to notice some features different from Santa Domingo. The dancers were lined up in two long lines and in between the two lines were four men with their faces painted black with small drums sounding out a staccato beat. They had a round fur cap on their heads, with a single feather sticking up in the center, and regular jeans and shirts with their moccasins. There was a huddle of older men in the center of the plaza dressed in fancy ribbon shirts. They were standing around a drummer who had a large bass drum. The older men were singing in unison to the beat of the big drum. It was like the sound of the earth and all the dancers were moving in time with the big drummer and the singers. The double line of dancers included people of all ages, from kids five-years-old to gray-haired elders.

Then I saw something I have never seen at other dances. Coming down the center of the plaza, winding back and forth between the two lines of dancers, was a man dressed totally in black with a black cowboy hat and black cloth covering his face. He had a horse, not a real horse, but a papier mache horse affixed to his body as part of his costume; the front of the horse in front of him, the back behind him. The horse was black and as he moved he acted as if he was riding the horse. He was accompanied on either side by two masked characters. They had colorful masks over their faces and different clothing with a coiled rope in one hand and a whip in the other. I first thought they are kachinas, and perhaps they are; they have an alien-like appearance and their masks covering their faces looked more like a bag over their head with a grotesque face painted on it. I have never seen anything like it or read anything about it. They went the length of the plaza and then turned around and proceeded back. When they reached the far end of the plaza, the drummers and singers reached a crescendo; the drumbeat got louder and faster and the sound of the rattles picked up the pace in a furious rhythm until it came to an abrupt end. The dancers stopped their movements and began to disperse. I feared the dance was over, but assumed that it was just a break.

As the dancers are dispersing I look at the far end of the plaza and see a sea of colors with turquoise blue floating above whites and blacks and reds. It is another troupe of dancers who have congregated there. The women all have turquoise tablitas on their heads and the blue of the turquoise dominates the colorscape; the men all have white skirts and the women have their black dresses highlighted with bright red. The first dancers have no sooner wandered off than this new set begins to proceed down the plaza in two lines. There are men, women and children in no apparent order except they are in two lines. A new drummer has appeared, along with a new choir of elders, all dressed much like their predecessors. The deep bass drum sounded out the rhythm in a fast-paced drumbeat as the sound of the elders' chanting filled the plaza. The plaza is like a sound chamber and the walls of the houses that line the plaza served as a sounding chamber to hold the tone of the drum and the sound of the songs. The two lines slowly proceed down the plaza, the men with their deer hoof rattles sounding in time with the chants and drum, making the primordial sounds of the people, a music like nothing else, an orchestra of aboriginal sounds, not the Western music of a symphony, not the guitar and bass of a rock band, rather something much older, more fundamental to our tribal heritage, closer to the earth, to nature, to human nature in its most basic, most original, most essential, most elemental, most vital elements. It gives me the shivers and touches something deep inside me, something in my solar plexus, something in my body that makes me want to sway and move with this symphony of sounds. The women dancers all have juniper branches in their hands and move them up and down with the same swaying movement I feel in my body. The men all have juniper in one hand and their rattles in the other. They slowly proceed down the plaza until they reach the far end where the line turns inward forming two more lines that proceed back, moving toward the other end of the plaza inside the outer two lines.

I see more black-faced drummers have appeared in between the four lines of dancers. The blackfaces have the same appearance as the previous group but are different people. Their smaller drums sound opposed to the deep bass of the big drum. I notice that while the men in the first group had their bodies painted a reddish earth tone, these men are painted a light turquoise blue on their chests and backs. Eventually the inner line of dancers works its way back to where they started and now the plaza is filled with dancers, filled with movement, filled with sound. It is a spectacle of sound and color and movement that thrills me and fills me with emotion; a wave of feeling passes through my body. It is a nostalgia that lifts a part of my being from deep inside and reminds me of something that I long to feel, to experience, something lost to me in the long ago of history, something beneath the surface of civilization, something that reaches back into my nature.

Now the two lines of dancers break up and begin a new series of movements, forming giant circles and moving in different patterns. Then they reform into the two lines and I see another set of characters have appeared. The black rider and his posse of masked accomplices have reappeared and are again working their way from one end of the plaza to the other, slowly winding back and forth between the lines of dancers. The masked rider, draped in black head to toe, rides his ersatz horse, moving its head like a hobby horse up and down, leaving me in wonder as to what it all represents. I know better than to ask any of the Indians standing around me. However, in the book *Pueblo Nations: Eight Centuries of Pueblo Indian History*, by Joe S. Sando, he indicates that the figure on horseback represents Coronado and that the two people accompanying him represent a Franciscan friar who came with him and Estavan, the black slave who was sent ahead to make first contact.

There are thousands of people watching the dance. There are lines of chairs all around the plaza, and behind them people standing ten or twelve deep. Then the porches and roofs of all the houses are filled with people. Behind the crowd watching there are people streaming back and forth. There are only a scattering of white faces. What voices I hear are all speaking in pueblo languages.

As the afternoon wears on we walk through the pueblo to see all the vendors. On one street we run into Otto and visit with him and Francine who are selling Zuni fetishes. Then we run into Andy Marion, one of the finest Navaho jewelers we have met. It is obvious that once the dances end there is going to be a huge traffic jam trying to get out of the pueblo so we decide to leave now, get ahead of the traffic and call it a day. I suddenly feel sad and upset at leaving, wanting to stay until the last beat of the drum but turn around and head back to the car.

THE GREAT HOUSE TOUR

CHACO CANYON: THE BROKEN POT - 2006

It takes half a day to drive from the Albuquerque airport through the ever-changing landscape of New Mexico to the turn off onto the unpaved back-roads that lead to Chaco Canyon. We had no sooner left the main highway when we found ourselves in an immense desert with nothing but sagebrush quivering in the intense sunlight as far as the eye could see. Then, after a few miles, the sage disappeared and there is nothing but the emptiness of the searing heat on the desert sand. I stopped the car and we got out to look at the landscape. The wind hissed as it scraped the seething sand over high-backed dunes in the distance. As we got back in the car I worried about getting through the sand as the road is little more than a faint track across the desert. Driving into Chaco Canyon is a process of initiation; first being smudged with sage and then sweating in the desert heat before entering the boundaries of Chaco Canyon. Before long Fajada Butte comes into view, a magnificent, monumental naturally-shaped gnomon. Fajada Butte stands at the entrance to Chaco Canyon, on a great plain where two canyons meet to form an even larger canyon that holds the fourteen Great Houses, all built a thousand years ago between 850 to 1250 CE. Fajada Butte is a huge column of stone, the Mount Kalish of the ancient Chacoans. It is bare rock, difficult to climb, with sheer stone faces on all sides. Yet from top to bottom there are petroglyphs and pictograms pecked and painted on the stone panels. The ground around the base is littered with pottery shards broken as offerings to the supernatural forces embodied in the stone.

Fajada Butte shoots up over four hundred feet out of the canyon floor and near the top is the most remarkable solstice marker in North America. There, behind three large stone slabs that lay propped against the walls of the butte, is a spiral petroglyph pecked into a sheer stone panel. The spiral has nine revolutions spiraling outward. In 1977, just a few days after the summer solstice, a research team including a woman named Anna Sofaer was doing an inventory of the petroglyphs in the canyon. They knew there was a spiral behind the large stone slabs and Anna Sofaer crawled behind the stones to make a drawing. While she was sitting in the shadow of the stone slabs a dagger of light fell slant on the shaded wall and, in a matter of minutes, moved down through the center of the spiral. She sat in amazement in a grail of quietude that surrounded this gift of light. She alerted other archeologists who went back to the site and observed that the light dagger was a solstice marker. When they returned at the winter solstice they were astonished to see two daggers of light appear and descend down the wall touching both sides of the spiral. And even more amazing discoveries were to come.

Just as the sun moves north to a standstill on the summer solstice and south to a standstill on the winter solstice, repeating this pattern each year, so the moon makes a migration to the north and south. In the seasons of the moon it takes just over nine years in its journey to the north and a corresponding time to return to the south, with standstills at either end of the journey. On the full moon nearest the moon solstice at the spiral on Fajada Butte there is a shadow cast by the light of the moon that falls exactly in the center of the spiral. In each subsequent year the shadow falls on the next of the nine spirals until, at the other end of its journey, the shadow falls on the far edge of the spiral. This one amazing marker creates both sun daggers and moon shadows. Once this remarkable site was documented and recognized as a solar and lunar marker people began to look for other markers at petroglyph sites all over the southwest and now more than three hundred have been documented, many associated with spirals. Anna Sofaer has gone on to lead a team which has investigated solar and lunar markers on numerous other petroglyphs and in the orientation of the various Great Houses. This discovery has sparked a new branch of archaeology called archeoastronomy.

There are eleven petroglyphs on Fajada Butte that exhibit solar features, with lights and shadows marking solar events. Of these, eight include spiral designs. These mark both solstices, winter and summer, and the equinoxes. Plus there are some that mark the midday and show the high point of the sun in the day. The ancients were obviously very well trained astronomers who were able to measure the movements of the sun, the moon, the planets and the stars. They created petroglyphs that were used to measure and mark the solar, lunar and planetary movement.

The great writer D. H. Lawrence visited the ruins in the American Southwest and intuited that the Indians retained a vast old religion which he considered greater than any of our modern religions. He sensed that before the birth of the modern religions, before the concept of monotheism, the people thought divine supernatural energy permeated nature and all matter was alive. There was direct, immediate, unmediated, ecstatic contact with the elemental forces moving in the vast reservoir of all the planes of existence; the upper world, the lower world and the human world.

The ancestral pueblo cultures were the only cultures north of Mexico to build with stone. The culture that arose in the San Juan basin constructed Great Houses as the major monuments of their civilization, which had its capital at Chaco Canyon. The Great Houses were built using stone and adobe that was sturdy enough to hold multistoried complexes. There were three phases starting about 800 CE with construction of the first Great Houses. This lasted about four hundred years and covered the San Juan basin, which comprises most of New Mexico and parts of Colorado, Utah and Arizona. The Great Houses were astronomically aligned and connected with major highways. The second phase was precipitated by a great drought that left most of the Great Houses without the agricultural resources to feed themselves and the people moved north to the Mesa Verde area of southern Colorado and to northern New Mexico, where they rebuilt their great cities.

However, this new building phase had distinct differences. In Chaco Canyon the Great Houses were palaces for the elite where the population at large gathered for ceremonies. Most of the population lived in smaller communities scattered through the area. In this new phase, the buildings were multi-storied residential villages where the population as a whole, not just the elite, lived. This phase lasted two hundred years before another series of droughts forced a move south to the Rio Grande Valley, where the people rebuilt, this time with adobe instead of stone, and created the pueblo culture which still exists today with the nineteen pueblos that line the Rio Grande, along with those that lay to the west (Acoma, Zuni and Hopi). It is remarkable that two of the ancient community buildings have survived at Taos and Hopi. All the pueblos of the Rio Grande had multistoried village complexes but only these two have withstood the ravages of time.

The most famous of all the Great Houses is Pueblo Bonito in Chaco Canyon. It is the largest of the fourteen Great Houses that were constructed in and around Chaco. There were other Great Houses constructed in the vicinity and there were many outliers with Great Houses scattered throughout the San Juan basin. The fourteen Great Houses in and around Chaco Canyon were the greatest achievement of pueblo architecture. Chaco Canyon was a great city with over three thousand rooms. Pueblo Bonito once stood four stories high and contained over seven hundred rooms. The great buildings are now thought to be gigantic cathedrals with over a hundred and fifteen kivas in all the buildings. Taken together, these subterranean ritual chambers were capable of holding up to ten thousand people. Pueblo Bonito itself includes at least twenty-eight kivas in the one building. The kivas were used to conduct rituals at the midpoint and extremes of the solar and lunar cycles. The people would gather from great distances to attend the rituals and make offerings. After the final mass migration brought the people to the Rio Grande Valley a new religious impulse arose involving the kachina cult.

We drove up to the parking area and went into the Visitor's Center. They have a great bookstore, with all the latest books about Chaco Canyon, and they have a schedule of the tours that are conducted by the Park Rangers. We quickly press on and go to Pueblo Bonito. We are just in time for the next tour and fall in with a small group to hear what the Ranger has to tell us about the Great House. He walks us through the designated walkways where tourists are allowed to visit and he points out all the main features. He showed us how the center wall served as a timepiece to show everyone when it is noon based on the shadow that the wall casts. When we are on the main plaza inside the building we see kivas everywhere. We aren't allowed to go into any of them but in every direction you look you can see the circular enclosures built into the building itself. Then we press on and go inside the building and see the inner rooms and the famous spot where you can look through three doors that are aligned. We end up at the front wall of the building and our guide shows us how the wall is aligned with the sunrise and sunset at summer solstice.

The building is built right up against the canyon wall and in one place a large piece of the canyon wall fell and destroyed a portion of the pueblo which still lies in ruins under the rubble of the fallen stones. There is an ancient stairway just behind the building and we walk up the narrow cut in the canyon wall to get to the top of the canyon. There is a great view from here looking down on the building and across the canyon to the great kiva that is directly across from us. We sit and rest for a few minutes at a spot where we can look down from above Pueblo Bonito. We can see people moving around on the sidewalks that go around the building. As we sit there, we notice that we can hear the people below us talking as they walk past a certain spot on the wall of the pueblo. There is a place where their voices are echoed up to us and we hear them as plainly as if we are standing beside them. We are delighted at this phenomenon and wonder if it was engineered as a communication device between the people in the pueblo and those up on the top of the canyon walls.

There is a lot to see and the day is getting late, so we head back down and take the car over to the great kiva. There, just across the canyon from Pueblo Bonito is one of the largest kivas ever excavated in the Southwest. It is sixty feet across. We marvel at its size and are able to actually go down into the kiva, a practice which was stopped after that year. The stone walls of the kiva are in great shape and there are a series of niches that go around the wall, and a stone bench that runs all the way around the inside of the kiva. There are four foundations that once held the great wooden posts that supported the roof. The fireplace in the center is well-defined and there is a channel that was once covered that served as a crawl space under the floor that runs from one of the entrances to the middle of the kiva. It is easy to image a costumed priest who uses the crawl space to appear in the mask of a god out of the smoke from the center fire. We sit in the kiva and marvel at the wonders of the ancient people who created these monumental buildings.

Pueblo Bonito was the largest building in all the Americas until the 1880s, when a larger building was erected in New York City. When early explorers first discovered the Great Houses in Chaco and elsewhere they assumed they were massive apartment complexes where large numbers of families lived. The assumption that the Great Houses were apartment complexes was quickly disproven when the first archaeologists determined that the great majority of the rooms didn't have hearths or proper ventilation. Then they decided the buildings were huge warehouses where goods were brought and stored for redistribution. Now they think they were monumental temples for religious worship and a palace where fifty to seventy people, the elite of the society, the emperor and the high priests, lived. The crowds of people came at solstice and equinox for great festivals. The exact nature of these ceremonies is lost in the ruins but the descendants of the people of Chaco still practice elaborate rituals to mark these solar events. These rituals, handed down for many generations, represent a distant echo of what was happening in the ancient days when Chaco was at its height.

The two largest Great Houses in Chaco sit side by side and are named Pueblo Bonito and Chetro Ketl. They designed the Great Houses to align with solar and lunar movements and to mark their standstills on the solstices. This was done in such a way that one of the main walls of the Great House would serve as a sight line for the sunrise and sunset on the solstice or equinox. In the ancient world at Chaco they considered that the sun had two houses, one in the north and the other in the south. These were the points along the horizon where the sun would rise and set in the same place for four days. When the sun arrived at its house at its northern standstill for summer solstice and then six months later, at its southern standstill for winter solstice, the people of Chaco Canyon, like their descendants at Acoma and Zuni, had great ceremonies and celebrations. People would come from miles away bringing offerings; things like corn meal, pollen, prayer sticks, arrowheads, fetish stones, turquoise, medicine bowls, seeds, and ears of corn. They put these things together in a ceremonial bundle that was offered to the sun. They would fast and use emetics and hold all-night dances, dancing in the plazas in elaborate costumes while the sun rested in its house for four days before starting its return journey. The ancient pueblo culture had a form of political-social organization with two moieties; the people divided into two equal parts, one concerned with farming, the other with hunting. Each moiety had its own leaders who were in charge of the entire society for half the year, from one solstice until the next, when leadership changed to the other moiety.

The people of Chaco Canyon interred their greatest leaders inside the monumental edifice of Pueblo Bonito. There, in the oldest section of the building, were tombs totally sealed from the outside world. The building itself is a crypt for the most important members of the society. When these graves were "excavated" they discovered the most important of all the burials, two men interred on a bed of sand covered with ash. There were turquoise beads and pendants in all four corners of the room. The bodies were covered with turquoise ornaments and beads, a shell trumpet at one side. There were shell ornaments inlaid with turquoise, rare minerals and ceremonial scepters. They found a basket inlaid with over twelve hundred turquoise chips with thousands more turquoise beads inside the basket. Just over this tomb was a floor made of wooden planks on which lay the disarticulated skeletons of fourteen people, seven men and seven women, who were surrounded by clay vessels filled with thousands of bits of turquoise, thousands of shell beads, ceremonial sticks and flutes. These people were presumably sacrificed to serve their departed leaders on their journey into the afterlife.

The architecture of some of the rooms in Chaco Canyon is designed with special places where the priest could "pull down the sun". Some of the fundamental principles of the ancient Chacoans survive, at least in part, shrouded in secrecy in shrines on remote and inaccessible buttes and mesas. They did ceremonies enacted in subterranean kivas where the sun was pulled down and directed through strategically placed openings, where it was refracted by crystals or collimated between upright stones to illuminate spiral petroglyphs, or bowls of water, or deer skins, or corn seed, or special chambers with markings of light or shadow. These rays of sunlight were used to show the middle of time, when the sun stops on its journey through the day, at noon, or when the sun stops on its journey through the year at each solstice. This was the time the people, guided by the priests, would give birth to the next cycle of life in the pueblo.

The search for the center was illustrated by the spiral design found pecked on rock walls all over the southwest. These multidimensional symbols represented the stars revolving in the night sky, a coiled serpent, the great winds, ancient migratory routes, whirlpools in a stream, the womb inside the female body and the earth itself. It was an iconic cosmogram leading to the exact center of the universe, the perfect midpoint where all things are in harmonic balance.

The Hopi and the Zuni both report that Chaco Canyon was the place of their ancestors. The excavations of Pueblo Bonito uncovered several mortuary chambers where they found a piece of cactus covered with cloth under one of the bodies. This same icon is still carried as an emblem of the priestcraft by the Hopi and Zuni. The excavations also uncovered eight large flutes and the remains of several Macaws. The Hopi have flute ceremonies that go on for nine days performed by the parrot clan. In 1910 the Smithsonian published a description of a flute ceremony. The ceremony began by building an altar in front of a spray of corn stalks. The altar held figurines of flute boy and flute girl, along with bird effigies, prayer sticks, rattles, medicine bowls, corn meal, ceremonial pipes, honey pots, bullroarers and feathered displays. Ceremonies were passed down, each clan having responsibility for enacting different rituals. This "modern" description is a distant reverberation, an echo, of the ceremonies at Pueblo Bonito.

The residents at Chaco Canyon were the rulers of a large empire covering five thousand square miles on the San Juan basin. There were hundreds of outlying communities, each with Great Houses and kivas. Their roads, cut into the desert floor, were thirty feet wide and ran straight as an arrow, some for hundreds of miles, many of them leading into Chaco Canyon from all directions. The construction of the roads required an immense labor force, as would the construction of the Great Houses in Chaco and elsewhere. The population had to be willing to dedicate a large portion of their labor to the state. The monumental architecture and the great systems of road could be built by the labor of the people as long as they respected the religious and political authority where the emperor was considered the divine authority over life and death. This system had been in place in Mexico and South America for many centuries. Chaco Canyon was the northernmost efflorescence of this great cultural phenomenon.

Anna Sofaer has determined that twelve of the fourteen major buildings in and around Chaco Canyon are oriented to the solar and lunar cycles. The Great Houses were designed and engineered so that the major architectural features were aligned in relationship to one another to create symmetrical geometric patterns. The monumental buildings, plazas and earthworks defy utilitarian logic and point to astrological principles embodied in the orientation of the buildings both toward the sun and moon and in relation to one other. This created cosmological calendars for the maintenance of ceremonial cycles. The buildings themselves are chronomic devices marking astronomical patterns.

Anna Sofaer's book, *Chaco Astronomy*, points out two places where there are large accumulations of broken pottery. One is on the top of the canyon wall just above Pueblo Bonito, which is at the nexus of the great road complex where all the roads come together at the heart of Chaco Canyon, and the other is at the northern extremity of the North Road, where it ends rather abruptly, about thirty miles north of Pueblo Bonito, at a steep drop-off.

Other shamanic cultures have funerary practices that involve placing the soul of the deceased in some convenient object, like a stone or a pot. Once the soul was in a safe place the priests responsible for their welfare in the afterlife conducted the necessary rituals to assure their passage into the upper world. Upon death the spirit could either descend into the underworld or be sent, often on a designated road, typically associated with the northern direction, to the upper world. The techniques for assuring that the soul goes to the upper world involve elaborate rituals and ceremonies. If the departed was in the underworld the priests had to rescue the soul. Once the soul was rescued it was placed where it could be held while the priests conducted the necessary rituals to get it to the upper realm. Sofaer provides ethnological information that indicates that ancient pueblo culture believed they could put the soul of the departed in a pot as part of a funerary ritual. Priests of the ancient pueblo were doing ceremonies that placed the soul of the departed in a piece of pottery which was taken to a special spot, such as at one end or the other of the Great North Road, where the pot was ritually broken, killed, and the soul was sent on its way into the upper realm. In this scenario, the Great North Road served as a launching pad or directional avenue for the souls of the dead on their way to the upper realms.

When the Spanish invaded the Southwest in the late 1500s, the archaeologists estimate there were eighty pueblos. There are nineteen today, these being amalgamations of the various peoples who had been devastated by the European invasion. They survived wave after wave of disease and cruel barbaric harassment by the Spanish, the Mexicans, and the Americans, all who did their best to eradicate pueblo culture. Their people were sold into slavery and severely punished any time they tried to practice their own religion or speak their own language. After four hundred years of occupation, the pueblos are finally able to live in relative peace, practice their own religion, speak their own language and educate their own children. Yet they are still under enormous pressure to become part of modern American society, which seeks to entice them to leave their ancestral traditions to assimilate and become part of the capitalistic consumerism that is our modern society.

In the Southwest, where the land is barren desert and the people had established cities, the culture has survived more intact than their fellow tribes to the east or west where they were forced to leave their homes and relocate, often to Oklahoma. In places like Hopi, Acoma, Zuni and Taos the people have maintained their traditions, their language, their religion and their medicine in ways impossible for the other tribes that have been either destroyed or devastated by the encroachment of modern American hegemony. In these isolated desolate places there are pueblos that have been continuously occupied for over eight hundred years. These are tribes that consist of only a few thousand members who have heroically held onto their traditional ways which were inherited from a great empire that covered much of what is now the Four Corners area of New Mexico, Utah, Arizona and Colorado.

A thousand years ago the ancestors of the modern pueblos were what we now call the Ancestral Puebloans. They created a culture that flourished under environmental conditions that were incredibly harsh, with extremely limited rainfall, blazing hot summers and frigid winters. Their culture evolved from nomadic hunter-gatherers to living in pit houses dug into the earth and later in multistoried apartment complexes built of stone and adobe.

Pueblo Bonito was built in episodes until it was abandoned about 1130 CE, after years of devastating drought. About fifty years later some people from Mesa Verde moved back to Chaco and built more kivas and resumed living there. The first excavations started with Richard Wetherill in 1896. He cleaned out ninety-two rooms. Then in 1921-27 National Geographic removed over 100,000 pounds of trash and dumped it in the creekbed that goes down the middle of the canyon. As a result, the periodic storms washed it all away in a devastating blow to future archaeologists. There were between six hundred and fifty to eight hundred rooms in the four or five-story structure. Then another sixty rooms were lost when a part of the canyon wall fell in 1941, taking out one side of the structure.

They currently think that the population of the entire canyon was three thousand people at its height and that as few as seventy-five, or at most two hundred, people lived in Pueblo Bonito. Most of the Great Houses in the canyon were built where small creeks came into the canyon, and only Pueblo Bonita is not associated with one of the smaller tributaries that flow into the wash that runs down the center of the canyon. The area gets about ten inches of rain per year, so the ancients created water basins everywhere they could.

They had three types of kivas associated with the buildings. The family kivas are the smallest and are only about twelve feet across; clan kivas go up to about twenty feet in diameter; and great kivas are from thirty to sixty feet across. They all have fireboxes in the middle.

By 1000 there were Great Houses all over the Southwest, all built with similar architectural features with core walls of stacked stone covered with adobe and great roof beams that supported the ceilings. The social and political organization that held all this together was centered in Chaco Canyon.

From there they built roads in all directions and established trade all the way into Central America.

The great kiva has its own solar alignments. There is a window on one side where on solstice morning the sun comes through and illuminates a niche on the opposite wall and that is the only day when the niche is fully lit. The wall is a near perfect circle, with multiple niches all around and if you draw lines connecting the opposing niches it creates a pattern that marked the exact center of the kiva where all the lines converge. The kiva has two doors, one on the north and one on the south, perfectly aligned with the compass points.

Much to the chagrin of the traditional pueblo religious leaders many of the ceremonies in the contemporary kivas have leaked out in published papers, starting in the late 1880s. The pueblos have enforced their secrecy with fierce determination, even with threats of death to any who reveal their secrets. But there are no shortage of accounts of various ceremonies and rites that are enacted in these chthonic chambers. These accounts tell of fasting from food and water for several days and taking herbal preparations that give you the runs and make you throw up so your body is totally free of any outside substances while you listen to a drummer and join in with dancers, some dancing on sounding chambers that are large stone boxes covered with wooden planks that create a dance platform. Inside the kivas the rhythm of the drums and the sounds of flutes and bullroarer would reverberate off the chamber walls. The room was incensed with sage smoke; at other times beams of light entered reflected by crystals or bowls of water to illuminate certain places and things. Finally, masked dancers who represented supernatural deities would appear, coming miraculously up out of the earthen floor, stepping out of a cloud of smoke, dancing with the dancers.

There was an ancient cultural impulse that started deep in antiquity and lasted until the European invasion of the Americas. It covered much of North and South America, ranging all over Mexico and Latin America and down into South America, particularly on the western slope of the Andes. It came north up the Mississippi Valley all the way to the Ohio River and covered all of what is now the Southeastern United States. It also came north out of Mexico and engulfed all the Southwestern United States as well. The characteristics of this cultural impulse include the belief that all the forces of nature can be personified as deities and the greatest of all these is the sun. They believed that to live in harmony with these forces it was necessary to propitiate them with offerings and sacrifices, the greatest and most powerful of which was human sacrifice. They also believed that the sun deity was manifest in human form as the emperor of their nation.

The earliest cultural dynamic based on these principles was the Olmec culture on the east coast of Mexico and the Chimo culture on the west coast of Peru. From then until the Spanish invasion, one culture after another would arise as a mighty empire. It would begin with a legendary leader who would form a capital city and build huge monumental temples, palaces and pyramids and conquer all the neighboring tribes. They would come to dominate a large geographic area and would last for a few hundred years before their demise. The most famous of these are the Inca, the Aztec and the Mayan. We have historical records to document their rise and fall of these three empires, but there are archaeological records of many others who came before.

The first American who came to Chaco Canyon, as far as we know, was an Army surveyor who had a Zuni guide who lead him into the canyon and showed him the ruins. When he entered the canyon, the Zuni guide told him the name of the canyon and the name of each of the buildings. So we, the Americans, did not discover the place, which was very well known by all the pueblo tribes, who did not consider it a ruin but a sacred site which they continued to use for ceremonial purposes and still do today.

Before about 650 CE there were no villages in the Southwest. People lived in scattered site residences called pit houses, with one room that was dug into the earth. After 775, the first villages appear and by 850 the population was shifting to village life with small pueblos with two or three pit houses, each accompanied by a suite of aboveground rooms and a series of storage pits nearby. Within the next hundred years something dramatic happened, culturally, and these people began to build the Great Houses.

Pueblo Bonito and the great houses at Chaco Canyon have been characterized as large apartment complexes, as tribute-gathering state capitals, as redistribution centers, as pilgrimage centers, as cooperative agrarian enterprises, as entrepreneurial production centers   and peer polity systems. What we know is that it was a long-lasting demographic center in the prehistory of the Southwest. Construction began around 800 CE and included large suites of tall rooms, much larger than other residences. These great houses required huge labor investments provided by a population living in scattered settlements. The residents of the great houses had differential distribution of prestige items and had distinctly different funerary practices. The privileged elites were taller and in better health than the population at large. All implying hierarchical institutionalized leaders ruling over centralized integrated regions. These regions included elaborate roads that were associated with shrines, Great Houses, and great kivas. They maintained their status up until about 1150 CE.

The great houses all over the San Juan basin shared certain characteristics. Architecturally they were all enclosed multi-room, multistoried buildings, with enclosed plazas. They were built with carefully laid core and veneer stonework and were associated with great roads and with great kivas. Excavations uncovered exotic artifacts, such as macaw feathers, copper bells, marine seashells, distinctive pottery styles, astronomical alignments and lots of turquoise. These great houses served as huge cathedrals and burial sites for the elite. They provided living spaces for a few elites while the rest of the population lived in smaller pueblos, with twenty or fewer rooms. These compounds included a kiva or pit house-type room for sleeping, storage rooms, mealing rooms, weaving rooms, living rooms with hearths and areas where they raised turkeys. They all had middens close by. These smaller communities with up to two hundred people were occupied for part of the year and the remainder of the year was spent in smaller residences in agricultural areas. The great houses were religious and political centers that dominated large regions with common ideational bonds and the residences of autocratic hierarchical rulers who extracted labor from the population. The people gathered at the great houses for ceremonies and festivals that included human sacrifices. Casa Rinconada in Chaco Canyon is one of the largest of the great kivas. To get to it we walked past two smaller sets of ruins. These were representative of the small living compounds with up to twenty rooms and three or four small kivas. At the height of the population in Chaco there were up to fifty of these compounds in the area. There were an equal number around Fajada Butte where the visitor's center is located now.

The earliest settled Puebloan peoples lived in pit houses. These were kiva-like structures which served as the primary living space for a matriarchic family unit. Once corn was introduced, they began to expand the living space with aboveground rooms and eventually these evolved into multi-room buildings. A family compound included a pit house as the sleeping quarters and kitchen where the family cooked the meals with the aboveground rooms for mealing, weaving and storage rooms. The next step was to have several families put their living spaces into a single compound where three or four families would live contiguously. Twenty rooms and four kivas in a compound would accommodate four families. The number of families could be estimated by the number of pit houses in the compound.   T h e s e compounds were the living quarters for the common people of the Chaco era. The elites had the great houses. The people in the compounds were the workers, the people that raised the corn and worked part of each year cutting stone, doing masonry on the great houses or building roads.

The ruling elite extracted labor from a large population to build the monumental architecture of Pueblo Bonito and the rest of the great houses in the canyon and beyond. The great houses in Chaco had a distinctive type of masonry that was replicated in the outlier structures. Archaeologists have documented over 225 great houses in the Southwest with Chaco canyon at the geographic center. These structures all have interior plazas with sunken kivas, rooms with T-shaped doorways, ceremonial artifacts such as wooden wands and stone phalluses, remains of exotic birds with colorful feathers and corn-based agriculture. They are multistoried complexes with hundreds of rooms, most of which were not residential. Many of these structures are associated with elaborate roads, often thirty feet across with low berms on each side. Many of the buildings have lines of sight to nearby mountains which are topped with fire shrines which could relay signals from mountain top to mountain top to other great houses hundreds of miles away. The great houses also include alignments to the solstices and equinoxes.

The first great houses appeared around 900 CE and included a warrior cult with deities that required human sacrifice, followed by cannibalism of the victims. This is thought to have been imported from the south. Other features of ancestral Puebloan society including reliance on corn, use of pottery and cotton cloth which was imported from Mesoamerica. Influences from Mexico include ballcourts, found as far north as Flagstaff, copper bells, macaw feathers, dental transfiguration and weaving techniques. The horned or plumed serpent and the death god Xipe were carried north by warrior cults who invaded the area after the break-up of the Toltec empire. They established their politico-religious system using ritualized violence including human sacrifice and cannibalism, as a means of social control to extract tribute and build monuments and roads. These rulers had a form of theocratic despotism that exercised absolute power and unlimited authority. Cannibalism is found in the archaeological record of the Southwest starting as early as 400 CE, and probably much earlier. Once agriculture became established, the society became characterized by rituals to assure the growth of corn, along with a yearly cycle of ceremonial observations, ancestor worship, communal social conformity, priestly authoritarianism, animal and human sacrifice, warrior societies and fertility rituals. Once the people settled into villages and tended their crops, weather magic to bring the rain was an important feature of their religious life.

The term taphonomy was coined to describe the study of postmortem bone distribution and modification. Archaeologists in the Southwest began to find human bones that showed definite signs of violent death and subsequent cannibalism. By studying the bones of animals that were butchered and prepared for cooking and comparing them with scattered unburied bones of humans, they were able to detect the same types of cut marks on human bones that were being prepared for a cannibal feast. Human charnel deposits found in the American Southwest were carefully compared to Mesoamerican remains where cannibalism was linked to ceremonies of human sacrifice, and they found the same types of bone breakage, cut marks, abrasions, and burn marks. By comparing animal bones processed for cooking with human bones from societies known for their cannibal practices with the charnel remains in the American Southwest, a very strong case has been made for the practice of cannibalism. Researchers have since found over three hundred sets of human bones at seventy-six sites in the Southwest where human bones provide evidence of this practice. Careful mapping of these sites and documentation of the ages of the bones show that cannibalism was clearly a part of the Chaco phenomenon. Evidence has been found at Pueblo Bonito, as well as numerous other sites in the Chaco sphere of cultural influence. By 300 CE Teotihuacan with its great pyramid of the sun dominated much of central Mexico. In 650 Teotihuacan was looted and destroyed. The next great culture to arise were the Toltec, who ruled the area with a militaristic theocracy that lasted until about 1000 CE. They were then succeeded by the Aztec, who came to power around 1300. All these cultures were dominated by warrior societies characterized by death cults that practiced human sacrifice and cannibalism.

AZTEC: THE RESTORED KIVA – 2015

Fifty miles north of Chaco Canyon is the largest ruin outside Chaco. Only Pueblo Bonito and Chetro Ketl are larger. The site includes a complex of three great houses now labeled Aztec West, East and North. Aztec West was excavated in 1916 by Earl Morris, a well-known archaeologist who grew up nearby. It has the classic D-shape design and well over 400 rooms and twelve kivas. Some archaeologists believe it was constructed to replace Chaco Canyon as the capital city of the culture after Chaco was no longer a viable place to live. The most common theory is that drought drove them out of the canyon sometime around 1150 CE and they resettled here, near the junction of the Animas and San Juan rivers. The crown jewel at Aztec is the reconstructed kiva. Earl Morris reconstructed it on the site where it was located. The great kiva stands in the plaza of Aztec West and protrudes 8 to 10 feet above ground level and is over fifty feet across. I've noticed other modern kivas at some of the living pueblos, like San Felipe, are similar, with about half the structure underground and the other half standing above ground. This one has entrances at the north and south while the living kivas have ladders with entrances through the roof. This kiva stands out because it has a series of rooms at ground level that surround the inner chamber. On the north entrance there is an elevated room with a large platform in the center of the room. The platform has an ominous feel and I sense that this could have been the spot where sacrifices were made. Although I have not found evidence indicating human sacrifice took place in the kivas, there is abundant evidence that human sacrifice was a part of the culture and was incorporated in the religious practices. The great kivas were where the major religious dramas were enacted. From the entrance room, which is at ground level, you have an incredible view down into the kiva which is sunk into the ground. There are four main columns holding up the roof and they are spaced equally inside the circle of the subterranean chamber. Stepping down into the kiva is an exhilarating experience. The ceiling is twenty plus feet tall with evenly spaced windows that look into the rooms that surround the chamber at ground level.

Only one of the three great houses at Aztec has been excavated. The eastern great house is in view of the excavated west house and the northern great house sits elevated on a ridge just above the other two. Plus there are numerous remains of other habitation sites in the vicinity. The area associated with the site extends for over two miles along the river valley and the terrace above the valley. Morris collected wood samples and made good use of the emerging science of dendrochronology to date the structures. The main construction phase took place between 1110 to 1120 CE. This site played a dominant role in the last phase of the cultural phenomena of the ancestral publeoan tradition. The site at Aztec flourished until 1275, when it was abandoned for still undetermined reasons.

SALMON: A CHACO OUTLIER – 2016

From Aztec we drove back to Farmington and spent the night. The next morning it was off to Salmon Ruins in Bloomfield, a few miles from the Aztec site. There, on the north bank of the San Juan River, only 45 miles north of Chaco, is another of the most outstanding post-Chaco great houses. It has a great house with over 250 rooms with a tower kiva at its center and a great kiva in its courtyard. It was once a three-story structure built around 1090 CE and occupied until 1280. It was excavated in the 1970s and has a nice museum where artifacts from the excavation are on display. It is widely assumed that both Salmon and Aztec were built as Chaco was becoming uninhabitable. The resources in Chaco Canyon, such as lumber for building and for firewood, were no longer easily available and soil fertility gave out and then extended drought created conditions that could no longer sustain the enormous infrastructure of Chaco. All the great houses in the canyon required labor and tribute. When the resources were no longer available in a viable fashion they moved north and started building Salmon and Aztec.

Salmon has the classic design and its masonry reflects the influence of Chaco. The rock work is exquisite. It has fourteen T-shaped doorways. We walk through the museum and down a path toward the ruins. The complex includes the old homestead of the Salmon family. The ruins were on land owned by several generations of the same family and they guarded the ruins and didn't allow them to be dug into by pot hunters.

The San Juan River is close by and floods the site from time to time. The walk goes through a grove of large cottonwoods and the great house backs up to a residential neighborhood. I was surprised to see pictures from the 1800s which show a desert landscape with no trees and no houses anywhere in sight. While the outline and dimensions of the building are apparent much of it has been backfilled to protect it, especially the great kiva. The rooms that are open and the tower kiva are magnificent examples of Chaco-type stonework in a beautiful setting. The river is close by and it seems apparent that the builders wanted to be near a permanent water source. The rooms on the southwest section are basically gone, the victim of floods. It is an interesting site and a vital part of the story of what happened at Chaco.

According to the 1978 architectural rendering there were no small kivas in the original design of the building. Now, as we walk through the ruins there are several places where small kivas have been built into the original rooms. A later influx of population moved in and redesigned the great house and put in aboveground kivas in some of the larger rooms. The T- shaped doors served as the main door to a family complex.

The culture that produced the great houses started at Chaco and then moved to Salmon and Aztec. Around the 13th century the people abandoned the great houses and moved to the Rio Grande River valley. This signaled a change in the cultural dynamics where the great houses, as ceremonial palaces, were no more. Once this paradigm no longer held, and the people moved to the Rio Grande, they built multistoried villages with clusters of large buildings that housed many different families where there was no distinct housing for the elites.

POSI: THE HOT SPRINGS - 2016

Posi is the name for a large ruin located at Ojo Caliente. It is adjacent to the natural hot springs a few miles southwest of Taos. Posi is well-known but is not visited as much as Aztec or Salmon because the ruins have not been excavated or restored. Posi doesn't fit into the same paradigm as Aztec or Salmon. It is a pueblo village and is not a great house. The people from Chaco Canyon migrated up to Aztec and Salmon but, once these new sites were deserted, the people moved to the Rio Grande River valley and the time of the great houses came to an end. After 1300, great house construction comes to a halt and they began building multistoried residential structures where the whole village could live in a series of buildings clustered together.

The famous hot springs at Ojo Caliente is now a spa and a hotel. A large spring pours out from under the mountain at a temperature of 104 degrees. The owners have channeled the water into a group of pools and have added other minerals to the natural iron ore in the water. There are hot pools with iron, mud, soda, Lithia and arsenic, along with saunas and comfortable lounge chairs and hammocks. The spa is in the Ojo Caliente River valley and the nicest of the springs is nestled up against a pure white cliff face composed of compacted volcanic ash. It is eroded into phantasmagoric hoodoos and peaks and points and has elaborate erosion lines that run over the face of it like wrinkles on the face of time. Just above the top of the cliff is the mesa top and on the lip of the mesa, looking down over the hot springs, are the ruins of the ancient village called Posi.

The spa is an elaborate operation which has been an attraction for centuries, first for the Indians, later for the Spanish and now for Americans. There are eleven different pools, each one marked to show the minerals in the water and the temperature. Some are private pools that can be rented or are just for guests who are renting a room; others are for everyone who shows up that day. There are about fifty motel rooms built in a courtyard configuration around the various pools so it is convenient to go from your room to the nearest pool. They have a restaurant which is the only restaurant for many miles.

It is the oldest natural hot springs resort in the United States, first opened in 1868. Long before the Spanish and then the Americans the hot springs were a meeting place where enemy tribes could come together without hostility. During the 17th century the Spanish made numerous attempts to colonize this region but were met with aggression by the Natives, who managed to keep them out of the area. There is a nearby mission church that was built in the late 1700s and you can still see holes in the walls where they put their rifles through to fight off the Comanche. However, after the Americans assumed control of the territory in 1848 the area came under the sway of westward expansion. When there were no more hostile Indians in the area people began to take note of the hot springs. The earliest accounts mention the green hue of the water which was colored by algae that flourished in the warm springs. Hints of the algae are still present in a couple of the pools.

The first Territorial Representative to the U.S. Congress was Antonio Joseph and he claimed the hot springs as his property and opened it to the public in 1868. A small village quickly grew up around it. Kit Carson, who left little territory in the area unexplored, was a frequent visitor. Two of the buildings in the complex are original architecture and they are listed on the National Registry of Historic Places.

After a morning of soaking in the various pools I get dressed and head for the Posi village site. The front desk has maps of walking trails and one of them goes to Posi. It is 1.3 miles round trip. It is just above our heads on the lip of the mesa. It is a hot fall day but the first of the fall colors are just starting to show up on the cottonwoods that line the river. Just behind the spa a trail leads up to the top of the mesa. There is a little bulletin board at the trail head; it has notices telling you to bring water and a warning about mountain lions and what to do if you run into one. It says to look them in the eye and walk, don't run, slowly away. The path to the top of the mesa is a bit rough but I scramble up to the top, which is an arid desertscape of low twisted juniper trees and cactus. What grass manages to grow is dry and brittle, scattered here and there. It is a sharp contrast to the lush river valley. The sky overhead is a radiant gleaming blue, clouds rack the horizon hazing the eastern sky a light mauve. I marvel at the utter silence, bask in it, amazed I can't hear any traffic or see any jet trails marring the depths of the sky overhead. Along the path I see some droppings, either deer or goat.

It isn't far before I come to a fence with an entrance sign saying not to pick up pottery shards or other artifacts. Then the path goes along a low rolling mesa with scrub trees and cacti nearly waist high. The trail isn't paved but it is well worn across the top of the mesa. I stop at one spot to enjoy the view: low mountains behind me and a panoramic view of the huge blue sky with a few feathery clouds, remote and motionless. I can see the river and admire the sensuous curves as it meanders down the valley. The mountains off to the north are snowcapped, gleaming cold and indifferent, the white tops glinting in the sun. Rain curtains hang at the base of the mountains, electrical impulses play in the darker recesses. A wild wind blows against my face and sings in the sparse bushes. I sit down for a few minutes to enjoy the vibe. A distant hawk circles lazily high above, riding weightless on the updrafts, then wheeling and sliding away disappearing in the distance. When the wind dies down nothing moves, I sit still and silent. In the distance a few sparse juniper trees on a ridgeline create dark outlines etched black against the horizon, an arboreal alphabet, a terma I long to decipher, a mystery writ large on the parchment of the sky. I feel giddy, knowing that generations lived on this spot and losing track of where the ancient world ends and modernity begins. After a few minutes sitting in the shade of one of the stunted junipers I glance down and see a big chunk of crystal; then I notice pottery shards scattered here and there littering the ground. I pick up the crystal, hold it up to the sunlight. It is hot from the baking heat on the mesa, translucent, glowing as the sunlight passes through it. It is about half as big as my fist. I lay it back down with the realization I have arrived at the village site. I am a bit surprised as there is nothing to see. If you didn't know what you are looking at you would have no idea you were standing in the ruins of a large village. Posi had over two thousand rooms in six main buildings with four big plazas and six kivas. Three of the buildings were on the edge of the mesa with a view down the river valley and off into a distant mountain range. Some of the buildings were three stories tall. Now they are rounded humps on the mesa top.

My brochure from the spa has a drawing of what the village looked like in its heyday. It showed the layout of the buildings with a path that goes through the main part of the village. I study the map and want to find each of the buildings. There are markers at five locations showing different features of the village. Here and there along the path there are a few exposed rocks, remnants of the pueblo walls. Every few steps there is a flat stone with a pile of shards on it. It seems to be a ritual to pick up shards and make a small collection on one of the rocks. With the help of the drawing I discern where the buildings stood and where the plazas were by the contour of the ground. The buildings are low mounds and the plazas are a bit lower and flatter but without a rendering it would be very difficult to recognize these features worn down by centuries of erosion and exposure.

The Tewa people in the nearby pueblos on the Rio Grande retain a living memory of Posi which they call Posi Ouinge. They translate this as "The Place of the Green Bubbling Hot Springs." They say that for many years the people were migrating and they had summer people and winter people and they lived in separate villages until the elders decided they should all come together and they came to this spot on the mesa just above the hot springs. They built the village around 1200 and lived there for about three hundred years, until an epidemic descended on the land and many people died. The elders held a council and said it was time to move on. They moved nearer the Rio Grande and after the Spanish arrived they moved again across the river, where they live to this day. Ruins of this size did not go unnoticed, even in their dilapidated state. Adolph Bandelier visited the area and surveyed it, as did Edgar Hewitt. The site has never been excavated so it stands now as the forces of nature have shaped it.

I explore around, climbing each of the low mounds that are the remains of the two and three story pueblo buildings. I come upon a depression in the earth that is perfectly round and twenty feet across, a kiva. I walk along the edge of the mesa enjoying the spectacular view looking directly down on the spa where the hot springs stream out from under the escarpment with the river winding down the valley and snowcapped mountains in the distance. I move through the whole site until I feel I have a sense where each of the buildings stood and can make out the plazas. There are piles of stone here and there and pottery shards litter the ground, thousands and thousands of pottery shards, many of them with designs.

Having been to the restored ruins at Chaco, Aztec and Salmon, where the sites are excavated and restored, it is interesting to see an undisturbed ruin. I sense the village buried just below me and imagine there are first story rooms with walls still standing. Here was a huge village that has never been excavated by an archaeologist. However, archaeologists have collected pot shards with the goal of identifying the artistic motifs and dating them to get a rough idea of the years of habitation at the site.

As I start back the heat is oppressive, even on the full moon of late September. I walked back with an image of pueblo walls and rooms filled with debris just under my feet, walking on the hidden ruins of the past. Here by myself in the undisturbed ruins of a great village I admired the spectacular landscape where they chose to make their home. Posi is obviously not a great house and represents the next stage in the history of pueblo culture, the stage in which the people moved into large plaza-oriented villages in multistoried pueblos, typically in a river valley where an entire village could live. This marked a political upheaval where the hierarchy of the past was no longer recognized. There was no Emperor with life and death control over the people living in a temple palace, no elite living separate from the rest of the people.

After walking back down to the spa and eating dinner, Susan and I join our friends Bill and Sandy and Susan's brother, Dave, and build a fire in the kiva fireplace in the corner of our room. Then, just as it is getting dark, we go out to one of the springs and ease into the hot mineral water. It just so happens that this is the night of the blood moon. The blood moon occurs when the moon is at its closest orbit to the earth and is thirty percent brighter than the typical full moon. As we lay in the hot pool we watch the moon rising over the horizon. It first appears as a striking reddish orange, bigger and brighter than I have ever seen. And to top it off there is a full lunar eclipse happening this night. We lay in the pool and, after the moon has climbed higher into the night sky, we watch the shadow of the earth move across the face of the moon and gaze, bedazzled, as the moon totally disappears and reappears.

This hot springs has been redone in the past few years. The place is full of people who are renting rooms in the hotel or coming to spend a few hours enjoying the hot springs. Once you check in at the desk they give you a bathrobe and the whole place is full of people in their white bath robes; they are in the restaurant eating meals in their robes, in the gift store and walking around from their rooms to the pools or between the pools and the saunas. The place makes me feel like I am in a high-priced trendy mental institution.

BANDELIER: FRIJOLES CANYON - 2015

A million years ago the Jemez volcano deposited over nine hundred feet of ash over what is now Bandelier National Park. The ash settled over time and compacted into soft stone. One main part of Bandelier is a beautiful little valley where Jemez Creek has cut through the ash and created high cliffs. The Indians found it a good spot and built two pueblos, one that was a circular building three stories tall and the other a set of buildings that were built flush against the cliff face. These were built after the end of the great house period.

It is a beautiful drive from I-25 to the park. It is one of those places in New Mexico where in the course of thirty miles you go through several distinct ecosystems. We started in a harsh flat desert and gradually climbed through sheer rock outcroppings into dense forest. Then we descended into a deep canyon and came to the visitor's center. There is a trail out of the visitor's center that is a mile and a quarter long and goes by the ruins. The people who inhabited them are closely related to the people now living in Cochiti Pueblo along the Rio Grande, so apparently they didn't move far.

The first thing you come to on the trail is an excavated kiva. You can walk right up to the edge of the kiva but are not allowed to enter. It was probably the ceremonial and social center for the people who lived in the pueblo. The roof is totally gone and all the plaster from the walls is gone as well. When it was in use it had a roof with a ladder sticking up. The roof was supported by six pillars and the supports for the pillars are still in place. It had a bench around the wall and murals covering all the walls. There were foot drums that dancers could stomp to make deep reverberating sounds to accompany the drummers. It was also a social space where people could weave or simply visit. The kiva is just a few yards from the outer walls of the main pueblo.

The main pueblo is called Tyuonyi and is a very impressive structure. It is circular and was two maybe three stories tall with up to four hundred rooms. This would have provided living space for up to a hundred people. When we are looking at the rooms at ground level they seem very small, most of them only six or eight feet long and four to six feet wide. These rooms were likely for food storage to keep two to three years' worth of corn and other dried crops stored for drought or hardships. There is a large plaza in the center of the building and there are depressions where three smaller kivas were located. The building must have been very striking when it was occupied. The outer walls were adobe covering a stone core and would have been quite imposing. The word Tyuonyi is a Tewa word that means "place of meeting" and it appears this village and the others located in the park were a dividing line between two language groups with Tewa speakers to the north and people speaking Keres to the south. The main building has been dated using tree rings to 1400 CE. It is intriguing to imagine what it must have looked like. The pueblo sits in the valley with long houses overlooking it up against the cliff face.

It is a short, but beautiful, walk from Tyuonyi to the cliff face. There are numerous outcroppings of volcanic tuff that stand out from the canyon wall and they have eroded into fantastic shapes. Some of the stones have a Swiss cheese look, full of holes and indentations. Others look like something out of a bizarre fairy tale. We follow the trail through this fantasy landscape and come to the canyon wall. There are rooms they call cavates in the cliff face, they were created by digging into the volcanic tuff of the cliff face with stone tools. The people built living quarters against the canyon walls and then made extra rooms by digging back into the cliff face. There are ladders you can climb into some of the cavates that are at the level of the second story. We climb the ladders and crawl inside the rooms where we can sit and look out over the village. The archaeologists say that the Indians plastered the inside walls of the cavates with adobe and then painted murals on them as well. One of the cavates still has some plaster with a zigzag design plainly visible. Another of the cavates has loom supports, with narrow beams protruding from the ceiling and depressions in the floor where the looms were set up. In prehistoric times the men did the weaving. In another there are three connecting rooms dug into the tuff.

From the vantage point inside the cave rooms you can look down on the main structure of the pueblo and the little creek. Just down from here the creek cascades over two waterfalls before it comes to the Rio Grande. The valley floor was used for growing corn, squash and beans and was irrigated with water from Frijoles Creek. Archaeologists have rebuilt a couple of rooms to recreate what it must have looked like when there were houses here. The adobe walls and exposed vigas give the buildings an organic feel where they nestle up against the base of the white tuff cliffs. There were houses built up against the cliff face in both directions. These look as if they could shelter a large population. They estimate that, at its height around 1400 CE, there were five hundred people living in this valley.

When the Jemez Mountain erupted it created obsidian and basalt. Based on the excavation at Tyuonyi the pueblo people used the obsidian for knives and arrowheads and the basalt for stone axes. The village may have been a manufacturing site for obsidian that was traded far and wide. Examples of this obsidian have been found far into Mexico to the south. It was evidently traded for live parrots and exotic feathers and even copper bells, all of which have been found in the excavations. There are parrots in the petroglyphs along the canyon walls.

As we continue along the trail, we come to the next part of the ruins, The Long House. The foundations of many contiguous rooms can be seen up against the canyon wall along this part of the tour. It is easy to see how many stories were built since they dug holes into the tuff to seat the vigas that supported the roofs, which then became the floor of the next story. There are lines of holes creating a distinct outline for each of the rooms built against the rock face. Plus there are cavates where they created extra rooms. Above the top level of the buildings are numerous petroglyphs; the designs include spirals, turkeys, a dog, parrots and zigzag lightning lines. The people here raised turkeys, primarily for their feathers which were used to make blankets and cloaks that were both water-repellant and warm. In one place there is a pictogram painted on the inner wall of one of the rooms that was discovered during the excavations when they peeled back a layer of adobe and found the painting on the earlier wall. It was on the back wall of a second-story structure and is now covered with Plexiglas to protect it. When we come to the end of the Long House the trails leads back about a mile into the canyon to a dramatic overhang. Then you have to climb 140 feet up a series of four tall ladders to get to a recreated kiva.

The whole site was occupied for hundreds of years and there is no explanation why the people left. When Don Juan de Onate colonized the area in 1598 Frijoles Canyon was deserted. However, after the pueblo revolt in 1680 some people came back and lived in the canyon for a few years. The land was eventually given to Mexican settlers as part of a land grant and it was inhabited until the 1880s. Adolph Bandelier first visited the canyon about that time and came back many times to explore the numerous ruins. By 1900, the land was preserved from homesteaders and in 1916 President Woodrow Wilson designated 22,400 acres as park land.

THE CLIFF HOUSE TOUR

MESA VERDE - 2016

The sky is a clear hot blue as Susan and I fly over the Sandia Peaks into Albuquerque. The area where Albuquerque sits was one of the most highly-populated areas in the Southwest before the Spanish invasion. The river valley, where it flows through town, was once lined with multistoried pueblos. They are long gone and, while local archaeologists have mapped the sites, most are completely destroyed by over 400 years of repopulation by wave after wave of invaders. I imagine the ghosts of the buildings as we come down for a landing and head out to see the great cliff dwellings in southern Colorado and Utah.

Two great cultures arose in prehistoric North America. The Mound Builders created great cities in the eastern half of this continent while the Ancestral Puebloans did the same in the Southwest. Both arose starting about 800 CE and both were gone by 1300. Chaco Canyon was the great capital city of the Puebloean culture; Cahokia, the equivalent to the east of the Mississippi River. Both required a refined tradition of engineering, architecture and astronomy, along with the combined labor of a workforce willing to carry out the vision that created these enduring monuments. Chaco Canyon holds twelve great houses in eight miles of canyon. Extensive surveys have been done to map the extent and placement of all the great houses scattered around the San Juan area and over 225 have been documented and mapped. There is still a great debate in the archaeological community whether these other great houses, obviously to some degree modeled on the great houses of Chaco Canyon, and often called outliers, were built under the domination of Chaco Canyon or simply emulated Chaco.

Just as Chaco was the capital city of a great culture, so too was Mesa Verde, and just as Pueblo Bonito is the largest of the great houses, so Cliff Palace at Mesa Verde is the most spectacular of the cliff dwellings. While cliff dwellings superficially appear to be great houses built under cliffs there are more differences than similarities and they represent two very different cultural impulses that are not directly related. Great houses were cathedrals where only a small handful of priests and/or chiefs lived. The population at large lived in scattered site residences in the surrounding countryside. The cliff dwellings are residential villages housing a group of living quarters, each one consisting of a subterranean chamber with a group of aboveground rooms. Just as great houses are located all over the Four Corners area, so cliff dwelling can be found wherever there are deep canyons with overhangs with adequate space for building. Cliff dwellings can be found all the way into Mexico.

Mesa Verde, located in southern Colorado in the Four Corners region, is a huge flat- topped mesa riddled with deep gorges. Mesa Verde includes about a dozen major pueblos tucked into the cliff faces. Mesa Verde is a remarkable geologic formation, bordered on three sides with sheer cliffs and on the south with a labyrinth of canyons. The top is flat and filled with trees. The canyons extend into the mesa like fingers. Each canyon is up to six hundred feet high with sheer stone walls. Here and there in these canyons are a variety of rock overhangs, many of them midway up on the canyon walls. The ancestral people took full advantage of these and built incredible stone buildings, many with towers that went from the floor to the ceiling. The greatest of all these is Cliff Palace with over 150 rooms.

The discovery of the Cliff Palace is one of the most remarkable stories in the annals of archaeology. It ranks with the discovery of Machu Picchu and revealed a civilization that was virtually unknown up until that time. In the mid 1880s the Wetherill family moved to southwestern Colorado from Pennsylvania. They ended up on a ranch at the edge of the Ute territory at the base of Mesa Verde. There were five sons and a daughter in a Quaker family. They didn't carry guns except to hunt for game and, before long, were accepted by the Utes, whom they befriended on several occasions. There was great suspicion and distrust between the settlers and the Utes, and with good reason. Both sides were capable of unprovoked attack at any time, but the Utes exempted the Wetherill family and even let them run their cattle in the maze of canyons that penetrate into the tableland of Mesa Verde. The eldest son, Richard, had to take much of the responsibility for running the farm as their father aged. He and another brother built a cabin on the edge of the canyonland where they could stay during the winter and chase down strays that wandered into the long fingers of the many canyons that emptied into the Mancos River drainage. The cabin was in the heart of the canyons and there was a Ute living nearby in a teepee who would come to visit. At one point he warned Richard that there were ruins of ancient villages in the cliffs lining the canyons and that he should not go near them, that if he did he would surely die. He emphasized that the Utes kept their distance from those places, which they considered the abode of the dead.

One winter the family had a visitor who was interested in seeing ruins and the Wetherills knew of an ancient village site on the banks of the Mancos River. While Richard took the visitor out for a tour, one of his younger brothers, Al, decided to go looking for other ruins. He headed up one of the largest canyons and late in the day, with the air full of snow, he looked across one of the canyons from a vantage point on the mesa and saw Cliff Palace. He reported it to Richard when they joined back up but the press of activities didn't allow for another visit that winter. The next winter, 1888, Richard and his brother-in-law, Charlie, were staying in the cabin looking for stray cattle when they came to the same place on the mesa and saw Cliff Palace in the distance, across a vast canyon. They quickly gave up on the cattle and began to figure out how to get across the canyon. When they were above the ruins they rigged up a ladder by taking two fallen trees, chopping off the branches about a foot from the truck, then tying them together and hanging them over the sheer cliff face. They used the branches like the steps on a ladder and made their way down into the ruins.

Once they were in the village it was as if the inhabitants had made a hasty escape and had left their household goods in place. They wandered from room to room and found hafted axes with the handles intact and large water pots and other pottery still sitting where they had been left. Richard immediately started calling it Cliff Palace for the grandeur of its architecture and the stonework in buildings that went up three stories under the expansive cliff. After a few hours, Richard had a hunch there were more ruins nearby and left Charlie and went looking and in a short time came upon another set of ruins in even better condition. There was a large spruce tree growing out of the wall in the front of the ruins and he called it Spruce Tree House. In one day Richard managed to discover and explore two of the greatest cliff houses that came to epitomize an entire ancient culture that was unknown at that time. It was a civilization that produced some of the finest stonework found anywhere outside Machu Picchu and the Yucatan peninsula.

Richard started coming to the two ruins every winter and digging. He quickly amassed a large collection of artifacts and a few years later put them on display in Denver. To his shock, the people in Colorado in the early 1890s had little interest in them. However, the next year he found the mummified remains of a child. He displayed it along with the artifacts the next year in Denver and the mummy of the little girl fascinated the people of Denver. The Colorado Historical Society ended up purchasing his collection for the sum of $3,000. He gave up farming and spent the rest of his life exploring the magnificent ruins of the southwestern United States.

He worked with the archaeologists of his day and quickly learned their techniques and applied them every time he discovered new ruins. He left his name scratched on the cliff walls at all the sites he visited. He found his way to Chaco Canyon and did the first excavations of Pueblo Bonito. He eventually ran into problems with the government, who decided they wanted to set aside the ruins and stopped him from digging and selling the artifacts. However, he was working with a large museum in New York and his finds were preserved at the museum and he kept field notes when he was excavating. Nonetheless, the government made him stop digging at Chaco Canyon. In 1910, he came to a premature end during a cattle dispute with the local Navajo that ended in a shootout. He is buried next to Pueblo Bonito at the base of the canyon wall.

Many years later two archaeologists who had become experts in the study of the cliff dwellings were exploring ruins in Mesa Verde and saw a small cliff dwelling that looked inaccessible as it was located high up on a sheer cliff face. They were mountaineers and made their way up the rock face and along a very narrow ledge hundreds of feet above the canyon floor and were able to get to the ruins. They thought they were the first to explore it but when they looked into the first room they saw a pencil inscription on the wall that read, "What fools these mortals be." R. Wetherill.

The park archaeologists have established dates for the construction of the cliff dwellings. They have taken thousands of tree ring samples and have beginning and ending dates for each structure. They have determined that the best-known cliff dwellings are dated from 1100 to 1280. The main exceptions were Long House and Step House, which had pit dwellings under their alcoves in 550 CE and 630 CE but then nothing up to 1100, when the villages we see now were constructed. They know from the tree ring dating that nearly all of Mesa Verde was deserted by 1300. [52] They are still not sure of the exact reasons. They assume it was a number of factors that came together, including: resource depletion of the wood and soil, severe drought, and warfare. There are signs in the archaeological record of war at several of the cliff dwelling, including reports of dead bodies unburied at the sites.

There are few places in the world with the concentration of ancient ruins comparable to Mesa Verde. Chaco Canyon is a rival; others are the Sacred Valley in Peru and the Vezere River in France. At Mesa Verde the Mesa Top Loop Road goes past seven mesa top farming communities, then comes to the canyon lip and follows the canyon toward its source. The road is studded with overlooks where you can peer across the canyon at the ruins of villages tucked under the canyon walls, one after another. They have names like Sunset House, Fire Temple, New Fire House, Oak Tree House, House of Many Windows and there, in the midst of them and sitting in a side canyon, is Cliff Palace. In a half-mile drive along the canyon lip we see nine cliff dwellings with Cliff Palace more or less in the center, all within a mile of Cliff Palace in either direction. This was the center of an empire, or perhaps more like a city/state with this canyon as the main capital.

At the end of the ridge that leads out to a point overlooking Cliff Palace sits the Sun Temple, with its tower close to the lip of the canyon. The confluence of canyons is filled with cliff dwellings in every possible alcove. The Park Service has metal signs with the names and locations of each of the ruins, so it is easy to see them. There is one overlook that looks across where two canyons merge with the Cliff Palace sitting in a large alcove. This area where these two canyons come together was the downtown of Mesa Verde with many more cliff dwellings than in any of the other eight canyon complexes that come up from the Mancos River into the mesa. Each canyon has its own cliff dwellings anywhere there was a rock shelter to house the buildings. Then there are all the people who lived on the top of the mesa. Taken together, the cliff dwellings in the canyons and the farming communities on the top made a huge metropolis in a spectacular landscape.

Richard Wetherill estimated there are at least 500 ruins at Mesa Verde, most of "inconsiderable size". He also reports numerous burials marked by low mounds covered with countless fragments of pottery. The archaeologists now estimate there are up to 5,000 archaeological sites at Mesa Verde.

There is only one motel inside the park and it is called Far View Lodge. When we check in we immediately understood why they call it Far View Lodge. It is one of the most spectacular views imaginable. Each room has a large picture window and a balcony. The view looks out across an immense horizon that stretches over the top of the mesa which is cut by a series of canyons, one after another as far as the eye can see.

CLIFF PALACE

Cliff Palace, only eighty miles north of Chaco Canyon, is the largest and most spectacular of all the cliff dwellings. It is one of the thirty-three cliff dwellings in Mesa Verde. One particular area, where Fewkes Canyon converges with Cliff Canyon, is the most fabulous complex of cliff dwellings that, in total, once housed 800 plus people. Cliff Palace looks out over a vast expanse where these two canyons come together. Cliff Palace was under construction from 1190 up until 1280. It was built using stone and wood, mortared with a mixture of mud and ash reinforced with chinks of small stone and pottery shards.

Cliff Palace has 150 rooms and twenty kivas. They believe that it was a residence for twenty-five to thirty households based on the fact that only twenty-five of the rooms have hearths. Those households were further divided into two groups by a solid wall just south of the Chief Speaker's Complex, probably denoting a clan distinction. The entire complex was fully developed and occupied around 1280 CE. I have a large architectural rendering of Cliff Palace from the book *Prelude to Tapestries in Stone: Understanding Cliff Palace Architecture* by Larry V. Nordby. I tape it up on the wall in our room and stand and study it every day while we are coming and going.

Excavations began almost immediately after its discovery in 1888. The Wetherill brothers and their ranch hands started digging into it soon after they discovered the immense ruins tucked under the great arch of the alcove. The first detailed description was done by Baron Gustaf Nordenskiold in his classic book *The Cliff Dwellers of the Mesa Verde*, published in 1893. He had the full cooperation of the Wetherills and hired their ranch hands as a crew and dug as many of the cliff dwellings as he could, taking detailed photographs. His excavations used the latest in scientific techniques including photographs, detailed drawings and architectural rendering of the sites. He carefully inventoried all the finds and preserved them. He collected enough artifacts to fill several railroad cars and when he packed them up to take them to Sweden the local Sheriff arrested him for trying to ship them out of the country. He hired an attorney who determined that, at the time, there was no law forbidding anyone from taking antiquities out of the country. Ironically, this helped lead to the first laws declaring that artifacts could not be taken out of the country.

When Nordenskiold did the first excavations at Cliff Palace he used letters of the alphabet to designate each kiva. This system has stuck and the kivas in Cliff Palace are still called by the letters he gave them. I have looked at the architectural rendering of Cliff Palace and tried to pick out the kivas that served residential purposes as part of a courtyard complex. In a residential kiva the top of the kiva was level to the ground and was incorporated in the courtyard with a suite of rooms that wrap around the courtyard. Kiva U has a complex of nine rooms. Kiva S has a complex that includes thirteen rooms and two towers, one round and one square. Kiva P has six rooms. Kiva M has eleven rooms in a horseshoe design on three sides of the kiva/courtyard. Kiva K has only three rooms in its immediate vicinity but one of these is a multistoried tower. Kiva J has seven rooms, Kiva E has six and Kiva D has six, plus a four-story square tower. Using this layout, I identified eight possible courtyard complexes in Cliff Palace. Each could have provided habitation for an extended family.

Jesse Walter Fewkes (1850 – 1930) was one of the first generation of archeologists working for the Smithsonian Institution and he excavated both Cliff Palace and Spruce Tree House. He surveyed the structures and saved them from decades of looting. He looked for hearths and other signs of habitation and estimated that only 120 people lived in Cliff Palace. He called them caretakers and thought other people would come for special ceremonies. The same is true for another of the major cliff dwellings at Mesa Verde, Spruce Tree House, which has 114 rooms and eight kivas.

He did the first professional excavations in 1909. He began the process of classifying the various rooms, noting the rooms that were plastered on the interior but not on the exterior, implying they were used for storage of grain, and those rooms with projecting timbers and pegs that served as storage for non-food items, like their closets for hanging clothes and bows and quivers.

The Public Works Administration (PWA) funded further excavations and mapping in 1935 and continued to 1943. The primary building materials are stone, mortar, plaster and wood, and were used to create six different room types: living rooms, food storage rooms, non-food storage rooms, mealing/milling rooms, ceremonial rooms and open space courtyards. Fewkes noted that primary habitation rooms had T-shaped doors that open into the courtyards. The granary rooms are easily distinguished by the fact they had to be sealed to keep out rodents. They were plastered on the interior walls and had entrances that could be sealed and need not be directly connected to living rooms. Milling rooms were likewise easily identified by the presence of mortars and stone milling bins. Only three such rooms have been identified at Cliff Palace. The kivas at Cliff Palace tend to have keyhole shapes with six tall pilasters around the outer edge. Cliff Palace has a kiva-to-room ratio of one to four while the average in Mesa Verde is one to twelve, leading Fewkes to believe it was a ceremonial site. The two southernmost kivas are connected by a tunnel. The kivas generally run from sixteen to twenty-four feet across. The open spaces, which are often the rooftops of the kivas, have multiple functions: first as social gathering spaces, next for dance or ceremonial purposes, and finally as a work space to process agricultural products or manufacture tools or weapons.

The opening in the cliff face where Cliff Palace sits is 324 feet wide, 89 feet deep and 59 feet high. Within this enclosure there are two circular towers and a four-story square tower. These are among the most distinctive architectural features in Cliff Palace. The four-story square tower still has a pictogram painted on the interior wall about three stories up. It is a red and white panel with a jagged design pattern still seen on Pueblo blankets.

Cliff Palace was not a simple residential complex; it was a special building in a special location. It stands in the middle of a complex of structures with the Sun Temple on the mesa top just opposite it. There is an array of other buildings up and down the canyon in both directions. The amount of work required to build it could not have been mustered without a hierarchic power structure that was able to command the labor force which had to be organized into masons, stone cutters, mortar makers and people to carry the immense amounts of rock, sand, clay and water needed to build it. The building itself was an architectural and engineering feat that required an educated class of design engineers with special training and the ability to command a substantial labor force.

We were determined to visit all the cliff dwellings that were open to the public and Cliff Palace was first on the list. You have to buy tickets at the visitor's center and we got our tickets first thing on arriving in the park. Cliff Palace is one of the most picturesque sites in the park and its symmetry and architecture make it famous around the world. We bought tickets for two visits during our time in the park since they only allow you an hour at the site. We were delighted to have a ranger who was a Native American and he gave one of the best descriptions of the culture we heard during our stay. Our next ranger experience at Cliff Palace was just the opposite. That's how it goes with the rangers.

The Native American ranger was very polite and answered everyone's questions in detail. He walked us into the site and along the prearranged trail that goes in front of the main buildings. Cliff Palace has been undergoing a lot of restoration for the past few years and they only open it for a few months of the year. The rest of the year they are working to stabilize some of the walls and buildings. Consequently, they only allow us to walk along a trail in front of the site and don't allow us to see inside the village except briefly at one end. At the end of the trail in front of the buildings the ranger let us stick our heads in a window and peer up into one of the towers. By looking directly up into the tower it is possible to see the pictogram that is still visible three stories up on the wall. It is painted on a batch of plaster that has survived the ravages of time for all these years. I was shooting pictures and the time we were allowed at the site passed very quickly so I was glad we had another ticket for a second visit later in the week.

BALCONY HOUSE

Balcony House was next on the list. Getting to Balcony House requires climbing a series of ladders, the tallest thirty-eight feet tall. Consequently, the Park Rangers don't allow anyone to visit Balcony House unaccompanied.

They schedule daily tours and sell tickets at the Visitor's Center. We meet our group at 9:30 AM and got a stern lecture from a female ranger warning us that, not only are there multiple ladders to climb, but we also have to crawl on our hands and knees through a very narrow tunnel. She reiterated that if anyone has fear of heights or is claustrophobic they better not go on this trek. She asks if anyone has a fear of heights and a half-dozen hands go up. About the same number raise their hands when she asked about the fear of closed spaces. But no one backs out and we head down a paved trail that takes us over the rim of the mesa and along a sheer cliff face. When we arrive at the first ladder, the guide says this is the point of no return. The ladder is made from three long tree trunks as uprights with rungs made from smaller tree branches that are bolted into the uprights. It is made for two people to climb at once and we start up it in pairs following closely one after the other.

I neglected to raise my hand when the ranger asked for a show of hands of people who have a fear of heights. However, when a ladder gets much taller than eight feet I begin to feel uncomfortable and looking up a thirty-eight foot ladder is a bit daunting. Going up the ladder I go into a state of one-pointed awareness. I focus on the rung in front of me and keep focused on it until I step up to the next rung, where I remind myself not to look down and stay focused on the rung of the ladder in front of me, one at a time. A part of my brain knows full well what I would see if I looked down. The ladder is sitting on a narrow ledge and the sheer canyon walls go straight down 400 feet. That part of my brain was reminding me that I was clinging to a ladder with nothing between me and the ground below. But I kept my attention focused on the next rung and one by one I made it to the top and stepped off on a ledge with a substantial metal fence separating me from the lip of the canyon. I repent my petty fears but it was a relief to get on the path which comes down to a small opening where we have to squeeze through. When we emerge we are in Balcony House and see immediately how it got its name. All the buildings in front of us have second-floor balconies. These are narrow affairs, about two feet wide laid on vigas that extend out with typical adobe style flooring. The whole site has two main complexes, each with a group of rooms and kivas.

Balcony House is the best preserved of all the ruins in Mesa Verde and the guide tells us very little restoration has been done. However, it is obvious that many of the rooms were built to extend up to the ceiling and have lost their top floors which have fallen into rubble. We can clearly see the outline on the roof where the walls terminated against the ceiling. In the main plaza of the first group of buildings we can see into several of the rooms. One of them still has the ceiling intact. I notice a small petroglyph and ask about it and she says that they have known it is there but I am the first tourist to notice it. She leads us up some ancient steps cut into the bedrock of the stone floor and along a path behind the first group of structures. Then we come out into the next smaller plaza, which has two kivas. The effort to build the kivas had to be immense. This section has twenty first-floor rooms and two kivas, probably housing two families.

At the far end of the plaza is a narrow cramped tunnel barely passable on your hands and knees. It is the only way out and would be a very effective defensive mechanism as only one person at a time can get through. It is about fifteen feet long and with light from both ends it is never quite dark in the tunnel. Once you get through there is another series of two shorter ladders and then we are back on the mesa top. While it is relatively simple to get into the site from the top of the mesa it would be a long climb to get into it from the floor of the canyon. Yet the ranger reported that there is an ancient path up the sheer cliff face. It is made of hand-holds which are little more than fist-sized holes cut into the stone so you can reach from one to the next to climb up the rock face. These were cut into the cliff face all the way up to the Balcony House. It is intriguing to imagine the people climbing up the sheer cliff face. From a distance the climbers would look like spiders climbing up the wall of the canyon. The ranger said they would carry everything they needed: firewood, water, food and game, whatever they required for their daily lives. They would strap it on their back and scurry up the cliff face to bring home their supplies from the floor of the canyon.

SPRUCE TREE HOUSE

Our next destination is Spruce Tree House. It requires no guide and is open to the public. It is only a short walk down the hill past the museum and visitor's center. It is one of the larger cliff dwellings at Mesa Verde with 114 rooms and eight kivas. When we arrive our guide from Balcony House is there, along with another park ranger watching over the large crowds that gather there. There must be sixty people milling around taking photos. I ask her if Richard Wetherill's initials are visible anywhere and she points them out. They are scratched onto the exterior wall of one of the rooms. I also see the numbering mark that Nordenskiold left by one of the kivas. I am disappointed to learn that only half the site is open. Some rocks fell from the ceiling in the other half after water seeping down weakened the roof and they closed this section for fear more rock would fall.

I see several T-shaped doorways and two reconstructed kivas, one open to the public. Many of the buildings still extend to the roof and it is a marvel of ancient architecture how they fit the buildings so snugly into the space. I want to see inside the reconstructed kiva and climb down the ladder. Looking down it appears quite dark but once inside the ambient light from the ladder hole illuminates the entire space. I take a few pictures and stand there watching, witnessing the people as they come and go, up and down the ladder. I am surprised that no one stays more than a minute or two before disappearing back up the ladder. The space feels warm and inviting. I imagine a small fire burning in the hearth and a family gathered around telling stories once the sun has gone down.

When I come out of the kiva I ask the ranger about petroglyphs and she shows me how to poke my head into one of the rooms. I can see turkey tracks carved in the stone and on a side wall there is a footprint of an infant pressed into the adobe plaster. She shows me a couple of places where painted designs are faintly visible on the walls. The place stirs my curiosity. Was it strictly a residential structure or was it a palace for a ruling elite or a ceremonial center with a small staff of priests who maintained a ceremonial calendar? I don't think there is a definitive answer. Fewkes thought Cliff Palace was a ceremonial center but the ratio of kivas to rooms makes me think this is a residential village. I know they were raising turkeys here for food and feathers because the early excavations found the evidence. I wanted to wander into the back rooms and explore the full area but the watchful eyes of the rangers restrained me, so I had to resort to studying the surveys done by Fewkes to see behind the walls. I take the kivas to be residential and the T-doors to be entrances into rooms with hearths. But the questions plague me: why did they build two- and three-story towers? When I compare the rooms in the cliff dwellings to the rooms in the great houses they are bigger in the cliff dwellings than in the great houses. Here all the rooms seem functional and have doors, and I can see each kiva has a group of rooms associated with it. Yet, a nagging doubt remains. The life of these people was ruled by a strict calendar of religious events, festivals and ceremonies. If this assumption has any truth to it, where did they go for these events? Did the local farming community gather under the cliffs for ceremony or did they, along with the people in the cliff dwelling, all go to the Sun Temple? Were certain of the cliff dwellings set aside for ceremonies and others strictly residential?

There are numerous places on the mesa where farming communities had small villages. Were the farmers a distinct class apart from the people living in the cliff dwellings? Were the cliff dwellings only for the elites while the farmers lived either on the mesa top or on the floor of the canyons?

PETROGLYPH POINT

There is a trail that leads from Spruce Tree House out to the end of the mesa where five canyons converge. There is a famous petroglyph panel at the end of the ridge. It is a two-and-a-half mile walk along a path that runs below the rim of the mesa along the wall of the canyon. It is a relatively easy walk but the trail is by no means smooth. It is unpaved and occasionally is a little rough but it is full of rewarding vistas across the canyon. The park service has produced a trail guide and from time to time we run into a numbered trail marker and stop to read the information they provide in the brochure. The path winds in and out of smaller side canyons and occasionally narrows and widens, depending on the terrain. It is a beautiful walk and we revel in the delights of seeing it. There was no one else on the trail as far as we could tell. We were on a narrow trail running alongside a steep canyon wall and opposite us, across the deep chasm of the canyon, we can see the rock faces, some of them over 400 feet tall with rubble at their bases. We can tell when we are getting near the end because we can see other canyons coming into the canyon we have been following and, as we near the end of the ridge, we come upon the petroglyph panel. From here we can see five canyons converging into one, like fingers joining in the palm of your hand. While we are sitting there studying the drawings the sound of a flute drifts over our heads with the breeze. It was clear as a bell and as beautiful as any recording by a professional Native American flute player. We looked for the source but didn't see anyone, hadn't seen anyone the whole time. Whoever it was did a beautiful job and we were mesmerized and touched at the remarkable coincidence of being there while someone unknown and unseen serenaded us.

The park service brochure told the story of two Hopi elders who had come to the panel and interpreted it as a map showing the migration of the people as they moved toward Mesa Verde. Some of the symbols were clan symbols showing how various clans had stopped off at different points along the route. Other images were said to be kachinas but this befuddled me since I thought the kachinas didn't start until after the breakup of Chaco and Mesa Verde and were a new cultural impulse that began after the people moved to the Rio Grande valley. The Hopi elders said the petroglyphs were places of pilgrimage. They called them sacred, hallowed ground where visions were sought and the spirit of the stone was made visible. They said people from different tribes were able to understand the language of the images. They were often located at the junction of trails and in these places even bitter enemies had to maintain their peace. The panels depicting spirals, concentric circles or eyes were observation points where markers on the distant horizon or displays of shadow and light created cosmographic seasonal clocks indicating the solstices and equinoxes. They were aesthetic inscriptions on canvases of stone, telling the story of their people.

SUN TEMPLE

The Sun Temple sits on the lip of the mesa opposite Cliff Palace. The point of the ridge where the Sun Temple stands affords a great view of Cliff Palace directly across the canyon. In all the literature, which is very limited, they say the excavations of the buildings in the Sun Temple found no roof beams. This led to the idea that the building was never finished. It is as likely that they never intended to put a roof on the structure. The building could have been an observatory open to the sky, where they observed the movement of the sun, moon and stars. It is a very special building and they put a tremendous amount of labor into its construction. It is unique in many ways. It was built out of large uniformly-shaped rocks and each rock is pecked so the outer surface is dimpled. It was excavated by Jesse Fewkes, who declared that no household goods were recovered from the site and the building was made for worship. It is a large D-shaped building with over one thousand running feet of stone walls. The walls are over four feet thick and are double-coursed with rubble fill between the inner and outer walls. There are the ruins of a tower just a few feet outside the main building. It is one of the sixty towers found at Mesa Verde. Unfortunately, little remains of the tower except the foundation and the first few courses of stonework.

The Sun Temple has a large inner courtyard with two round rooms, like towers, about eight feet tall, one on the east, one on the west. The main entrance to the whole complex is on the south wall. All around the exterior of the building are fourteen, narrow interconnected chambers which are four-feet wide and twelve to fifteen feet long. Each one has a doorway into the next chamber so each chamber is connected to the next all the way around the building. The building is completely closed to the public so the best we can do is walk around the outside, but that is impressive enough. In the back of the building, on the north side, there are some exposed boulders against the exterior back wall and we climb up on them and look down into the courtyard and see the remains of the two towers. Each of the towers has a narrow entrance on the south side.

One of the strangest features of the building is on the southwest corner where there is a niche in the outside wall. Inside the niche is a flat stone with a series of ruts that radiate out like rays from the center. There is speculation that it was some kind of sundial. There is an indentation in the center where they think a stick was placed. The stick would cast a shadow that moved around to mark time as the shadow moved. However, the little hole in the center is very shallow and doesn't appear deep enough to hold a stick upright. It is very mysterious. It was elaborately designed and placed dramatically in the architecture of the building. Its function is still undiscovered. Frank Waters said that it was a grooved dial that was used to measure the progress of the sun on the southern horizon and that when the shadow of the sun reached certain of the grooves it marked the time for certain rituals. He said these rituals required the preparation of herbs and other medicinal plants. He thought the fourteen chambers around the edge of the main building were used in the preparations needed for these rituals.

While very little is known about cliff dwelling religious practices, one interesting remnant has survived about the rituals and ceremonies conducted at the Sun Temple. According to Frank Waters [53] the Navajo have preserved a fire ritual that was passed down to them by the people who lived at Mesa Verde. Mesa Verde was abandoned by the year 1300 and the exact location where the inhabitants fled is still a mystery, although it appears that the Hopi and the Zuni are related to the Mesa Verde people. How the Navaho learned the ritual is a separate mystery. The Navajo were not in the area until several centuries after Mesa Verde and Chaco had been abandoned. Yet they may have found a band of descendants from Mesa Verde who knew the fire ceremonies and adopted them. The same ritual described to Frank Waters by the Navaho has also been described by Cushing as part of Zuni culture.

Both cultures tell the story that at a certain time of the year everyone would extinguish their household fire and sweep out the ashes. Then the priest would go through elaborate rituals to start a new fire. As part of this ritual the priest had to find a cottonwood tree that had been struck by lightning. The priest would make offerings to the tree and then construct a fire stick consisting of a straight stick, like a long pencil, and a flat base. The point of the stick was inserted in a small hole in a flat base where the drill stick could fit. This fire starting device was the Indian version of a match. The stick was twirled between both hands until the friction between the two pieces of wood heated up enough to smolder. Then they used dried bark as tinder to start the flames. During the process of starting the fire certain songs were sung and these were passed down to the Navajo singers and now, even today, as they start a new fire they sing these songs.

Waters indicates that the sun was considered the "father of all life". It was the source of all fire. It was represented in the light that came from the sun, and from the lightning that carried fire with it to the earth and from the flint rocks which held fire so that when they were struck together fire was released. In the Navajo fire ceremony, which Waters claims was derived from the ceremonies conducted at the Sun Temple, they would have a young man on the east side, a young woman on the west, an elderly man in the south and an older woman on the north. As the priest twirled the fire drill the people would sing,

The fire of darkness appears

Long life fire appears

Moon fire appears

Darkness fire appears

Dawn fire appears

Sun fire appears

Long life fire appears

Happiness fire appears

Sunlight fire appears [54]

When the fire began to smolder, cedar bark was fed from the east, oak bark from the south, pinon from the west and scrub oak from the north. When these ignited, wood from the lightning-struck cottonwood was used to feed the flame. As the flames appeared,they would sing,

To the fire of Emergence Elders he added fuel

To the fire of Emergence Young Men he added fuel

To the fire of Emergence Young Women she added fuel

To the fire of Emergence Children they added fuel

Now to the fire of Tree Woman, of trees of all kind,

To this they added fuel

To the fire of long life of happiness they added fuel

Nicely they added fuel [55]

Once the fire was going everyone in the community would come and take some of the fire and go to their hearth and restart their own fire. The ethnologist who recorded and translated these songs, Father Berard Haile, said the Sun Temple was called the House of Flint or the Flint Corral. He said the western tower was associated with the female aspects of the Flint Way and the eastern tower was the male Shooting Way. He says there are fourteen groups of respondents in the ceremony and that the fourteen chambers of the Sun Temple were associated with these groups. Each group was responsible for manufacturing ritual flints and other preparations needed for the ceremony. In the oldest myths, the female earth was impregnated by the masculine force of the sun and from this all life came forth on the surface of the earth. The Temple was the vessel that held the enactment of these ancient legends. In the Navajo ceremonies, they used flint arrowheads to create a circle around the place where the new fire is kindled.

LONG HOUSE

We were up early to experience the sunrise over the mesa; then, we were off to Long House. It is only a twelve mile drive but it takes forty-five minutes to get to Long House at the end of the mesa. This drive is one of the most spectacular anywhere in the country. The twelve miles include views off the lip of the mesa and across the Montezuma Plains to the snowcapped mountains in the distance. There are sheer rock walls below us at every curve. In other spots, the ridge gets very narrow and there is a steep drop-off on either side. There is not a straight quarter-mile from the beginning of the road to the end. The road goes across Wetherill Mesa and comes out along the edge of Rock Canyon and leads to a parking lot and a building where locals sell soft drinks and snacks. A group of about thirty people gather for this tour. We proceed down a paved path for a mile through a forest of burnt trees, scorched from one of the many forest fires that have ravaged the area. Their trunks look skeletal and gloomy on the landscape, but this burnt world soon passes and we enter a living forest of juniper and cedar. At one point we walk by a gnarled juniper tree, its bark convoluted with whirling patterns, and the ranger says it is 1300 years old. We come to a gate and down steps leading to a paved walk that goes over the lip of the canyon and along a winding path around the end of a ridge. At the end of the ridge Long House comes into view. It fills a huge alcove set back in the main canyon. One of the first sites we come to is a small kiva. I notice that it is constructed with carefully-crafted stone blocks and that each block is dimpled like the stones used to build the Sun Temple. This must have been a special building for them to go to so much trouble in its construction. Another unusual feature is that it has dual wall construction with rubble fill between the two walls. This is the same construction technique we saw at the Sun Temple but nowhere else on Mesa Verde.

The entire complex under the long alcove has fifty rooms, of which fifteen are round chambers, some subterranean kivas and some round towers. One of the highlights of Long House is that we get to go into the ruins and walk through the village. In many of the ruins we have to look from a vantage point across the canyon or be content to walk in front of the village without going through the inner streets and plazas. The ranger supervises while we climb a ladder and make our way along a designated trail to the back of the village. This is the deepest point under the alcove where the roof meets the floor. At one spot in the back there is moss growing and then we see a small seep with a trickle of water that comes out into a small basin that is surrounded with dark green moss. Along with the main basin that collects the water they had hollowed out a series of smaller collecting pools where they could dip out water. From the back of the village we can see that several of the buildings still have intact roofs and one of them has a ladder we can climb and get a better view of the roof. However, they won't let us get off the ladder to enter any of the upper-story rooms.

Another distinctive feature of Long House is the main plaza. It sits on the ground level in the center of the village and has stone walls on two sides and the sheer rock face as the back wall. The plaza has two large footdrums and another square stone box right in the center of the plaza. The ranger mentions that the stone box sits directly beneath where water falls from the top lip of the canyon, and thus functioned as a cistern.

The village actually has two levels with another group of buildings in a smaller alcove high above the floor of the main village. There are a series of small rooms which are presumably for storage since there isn't enough room to stand up in them. It was investigated by Gustaf Nordenskiold, who spent two days constructing a scaffold that was little more than a tall tree trunk with stubs of some limbs left on for handholds. He described climbing up there as a risk to life and limb, and when he went to the top he found very little for his trouble. Richard Wetherill had already been there and "collected" the artifacts that were laying in plain view on the floors of the rooms. Nordenskiold examined the structure and found a series of small windows which he assumed were for defense so archers could rain down arrows on attackers. This idea no longer resonates and now they call them granaries and think the upper stories of the main buildings probably reached up high enough to give easy access to the upper ledges. There are no petroglyph panels at the site but there are a few handprints and a couple of prayer sticks wedged into the cliff.

STEP HOUSE

Step House and Long House share the same parking lot. It has two clearly-marked trails, one to Step House and one to Long House. We follow the trail to Step House, where we find a ranger watching over an impressive cliff dwelling under a roof of stone in a canyon wall. The ranger points to some pictograms on the high ceilings, where we see several four-pointed stars. We wondered if it was some sort of star map. It is a wonder to behold since it would have required elaborate scaffolding to get to the place where they were painted on the ceiling. Compared to Cliff Palace and Spruce Tree it is much smaller, only about ten rooms with two kivas. We explored as much as possible before returning to the parking lot.

THE FIRE TEMPLE

The Fire Temple is the last site at the head of Fewkes Canyon and I had seen a reference to it having a plaza much like the one at Long House. There is no tourist access to the Fire Temple. It is located on the canyon floor and tucked under an overhanging ledge, but it is clearly visible from one of the pullovers on the lip of the canyon. Sure enough, looking down on it from the canyon top it was easy to see the plaza with the two footdrums with a large fire pit between them with stone walls on two sides and in the back. Even from across the canyon, we can see the back wall of the plaza still has a visible coat of white plaster. There are faint murals visible on the plaster.

FARVIEW

Just past Far View Lodge heading toward the Archaeological Museum is a pull-off for the Far View Community. It consists of a trail that goes by six mesa top sites, five pueblos and Mummy Lake. This community started around 900 CE and was developed until the whole place was abandoned about 1300. The archaeologists have located fifty different villages, all within a radius of a mile of this site. With its many villages and the cliff dwellings in the gorges, this area was densely populated. That immediately raises the issue: what was the difference between the people living on the top of the mesa and those living in the cliff dwellings in the gorges? And why go to all the trouble of carrying the building materials up and down the sheer cliffs when you could be living on the mesa top with much easier access to building materials along with food, water and fuel?

The first structure is called Far View House, then comes Pipe Shrine House, followed by Coyote Village, Far View Tower, and Megalithic House. Far View House is beautifully constructed with dimpled stones. There is a spiral design on a prominent stone on one side. It is obviously a special place. It has a commanding view; we can see a line of canyons cutting across the mesa and off in the distance Ute Mountain stands tall. When Jesse Fewkes excavated the site in 1916 he named it Far View in honor of the expansive vista. The structure was two stories tall and, like most of the cliff dwellings, the tree ring dating shows it was built and occupied from 1000 to 1300 CE. There were 40 rooms on the first floor and more on the second floor but it is impossible to tell exactly how many. There were five kivas, four built into the main structure and one just outside in the main plaza. The main kiva in the building is larger than any of the others. In one of the kivas they found twenty layers of plaster. If the site was occupied for 200 years that means they were refreshing the plaster and the murals every decade. Far View House must have been for the elites or for ceremonies as well as residential purposes since it was built with dimpled stone blocks and has some of the finest stonework.

The next building, about the same size, is named Pipe Shrine House. It sits in sight of Far View House. It has four main residential structures, each with multiple rooms. It is made of stone but the stonework is not as nice as Far View House. A few hundred feet away is the third site, named Far View Tower. It consists of a two-story tower in a complex with three kivas and sixteen rooms. The rooms are all single-wall construction but the tower has double walls.

The next site, Megalithic House, is protected by a metal roof. We enter and look around. There is only one complex of rooms and a kiva, but the kiva has a tunnel that connects it to one of the other rooms. One of the walls in Megalithic House has some large stones built into the first run of stonework, hence its name. Fewkes reported that he found the same kind of "Cyclopean walls" in other sites around Mesa Verde. This site has nine rooms and the kiva. This structure is a classic clan or family unit in one building.

It is a remarkable gathering of small villages or clan structures, all within easy walk of one another. I am surprised that here at Mesa Verde, with cliff dwellings in so many canyons, we find these village-type structures. The presumption is that these were farming communities living on top of the mesa to watch over the crops.

The last in the line is called Coyote House. When we walked up to the site there were four men in ranger suits working. We watched them putting new mortar in one of the kiva walls. One of them invites us to enter the site and we did. One room has a distinctive feature with five mealing bins lined up, one beside the other. It also has a round tower that anchors one corner of the site. When they finished and everyone climbed out of the kiva I asked if any of them were archaeologists. A tall man, lean and deeply tanned with a white beard, said he was an archaeologist. I asked, "One of the big questions I have is about the difference between the cliff dwellings and the great houses. Are the cliff dwellings just great houses built under the alcoves in the canyons or do they represent a totally different culture?"

He thought for a moment and said, "Great houses are typically multistoried structures but really there isn't much difference. Maybe a difference in style of stonework or masonry. But I would have to say that cliff dwellings are not just great houses built in an alcove."

I continued with my questions. "How do you compare the people from Mesa Verde with the culture at Chaco?"

"It's hard to say, you know we can look at the different kinds of stonework that they used at Chaco and compare it to here, or we can look at pottery styles and see if they are distinct, or we can look at the flint knapping techniques but the problem is we can find examples of Chaco-style stonework here at Mesa Verde, both here at Far View and in the cliff dwellings, and we can find different styles of pottery design that show up here but then they show up at some of the Chaco outliers and the same for the flint points. So there is no good answer."

One of the kivas at this site has very unusual timbers in sets of two that stretch between the pilasters so I ask, "Do you have any idea about why they have those timbers in that kiva, I've never seen that anywhere else?"

"It is really unique. I haven't seen it anywhere else either. We are just guessing but it could have been for drying meat or hides, or for hanging ceremonial garb."

"We have been exploring the various cliff dwellings in the park and it is amazing to see these structures here at Far View since they obviously aren't cliff dwellings but they must be part of the Mesa Verde cliff dwellers' culture?"

"Yes, it is assumed that these were agricultural communities growing corn on top of the mesa."

"What is the difference between the people in these dwellings and those living in the cliff dwellings? Were the cliff houses for elites or only for ceremonies where only priests and elites could live?"

"That's hard to say, it is one of the big questions here at Mesa Verde and we still don't know the answer but some people believe that the people in at least some of the cliff dwellings were ritualists and in a different class than the people on the mesa top. But there are places here on the mesa top that could easily be designated as ceremonial sites, so it is still up in the air."

The rest of the crew had gathered up the tools and put the trowels and equipment into a big bucket and it looked like they were ready to call it a day. I could see these guys were ready to take off so I asked one last question. "Well what is there here at this site that is special? Are there things we should notice here that don't show up at other sites?"

"Well the timbers between the pilasters in that kiva are the most special thing here, plus the series of mealing bins that are very well preserved; otherwise it is all pretty much standard with the rest of the buildings in this area."

"Well thanks for spending a few minutes with me."

With that they headed back the path. Susan and I stayed a while longer walking through all the rooms and enjoying having the site to ourselves. Then we followed our guidebook and walked over to Mummy Pond. It is a beautiful site which was a water catchment area. It is quite large and has thick stone walls that appear perfectly round. On one side there is a double wall and the stonework is exquisite, with about ten feet between the two layers of walls and the area between the two walls filled with dirt. It would have made a substantial dam to hold the water in the pond. On one side of the circle is a beautifully built entrance designed to catch the runoff from the rainwater. The stonework reminds me of some of the great Inca stonework we had seen in Peru. The stones are uniform and are carefully cut and laid up like blockwork and even today have hardly deteriorated. The entrance is a spillway that conducts the rainwater from the mesa top into runoff channels that empty into the large pond. I read that it held water for hundreds of years after its construction and I could easily believe it. There are other areas that are terraced to hold back the water and save the soil that would have been lost in the runoff. These check dams were used to build up agricultural areas, which would have not have been feasible otherwise. It required up to 350 pounds of corn to sustain each person for a year. No matter how you figure it, it would require many acres under cultivation to meet the needs of all the people living in Mesa Verde.

RANGERS

There are rangers stationed at all the sites to make sure the hordes of tourists don't damage the sites or get into restricted areas. We had some interesting rangers. The young Pueblo Indian had the most enlightened point of view about the sites and presented the information from a Native American perspective. They give the rangers some training but they move them around from site to site and then from one National Park to another. I wanted to question the rangers in detail but quickly came to the realization that their information was very limited and that anyone who took the trouble to read a few books about the sites knew as much as the rangers. However, the rangers were, for the most part, very nice and were quite willing to share everything they knew. However, we did come across one exception to this rule.

One morning we got up early and drove out to Cliff Palace for one more visit. It is exciting to drive around the edge of the canyons to the parking lot and walk down to the overlook where the tour begins. It is a short walk from the parking lot to the overlook and even though we are fifteen minutes early there is a crowd gathering. They let 40 people go on each tour and in the next few minutes the place fills up and a female ranger appears. When the clock was straight up on the hour she called us together for the ranger speech. She introduces herself as Lucille and then says that "they" always insisted that she give everyone a warning.

"So listen up," she says, "we are going to be out in the hot sun and we are going to be hiking up and down some steep trails and have a long way to go to get down there and then a long way back, so if any of you people have a bad heart you better not be out here. They gave me some CPR training." Then she pauses, "But I have forgotten most of it and sure don't want to try to use it so I don't want anybody having a heart attack or getting heat stroke. So just turn around and go back if you don't think you can make it. Don't forget, you've been warned."

That said, she moved on, "Now I'm from the Appalachian Mountains in East Tennessee, what people call the Bible Belt, and if you have any questions about the Great Smoky Mountains I can probably give you a good answer. They have been training me here and I can tell you this site was built 12,000 years ago."

I was shocked at such a blatant error, but also amused. She was obviously confused; these ruins were built during the 1200s, but I didn't raise my voice. However, someone a bit bolder spoke up and said, "Don't you mean in the 1200s?"

"Oh yeah dude, that's right, that's what I meant to say, so when I say 12,000 I want all you people to understand that means 1200 not 12,000." I smiled; well at least she would fess up and correct herself.

Then we started down the path. As we walked along I told her Susan and I are from Tennessee and talked to her about the Smoky Mountains. It is a beautiful morning, hot as blazes with a clear blue sky overhead. It didn't take long before the site came into view. I stop to take pictures and then we all gather on the walkway at the entrance to the site. Lucille starts in again, "We don't know much about this place or these people but we do know the women were in charge. That's right all you men, listen up here. The women definitely ran the show, if any of you guys act up today you are in the wrong place. Back when the Indians lived here all a woman had to do was take your stuff and throw it out the door and you were divorced. How do like that?" She thought for a minute and went on, "You might be able to take a couple of tools but that's it and then you had to go back to your Momma's house and see if you could live there. When a couple got hitched, the man had to move into the wife's house and if she got tired of him he was out, just like that."

As we walked along the front of the site I found myself next to Lucille so I said, "I want to take pictures of a part of the village called The Chief Speakers Complex, can you identify that building?"

"Do you really want to know?" she tossed it back to me.

"I want to get pictures of it from several angles, so I suppose so."

"Well listen dude that is part of my presentation but it doesn't come till later so I don't want to give it away just yet."

I was a bit surprised but pushed on. We walked from one end of the village to the other. She had us stop at one of the kivas and then told us that the sipapu, the small hole at the center of the kiva, was the same thing as a cross to the Christians. She was talking about an excavation that had taken place and she kept referring to the "refugee" piles where the archaeologists were digging. At the end of the walkway I could see a place a little further up the path that I thought would give me good light, so I went up there to take a few more shots. The group was below me, about 40 or 50 feet away, and I wasn't paying any attention to them.

However, Lucille was down there telling the group. "There's this dude who wanted to know about the Chief Speaker's Complex and now he isn't here." She spotted me and called out, "Hey dude, hey dude." My concentration was elsewhere and I didn't hear her. Lucille looked around, "Who owns that dude?" Now Susan wasn't willing to claim ownership since we don't think of each other as possessions, but when Lucille went on about it Susan finally told her, "His name is Michael."

So Lucille yells out, "Hey dude, hey Michael."

Hearing my name brought me out of my reverie and I put the camera down and looked down at the group. Lucille yelled, "Hey dude, come down here, you want to hear this part." I waved and walked down the path to join the group.

She started in, "Now this is the best place to see the Chief Speaker's complex. Look over there where you see those windows that look like the eyes and nose of a face and that is it." It is a complex of rooms that has a round tower and a square tower with a plaza at their base and more rooms than anywhere else in the village. And from here there are three windows that are positioned about right to look like the eyes and nose of a face.

One of the people in the group asked, "Where did people go to the bathroom? Did they have bathrooms in the village or outhouses or what?"

"Well what do you think they did dude?" She looked at the guy who asked the question.

"Hum, I don't know maybe they just walked over to the edge and did it off the edge."

"Just imagine" she said, "just think about that." And she went over to the edge of the walkway and stuck her butt out over the edge and squatted down a bit. "Now can you imagine those Indians looking this like, I don't think so dude."

This was her way of dealing with questions. She would toss it back to the group and ask if anybody knew the answer. There were always a couple of people willing to venture a guess and she would make fun of their answers. That seemed to take care of that issue and we could see the next tour group entering the other end of the village. When Lucille saw them she announced, "Time to go people. Now listen up everybody, I know lots of stuff about this place but I don't want to tell. They told us all about it but said we shouldn't tell all the secret stuff but there is stuff you could see from right here that I'm not going to show you." I assumed she was talking about a pictogram that is in one of the buildings, but who knows. Lucille announced we should all head back to the parking lot. It was the strangest, funniest ranger experience of the trip. Lucille was a ranger who gave away no secrets.

The next morning it was time to head back to Tennessee. I wanted to stop at the Research Library in the Visitors Center to look at any archaeological reports about the Sun Temple. It was the most intriguing of the sites and I wanted to study it in more detail. But the library was not open to the public. So that was a lost cause and we pressed on. Our route took us by Monument

Valley and we took the eight-mile drive through this park. It is another spectacular drive through sheer stone monuments with exposed rock faces on
mesas and buttes. There are numerous pinnacles and colored hillsides with
bands of red and black and white, monuments to the forces of nature.

Then it was back to Albuquerque and the flight to Nashville. On the plane
I was looking down on America from a great height with an eye for another
kind of seeing, watching through time, hoping to find that still center of
human nature, where I am able to observe all the manifestations of human
nature, to study the ancients and their culture and myself in mine, and feel
that ephemeral spark of life, a flame, a light to carry on.

CONCLUSIONS

The earliest habitation sites in the San Juan plateau were pit houses. They were semi-subterranean one-room structures built with a circular design, inset about four to six feet in the ground, with raised walls and a dirt-covered roof. Pit houses marked the transition from nomadic hunter-gatherer bands to settled agricultural settlements. From 200 CE up to 900 CE pit house communities began to develop. Eventually, they began to add aboveground rooms for additional storage, with the pit house serving as the nighttime residence. In the earlier phases the roof was raised above ground level, but as the courtyard complex developed, the roof was lowered to ground level to add to the courtyard. Family or perhaps clans began to occupy contiguous units rather than living in scattered site pit houses. Over time the pit house evolved into the kiva, which was residential rather than ceremonial. At first, some archaeologists assumed that kivas were strictly ceremonial and served as a communal religious structure where people could come together for ritual and ceremony. Now, however, in light of the idea of the kiva evolving from the pit house, as well as ethnographic and historical information that shows people sleeping in the kivas as part of their residences, the tide has shifted.

Each of the modern pueblos has several kivas aligned with the clan structure of the village. These kivas are strictly ceremonial. Much of the preparation for the dances takes place in the kivas and dancers do all-night ceremonies in the kivas. As these subterranean chambers changed from residential pit houses to their current ceremonial usage, they evolved from a small one-room chamber for sleeping and staying warm into rooms up to sixty feet across where large groups of people could come together to dance and celebrate. As great houses and cliff dwellings developed, kivas were built for strictly ceremonial functions. Smaller kivas retained their residential function when they were associated with a block of rooms that served as the household of a family unit.

The first contact between the Spanish and the pueblo people marked the end of the prehistoric period and the beginning of the historical era in the Southwest. The Spanish kept detailed records of their invasion forces, and after Coronado's disappointing entrada in 1540 it wasn't until 1581 that the Spanish recorded their next expedition into this region. This force was led by Fray Augustine Rodriguez. His chronicler, a man named Gallegos, wrote that they spent most of their time exploring along the Rio Grande and visited 57 pueblos This expedition was the first to observe the use of prayer sticks and to hear about the Snake Dance. They described the pueblos as filled with food and thought the pottery and weaving to be better than in Spain. During their entrada, the Spanish demanded food from all the pueblos. They soon encountered hostilities and by January 1582 made a hasty retreat to Mexico, leaving three priests behind.

The entrada had no sooner left the pueblos than the three priests were killed by the Indians. The Spaniards, recognizing the dangers, and the opportunities, organized another entrada as a rescue party under the leadership of Don Antonio de Espejo and Fray Bernardino Beltran. They set out in November 1582 with fourteen men in armor, one priest, a herd of horses and thirty Indian warriors. Espejo wrote an account estimating the population along the Rio Grande to be around 12,000. [56] The Indian's first response to this entrada was hospitality but, once they came to understand the mission of the Spanish, their cooperation turned to hostility. The Spanish were there to terrorize and enslave the Indians. When Espejo's continuing demands for food and supplies, and his greed for silver and turquoise, were refused he rounded up thirty Indians, forced them into a kiva and burned them alive.

He described kivas being used as living quarters, especially in the winter when they could be heated with a small fire. The chronicles describe, "houses two, three or four stories high, each house being partitioned into a number of rooms; and in many of the houses there are estufas for the winter weather. In the pueblos each plaza has two estufas, which are houses built underground, well sheltered and tightly closed with benches inside to sit on...some of the natives are clad in cotton blankets, buffalo hides, or dressed chamois skins. The women have cotton skirts, often embroidered with colored thread, and over the shoulders a blanket like that worn by the Mexican Indians." [57] Espejo estimated the population at Zia to be about 4,000 men and boys and the pueblo to have up to 1,000 houses. He visited both Hopi and Zuni and explored for silver. He found little in the way of gold or silver and by the end of 1583 was back in Mexico. He died two years later in route to Spain, where he hoped to get permission to establish a colony along the Rio Grande.

The next entrada arrived in 1590 and was led by Gaspar Castaneda Sosa, who was accompanied by 170 colonists. The chronicle of this entrada provides an eyewitness account of the architectural features of the pueblos around 1600. This is one of the oldest surviving accounts of first contact between the prehistoric pueblos and the historic Spanish empire. Sosa was met with immediate hostility. The guns and horses and armor of the Spanish were overwhelming against the arrows of the pueblo warriors. So the people developed a new strategy. When they knew the Spanish were coming they abandoned their pueblos and fled to the hills where they would gather at a mesa top that was easily defensible. The Spanish would raid the food stocks and move into the pueblo.

Sosa reported that each home contained two storage rooms for corn, beans, chilies and calabashes. The houses each had abundant pottery, including beautifully done cups, like our coffee mugs. He described the architecture of the pueblo as four and five stories tall, with entry to each unit via a ladder through the roof. Sosa reported, "Each floor of every house has three or four rooms, so that each house as a whole, counting from top to bottom, has 15 to 16 rooms...Every house is equipped with facilities for grinding corn, including three or four grinding stones mounted in small troughs and provided with pestles, all the rooms are white washed." [58] The entrada proceeded from pueblo to pueblo. Prior to this latest entrada, Sosa had neglected to get the permission of the Mexican authorities who, once they figured out what was going on, sent troops to track him down and arrested him. Consequently the Spanish were forced to return to Mexico and Sosa's attempt at colonization failed.

This effort was quickly resumed when in 1598 Don Juan de Onate headed north with over a hundred soldiers. He intended to colonize with this expedition and brought along wives and children and a contingent of ten priests. They supported themselves by raiding the pueblos for corn and food. As before, when the Spanish approached each pueblo the Indians would desert the entire pueblo. That summer Onate called representatives from all the pueblos and informed them that they were henceforth servants of the King of Spain and were expected to pay tribute and to become good Christians.

The Spanish colonists considered agricultural work under their social status. The Indians were enslaved to work in their fields and when that wasn't enough to feed themselves, the Spanish raided the pueblos and took additional tribute. In 1601 Onate went back to Mexico on business and over half the colonists deserted, fearing starvation. The Indian's food reserves were quickly depleted and the Indians faced starvation as well. Onate returned and stayed until 1610, when he was recalled. But after this there was no stopping the rapid colonization of New Mexico. Santa Fe was chosen as the capital city and built with slave labor. When Indians revolted they were punished severely. When the Acoma pueblo revolted, Onate attacked and, upon taking control, ordered that all the men be punished with the amputation of one foot and twenty years of forced labor. After Onate's departure, New Mexico became a royal colony and a vigorous missionary effort to convert and enslave the pueblos was instituted.

By 1621 the authorities had to intervene with rules about the exploitation of the Indians, although these had little effect. A series of governors of the territory used their office to become rich on tribute collected from the Indians, who were forced into sweat shops in Santa Fe. By 1631, missionaries were in twenty-five of the pueblos and they used forced labor to build large churches. In 1632 the priests at Zuni were killed and when the government sent troops the Zuni retreated to the top of Corn Mountain and waited them out. Other priests were killed at Taos and there was a general attitude of revolt, which finally led to the pueblo revolt of 1680. Wave after wave of plague also struck the area. The population of at least 50,000 was reduced to less than 20,000 by the late 1600s. The survivors banded together and were successful in driving the Spanish completely out of New Mexico in 1680. This lasted for ten years before the Spanish returned in force and established their rule with even more cruel and torturous practices.

A Spanish priest described a typical pueblo household in 1776: "The ceilings are quite low... and the arms of the men and harnesses of the horses are hung from stakes ..." [59] These ancestral pueblo households had stakes protruding from the walls to hold their bows and quivers and blankets and hides as well as other storage rooms for "sacred regalia" used in the dances and ceremonies.

The archaeological and ethnographic literature, along with visits to the sites, provides an idea of the effort it took to build the great houses, the cliff dwellings and the multistoried pueblos. Yet there is a lot to learn about the political, cultural and religious motivations that created them. The descendants of the people who built the great houses and cliff dwellings are still alive and, after a thousand years, there are still tribal memories that survive. And after over a hundred years of archaeological and ethnological investigation there are still many mysteries to be solved.

Empathy with the pueblo people and a curiosity and concern with the literature can only take you so far. There are plenty of professional scholars who have spent a lifetime studying these issues. Different theories arise in the literature, typically to be replaced by the next generation, who add a bit more information with extended surveys and more excavations. These scholars write academic articles that gather dust in University libraries and book-length studies illustrated with tables and maps.

All these years of study have led to the observation that the cliff dwellings are divided into family compounds in which each family unit consists of, at least, a kiva, a living room with a hearth, storage rooms, a courtyard and a room to mill corn. The cliff dwellings appear to be primarily residential complexes, although they certainly include ceremonial spaces and plazas. The great houses have a different architectural configuration, more like a cathedral with living units for the elites. Many of the rooms in the great houses are for architectural support and are not living or storage spaces. In the cliff dwellings they could not afford the luxury of rooms that serve only to support what is above them. The space in the cliff dwellings is limited by the dimensions of the alcove and the residents' designed their rooms to take full advantage of that space. Another difference is that in the great houses the rooms are stacked one on top of another in a stair-step fashion and they used ladders to get from one story to the next and each housing unit had access through the roof with a ladder. However, in Mesa Verde Gustav Nordenskiold reports they found no ladders in any of the dwellings. He found lots of wooden artifacts that were well preserved but no ladders. Again archaeologists had first assumed that the residents in the cliff houses used ladders to gain access to the upper rooms and to get from one level of the multileveled structures to another. However, no evidence for this has been found. Instead there were niches cut into the stone which people used as hand and toe holds to climb around without the use of ladders.

There are obvious differences between the great houses and the cliff dwellings and the multistoried pueblos. The evolution of the architecture can be traced in the archaeological records. It began with pit houses and evolved into courtyard complexes, and then into the great flowering of culture that created the great houses and the cliff dwelling. But by 1300 both the great houses and the cliff dwelling were abandoned and the people moved to the Rio Grande valley and build the multistoried pueblos. This marked a new shift in cultural dynamics. The multistoried pueblos were villages and there was no distinction between the houses of the chiefs or priests and the housing for the rest of the people. The labor required to build the great houses and cliff dwellings was conscripted from the population at large. The labor to build the multistoried pueblos was communal. This would seem to mark the end of the autocratic despotism of the great houses. Once the transition was accomplished from the great houses to the pueblos on the Rio Grande, the kachina cult sprang up and added a new religious impulse that distinguished the pueblos from the great houses and cliff dwellings.

The great flow of cultural impulses that created and sustained the traditions that built these marvels of engineering and architecture endured for over a millennium. Can these monuments and all these studies tell us something about our own human nature, about its plasticity and its multitudinous expressions? What is it about our past, its extremes of societal cruelty, the evolution of political systems, the rise and fall of religions, the art and architecture that survives, that stirs us, that reminds us who we were, who we would have been had we lived in that era? Can we examine the trash piles of the past to see what kinds of people we were in those previous incarnations? What was ordinary for them seems horrendous to us. Will what we do today seem equally horrendous to future generations? Did they see themselves as advanced in their time as we feel today? Will our wealth inequality, rabid greed, environmental degradation, mass incarceration and conservative political ideology seem as barbaric to future generations as the forced labor, human sacrifice and theocratic authoritarianism that created the great houses and cliff dwellings seem to us now? Time will tell.

POSTSCRIPT

HISTORY AS CONTINUING CASTASTROPHE

It is an old cliché that history is written by the conquerors. In the history lessons I learned in school they taught Columbus discovered America in 1492, and then nothing much happened until the Pilgrims landed in 1620 and American history begins. There is a huge untold tale hidden behind this myth. It is a tale that reaches deep into prehistory, its beginnings only slowly coming to light; a story that reaches back at least 20,000 years with wave after wave of people coming from different directions.

For many decades it was believed the first natives came to America across a Siberian land bridge about 4,000 years ago, then that got pushed back to 10,000 and 12,000 and 14,000 years ago. Now sites have been documented that are over 20,000 years old. By the time the European invasion began there were native peoples in all parts of the Americas, from the Arctic in the north to the tip of South America.

The earliest record of the first Europeans to come to America tells of Vikings coming to America around 990 CE. In 985 a Viking named Erik the Red was exiled to Iceland where he ended up in a violent feud which resulted in him heading out in his ship to the west. He ended up in Greenland where he founded a colony that grew to over a thousand people. It was there he had a son named Leif. Leif became famous after he was on a voyage from Norway to Greenland when he lost his way and ended up in a new land. He eventually made his way back to Greenland and then returned with thirty-five settlers. They worked their way down the coast until they came to an island where a river filled with salmon entered the sea. They built houses and established a colony. When they explored inland they discovered wild grapes and began making wine, which they exported back to Greenland. As a result they named the land Vinland or "Land of Wine".

Leif's brother, Thorvald, came to Vinland and became the first recorded European to make contact with the Native Americans. As they were going up the river they came upon three boats made of skins filled with Native Americans. They killed all of them but one, who soon came back leading a large number of boats in a counterattack in which Thorvald was killed. The two groups soon sorted it out and made peace and began to trade. The Vikings called the Native Americans "skraelin", an archaic word that means "wretched". Thorvald's widow, Gudred, remarried and gave birth to the first European child born in America in recorded history, a boy named Snorri.

Nearly five centuries would pass before the next wave of Europeans landed on these shores in 1492. When Columbus returned from his first voyage, he was given a hero's welcome and rewarded with seventeen ships and a contingent of fifteen hundred men for his next expedition. He sailed across the Atlantic in twenty-one days and came to the Greater Antilles, where he picked a spot to found a city on the Island of Hispanola. He named the first settlement La Isabella after the queen who sponsored him.

The Indians on the island called themselves Tainos. They produced beautiful pottery with zoomorphic figures on the handles. They carved stone, bone, wood and shell statuary. They practiced elaborate rituals and ceremonies and lived in large formally-arranged villages with plazas, dance grounds and ball courts. There was rigid social stratification, with paramount chiefs who could command life and death, as well as labor and goods. They flattened their foreheads, painted their bodies and tattooed their faces. They used ear and lip plugs along with nose ornaments. They cultivated corn, sweet potatoes, beans and cotton. They had canoes that held a hundred and fifty people and traveled throughout the Caribbean. They presented Columbus with cotton fabric, gold ornaments, wood carvings and feathered cloaks. The art, economics and politics were all intimately tied to their religion, which included belief in an afterlife, creation myths and myriad supernatural forces. They fasted, danced, purged, chanted and used psychedelic drugs in a religious context. Chastity was not a virtue and there is explicit sexual imagery in their art and cosmology. Columbus reported that they were, "guileless and generous with all they possess." [60] Within less than a year open hostilities were an on-going part of life. When captured by the Indians the Spaniards were ritually sacrificed as offerings to the gods. Within two years Columbus attacked the major towns and enslaved all his captives. Over five hundred Tainos people were shipped back to Spain and sold into slavery. The rest of the population was forced to pay tribute four times a year and began to die of new, unknown diseases. Many Tainos fled from their homelands to escape capture, death and disease, and by 1515 the native population of the islands was reduced from nearly one million to less than fifteen thousand.

The Spanish began an intensive colonization and made Cuba the next major headquarters. From there they launched voyages of discovery in every direction. In 1511 a Spanish vessel bound for Jamaica sank in a storm and twenty survivors escaped in a small boat with no provisions. They drifted for thirteen days during which half the crew perished before gaining the distinction of being the first Europeans to come ashore in the Yucatan. They were immediately captured by the local natives, who sacrificed five of the captives in religious ceremonies and cannibalized them. The remaining five managed to escape and fell into the hands of a neighboring chief who made them slaves. Three of the five got sick and died, leaving only Gonzalo Guerrero and Geronimo de Aguilar, who both learned the language of their captors and adapted as best they could. Aguilar kept a breviary and maintained a calendar. Guerrero was taken to the capital city and presented to the ruler, who ended up putting him in charge of the army. He was very successful in this new position, defeating all enemies by employing European military strategy. He married and had children, let his hair grow, pierced his ears, and adopted Mayan fashion and Mayan religion.

Six years later, Hernandez de Cordoba arrived at the Yucatan with three ships in search of slaves, since the entire Indian population of Cuba had either died or left the island. They quickly found their way to one of the largest cities on the coast, where the local chief attacked them, killing twenty men and wounding another fifty. The Spanish managed to capture a few items of gold which, on their return to Cuba, fueled a fervor for conquest. In 1518 Hernando Cortes set sail with five hundred men and horses. Upon his arrival on the coast of Mexico he burned his ships and proceeded to sack every town he came to. Eventually, he captured a chief's wife who told him there were other bearded men in the Yucatan. He wrote a letter which Aguilar eventually received. Aguilar immediately went to Cortes, who put him to work as his translator. Guerrero stayed with his adopted tribe and was the first European to go native. Cortes went on to conquer the Aztecs and built his capital city on the ruins of their capital city.

In 1538 Hernando de Soto landed in Tampa Bay with seven hundred and thirty men, two hundred and twenty horses, a pack of dogs and a herd of pigs. He had been part of Pizarro's army of conquest in Peru and used his portion of the plunder to equip his expedition to La Florida, where he hoped to found a colony and find riches greater than those of Peru and Mexico. His method was to capture some Indians, torture them to reveal the location of the next large village and force them to guide him to its location, where he and his men would steal all the food, capture as many Indians as possible, use the women as sex slaves and cut off the hands and noses of the men. Captives were fed to the dogs at the slightest provocation. Each side considered the other savage barbarians. Both were right. De Soto would capture the local chief and reveal things he had learned from other captives and lead him to believe he had supernatural insight. He would hold up a mirror to his face and tell the chief that this image was a magical double which could visit the chief and spy on him.

De Soto traveled north into Tennessee, then west into the lands across the Mississippi River. He continued until he was finally discouraged and turned back. When he made it back to the Mississippi River he became ill and died. After his death, a local chief who had become an ally sent two young men to be sacrificed to serve as guides and helpers for de Soto in the land of the dead. Desoto's captain sent them back to their tribe. One refused to go, saying he preferred to be a slave of the Spanish, a very unwise decision since the slaves all died of starvation and disease. After de Soto's death, the army went down the river to the gulf, where they built a primitive forge and melted all the iron to make spikes and built enough boats to travel around the coast until they came to a Spanish settlement on the coast of Mexico. Only three hundred men survived. About the same time de Soto was invading the Southeast, Friar Marcos, seeking the Seven Cities of Gold, stumbled upon the Zuni in the Southwest. Coronado quickly followed in his wake and explored the pueblo culture. He made it into the Great Plains before turning back.

In 1565 Pedro Menendez founded Saint Augustine, the first European settlement in the United States, a half-century before the Pilgrims gave a thought to coming across the ocean. The Spanish and French were both securely established on this continent before the English made their first settlements. Conflict was inevitable between these three groups of invaders and the natives.

From the earliest contact with the Vikings, to the final conquest of the Sioux and Apache in 1890, the European invasion of America was one of utter devastation for the indigenous people. They were ravaged by wave after wave of disease for which they had no resistance. Those who survived disease and war bonded together and fought the invaders while continuing their own inter-tribal warfare. This history is slowly coming to light, replacing the American myth of Manifest Destiny. The invaders were crazed Aryans whose massive rapacity brought wave on wave of insane violence that was driven by Semitic scriptural justification. They thought themselves reenacting Hebraic myths of god-driven conquest, their eyes blinded by their own ignorance and greed. Crazed, mindless and pale-skinned, they were filled with longings that no restitution, save the deepest darkness of history, could appease.

The Indians told their history in their myths that recount their creation story of how they emerged from the earth, travelled on great adventures and settled to find their way in relationship with the animals and the forces of nature. They developed traditions radically different from the Western mindset. We have only recently been able to cut through our own prejudices to see that their story is just as vital and meaningful as our own. There are lessons to be learned about a way of life that doesn't exploit and destroy the environment. Their ways certainly can't be emulated; they were fraught with inter-tribal violence, with a justice system based on revenge and a religion of sacrifice. Yet they had an original relation to the earth as the mother of life and the sun as the father, and they felt a responsibility to live in harmony with these mysterious forces and to establish a reciprocal relationship that does not exploit nature for personal gain, a lesson we have been loath to learn and one that, unheeded, will have a steep toll.

On our return to Tennessee I felt divested of my own history, feeling that it was myth in the worse sense of the word. Civilization has been in decline since the Paleolithic period. All our vaunted progress, bullshit. Where has technological development gotten us? It's been a downhill slide on a slippery slope for the past ten thousand years. Techno-industrial capitalism has been devastating to the environment, to say nothing of militarization and nuclear proliferation. Homo erectus lived on this planet for two million years; Homo sapiens have been here two hundred thousand years and the prospects don't look good. Our ancestors were not ignorant cave dwellers. Hunter-gatherers were inventive, attuned to their environment, living in socially-connected egalitarian bands. They had no bosses and no cops. Everything was owned in common; their bodies were sturdier, their brains larger. Those who survived their infancy lived as long as we do now. Their diet was better than ours; they had less disease, less emotional stress. They worked fewer hours and participated in more music and dance. Where has our civilization gotten us? We are pitiable domesticated versions of our Paleolithic ancestors.

I walked through the woods behind our house, feeling an alienation from life in America. Our modern cities are covered in a haze of pollution; I am a witness to a devastation I want nothing to do with yet can't escape. I long for the stars, for nature, for clean water and air and unspoiled countryside. Instead, I howl down the ragged oblivion that shrouds our future, knowing the toll to be paid for our lifestyle is one of desolation and destruction in future generations. My people seem like pathetic, bald, bipeds who have made a world that cannot lead to any good end. I feel a door shutting behind me.

ENDNOTES

1. Cushing, Frank Hamilton, *Zuni Fetishes,* Introduction by Tom Bahti, Facsimile Edition by KC Publications, Las Vegas, Nevada, 1994. p. 17.

2. Bunzel, Ruth L., *Zuni Katchinas, 47th Annual Report of the Bureau of American Ethnology,* 1929-1930. p. 941.

3. Ibid. p. 851.

4. Smith, Watson, Woodbury, Richard B., Woodbury, Nathalie F.S., *The Excavation of Hawikuh by Frederick Webb Hodge: Report of the Hendricks-Hodge Expedition, 1917-1923.* Contributions from the Museum of the American Indian, Heye Foundation, Vol. XX, Museum of the American Indian, Heye Foundation, New York, 1966. p. 14.

5. Flint, Richard and Shirley Cushing, Edited, Translated, and Annotated by, *Documents of the Coronado Expedition, 1539 to 1542.* Southern Methodist University Press, Dallas, Texas, 2005. p. 2.

6. Hodge, Frederick Webb, *The History of Hawikuh New Mexico: One of the so-called Seven Cities of Cibola, Vol. 1.* The Frederick Webb Hodge Publication Fund, The Museum of the American Indian, Heye Foundation, Los Angeles, CA. 1937. p. 111.

7. Ibid. p. 388.

8. Ibid. p. 76.

9. Flint, Richard and Shirley Cushing, p. 260.

10. Bunzel, Ruth, *Zuni Ritual Poetry*, Smithsonian Institution, 47th Annual Report of the Bureau of Ethnology, 1929-1930, p. 142.

11. Ibid. p. 144.

12. Ibid. p. 156.

13. Stevenson, Matilda Coxe, *The Zuni Indians: Their Mythology, Esoteric Fraternities, and Ceremonies*, 23rd Annual Report of the Bureau of American Ethnology, 1901-1902, The Rio Grande Press, Inc. Glorieta, NM, 1970. p. 24-26.

14. Cushing, Frank Hamilton, *Zuni Breadstuff,* Museum of the American Indian, Heye Foundation, 1974, p. 315.

15. Mails Thomas, *Dancing in the Paths of the Ancestors: Book Two of The Pueblo Children of the Earth Mother*, Marlowe and Company, NY, 1983. p. 235.

16. Wright, Baron, *Kachinas of the Zuni*, Northland Press, Flagstaff, AZ, 1985. p.39.

17. Cushing, Frank Hamilton, *The Selected Writings of Frank Hamilton Cushing*, Edited with an introduction by Jesse Green, University of Nebraska Press, Lincoln and London, 1979, p. 83.

18. Ibid. p. 87.

19. Ibid. p. 88.

20. Ibid. p. 320.

21. Stevenson, p. 231.

22. Ibid. p. 253.

23. Ibid. p. 253.

24. Ibid. p. 260.

25. Ibid. p. 255.

26. Bunzel, p. 899.

27. Ibid. p. 893.

28. Ibid. p. 863.

29.Ibid. p. 963.

30. Ibid. p. 965.

31. Ibid. p. 965.

32. Ibid. p. 965-966.

33. Ibid. p. 974.

34. Ibid. p. 862.

35. Ibid. p. 248-249.

36. Parsons, Elsie Clews, *Pueblo Indian Religion*, Bison Books, University of Nebraska Press, Lincoln and London, 1939, 1996. p. 752.

37. Fergusson, Erna, *Dancing Gods: Indian Ceremonials of New Mexico and Arizona*, University of New Mexico Press, 1931. p. 95.

38. Ibid. p. 98.

39. Ibid. p. 100.

40. Ibid. p. 107.

41. Tedlock, Barbara, *The Beautiful and the Dangerous; Dialogues with the Zuni Indians*, Penguin Books, NY, 1992. p. 228.

42. Ibid. p. 227.

43. Ibid. p. 225.

44. Ibid. p. 227.

45. Ibid. p. 247.

46. Ibid. p. 249-250.

47. Mails, p. 244.

48. Bunzel, Ruth, *Zuni Ritual Poetry*, Smithsonian Institution, 47th Annual Report of the Bureau of Ethnology, 1929-1930, p. 215, 219.

49. Wright, Baron, *Kachinas of the Zuni*, Northland Press, Flagstaff, AZ, 1985. p. 164.

50. Bunzel, p. 264.

51. Parson, Elsie Clews, *Taos Tales*, Dover Publications, NY. 1940, 1996.

p 50.

52. Nordby, Larry V., *Prelude to Tapestries in Stone*, Colorado Historical Society 2001, p. 114.

53. Waters, Frank. *The Masked Gods*, Ballantine Books, NY. 1950, 1970., p 440.

54. Ibid. p. 439.

55. Ibid. p. 439.

56. Ortiz, Alfonso, *The Pueblo*, Chelsea House Publishers, New York, NY. 1994. p 30.

57. Ibid. p. 30.

58. Ibid. p. 33-34.

59. Ortiz, p. 58.

60. Deagan, Kathleen, and Cruxent, Jose Maria, *Columbus's Outpost among the Tainos*, Yale University Press, New Haven, 2002. p. 3.

BIBLIOGRAPHY

Bandelier, Adolph F., *The Discovery of New Mexico by the Franciscan Monk, Friar Marcos de Niza in 1539*, Madeleine Turrell Rodack, Translator and Editor, University of Arizona Press, Tucson, Arizona, 1981.

Benedict, Ruth, *Introduction to Zuni Mythology*, Columbia University Contributions to Anthropology, SSI, Columbia Press, 1935.

Bunzel, Ruth L., *Zuni Katcinas: An Analytic Study*, 47th Annual Report of the Bureau of American Ethnology, 1929 -1930, reprinted by The Rio Grande Press, Glorieta, NM, 1984.

Bunzel, Ruth L., *The Zuni: Southwest American Indians*, Forgotten Books, KY, 2008.

Cushing, Frank Hamilton, *Zuni Breadstuff*, Museum of the American Indian, Heye Foundation, 1974.

Cushing, Frank Hamilton, *Zuni Folk Takes*, The University of Arizona Press, Tucson, 1988.

Cushing, Frank Hamilton, *The Selected Writings of Frank Hamilton Cushing*, Edited with an introduction by Jesse Green, University of Nebraska Press, Lincoln and London, 1979.

Cushing, Frank Hamilton, *Zuni Fetishes*, Introduction by Tom Bahti, Facsimile Edition by KC Publications, Las Vegas, Nevada, 1994.

Deagan, Kathleen, and Cruxent, Jose Maria, *Columbus's Outpost among the Tainos*, Yale University Press, New Haven, 2002.

Fergusson, Erna, *Dancing Gods: Indian Ceremonials of New Mexico and Arizona*, University of New Mexico Press, 1931.

Flint, Richard and Shirley Cushing, Edited, Translated, and Annotated by, *Documents of the Coronado Expedition, 1539 to 1542*. Southern Methodist University Press, Dallas, Texas, 2005.

Green, Jesse, Edited by. *Cushing at Zuni: The Correspondence and Journals of Frank Hamilton Cushing, 1979 – 1884*, University of New Mexico Press, Albuquerque, 1990.

Hodge, Frederick Webb, *The History of Hawikuh New Mexico: One of the so-called Seven Cities of Cibola*, Vol. 1. The Frederick Webb Hodge Publication Fund, The Museum of the American Indian, Heye Foundation, Los Angeles, CA, 1937.

Hodge, Gene Meany, *Kachina Tales From the Indian Pueblos*, Sunstone Press, Santa Fe, NM, 1936.

Jones, Hester, *Zuni Shalako Ceremony*, Kessinger Legacy Reprints, original by The School of American Research, U. of N. M., 1931.

Mails, Thomas, *Dancing in the Paths of the Ancestors: Book Two of The Pueblo*

Children of the Earth Mother, Marlowe and Company, NY, 1983.

Mindeleff, Victor, *A Study of Pueblo Architecture: Tusayan and Cibola*, Map 27, "Plan of Zuni Pueblo". Eighth Annual Report of the Bureau of Ethnology, Washington, 1891.

Nordby, Larry V., *Prelude to Tapestries in Stone*, Colorado Historical Society, 2001.

Nordenskiold Baron Gustaf, *The Cliff Dwellers of the Mesa Verde*, Mesa Verde Museum Association, CO, 1990.

Ortiz, Alfonso, *The Pueblo*, Chelsea House Publishers, New York, NY, 1994.

Parsons, Elsie Clews, *Pueblo Indian Religion*, Bison Books, University of Nebraska Press, Lincoln and London, 1939, 1996.

Parson, Elsie Clews, *Taos Tales*, Dover Publications, NY. 1940, 1996

Sando, Joe S., *Pueblo Nations: Eight Centuries of Pueblo Indian History*, Clear Light Publishers, Santa Fe, NM, 1992.

Schaafsma, Polly, Edited by, *Kachinas in the Pueblo World*, University of Utah Press, Salt Lake City, 2000.

Sei, Toshio, *Kachinas and Ceremonial Dancers in Zuni Jewelry*, Schiffer Publishing, PA, 2012.

Smith, Watson, Woodbury, Richard R., Woodbury, Nathalie F.S., *The Excavation of Hawikuh by Frederick Webb Hodge: Report of the Hendricks Hodge Expedition 1917- 1923:* Contributions from the Museum of the American Indian, Heye Foundation, Vol XX, 1966.

Stevenson, Matilda Coxe, *The Zuni Indians: Their Mythology, Esoteric Fraternities, and Ceremonies,* 23rd Annual Report of the Bureau of American Ethnology, 1901-1902, The Rio Grande Press, Inc. Glorieta, NM, 1970.

Tedlock, Barbara, *The Beautiful and the Dangerous: Dialogues with the Zuni Indians*, Penguin Books, NY, 1992.

Tedlock, Dennis and Barbara, *Teachings from the American Earth: Indian Religion and Philosophy*, Liveright Press, NY, 1975.

Wright, Barton, *Kachinas of the Zuni*, Northland Press, Flagstaff, AZ, 1985.

Wright, Barton, *Patterns and Sources of Zuni Kachinas*, Harmsen Publishing, Denver, CO, 1988.

CPSIA information can be obtained
at www.ICGtesting.com
Printed in the USA
LVHW112243060319
609133LV00001BA/12/P